RISK MANAGEMENT FOR ACADEMICIANS AND PRACTITIONERS

THE BOOK CATERS TO THE NEED OF BOTH BEGINNERS AND EXPERIENCED RISK MANAGEMENT PROFESSIONALS

SONJAI KUMAR

JAI KUMAR VERMA

This book is dedicated to my father Shri Jai Kumar Verma who was instrumental during my early days of development and inculcated foundational habits that I relish today.

Contents

Preface

This is my second book on risk management. I wrote my first book **"Risk Management in Current Scenario"** in 2017-18. That book was the culmination of my thoughts, readings of risk-related matters, talking to other risk professionals, and experience that I gained at that point in time. At that time, risk management was a bit at an early stage in India, so the reason was obvious. One feedback that I got from my previous book was that it was not covering the fundamentals of risk management. Perhaps, the reason was, that there were not too many people looking for risk management education.

However, things over the last four and five years have changed gaining momentum toward corporates adopting risk management as well as providers offering risk-related courses. But, I still have to find one book in India that can cater to the needs of the masses who could gain risk management knowledge with confidence. Considering this gap, this book covers the fundamentals of risk management in the first half of the book and also covers the challenges and issues faced by risk management professionals in the second half of the book.

Therefore, the book caters to the need of both beginners and experienced risk management professionals.

The blend of the two also comes from my continuous efforts in gathering risk management knowledge while lecturing on the subject and gaining practical knowledge working in the industry. Also, over the last two years, while reading for my research towards my Ph.D. journey I gained new knowledge about risk management. Also noted is the relationship between risk-based capital and the emergence of enterprise risk management (ERM).

According to my study, there is a strong relationship between the beginning of ERM as a consequence of the adoption of risk-based capital (RBC) both in the US and Europe in the banking (due to Basel) and insurance sector, however, in the academic front, such relationship is yet to be proved. One chapter is dedicated to this, however, my earlier effort has challenged that the development of ISO 31000 and COSO are independent of RBC development. More digging is required.

The first ten chapters cover the fundamentals of risk management. Anyone without any background of risk management can gain a good understanding of the subject. After chapter 10, different issues are discussed such as challenges with corporate governance, the three lines of defense model, the development of risk culture, etc. The challenges mentioned in the book are not only faced in India but also in different parts of the world, that I gathered from reading various academic research papers and global surveys. There are also discussions about the various life insurance risks and their management. Few chapters are dedicated to the development of digitalization and how it can influence risk management. The classic example is how driverless cars are going to change motor insurance. The final chapter is given on flow charts that I used to prepare for a high-level understanding of various concepts of risk management. I have shared through this book everything I learned up to this point in time.

Have a good read and do not forget to respond to
sonjai_kumar@hotmail.com

Acknowledgements

I would like to thank my parents for always backing and encouraging me. The credit is much greater for my wife allowing me to spend long hours on my passion for writing. My Son has always given short but constructive feedback that I never ignore. My niece has always been considerate and passionate about my work.

I would like to thank all the individuals that have helped me either directly or indirectly.

Thank you everyone.

ONE

Introduction to Risk Management

Introduction

The chapter covers the fundamentals of risk management begining with the definition of risk, benefits of risk management, principles of risk management, differences between risk management and enterprise risk management, corporate governance, risk management framework, risk management process and types of risks.

This chapter is based on my reading of various risk management contents and experience gained over the working period.The insurance and banking sector examples are shared to back the concept.

What is Risk

According to ISO 31000, the definition of risk is "The effect of uncertainty on objectives." This definition is about the uncertainty that arises in the future, and the risk is objectives may not be met due to the uncertainty. Therefore, for risk to happen, both the condition of "future" and "objective" must be met for risk to exist.

For example, if a person's objective is to go for a morning walk in a nearby park and find his car's tyre punctured does not have any impact on meeting his aim of going to the park. So, the risk of a car's tyre puncture has no effect; there is no risk. But, on the other hand, if the same person is to go to the office using his car, finding the tyre puncture has an impact. So, a person's objective has a significant effect on whether risk materializes or not. Similarly, if someone is living in New York, have no impact on risk if it rains in London.

Similarly, "future" significantly impacts whether risk occurs or not because uncertainty arises due to an unknown future. For example, if there exists no tomorrow, there is no risk even if an objective exists. For instance, if someone is on his deathbed and wants to be a millionaire (objective) presents no threat to him, as his life is very short and almost has no future, and therefore, there is no uncertainty, so no risk exists for him. However, if a 40-year-old man wants to be a millionaire, the future presents a chance that he may not be a millionaire because of uncertainty.

Therefore,

Risk = Uncertainty due to future + Not meeting Objectives

Risk Management

Risk management is to help organizations identify, understand and manage their risks and opportunities, and thereby increase the likelihood of achieving their objective by reducing uncertainty

The above description of risk management results from the way risk is defined above because the management of risk helps identify the risk, which helps in understanding its likelihood and severity and helps understand the threats and opportunities that uncertainty presents and thereby helps in meeting the organization's objectives.

It is, therefore, imperative to have a complete understanding of risk. For example, Kodak is a classic case of failure to understand strategic risk management and lacks a vision for approaching risk. Kodak dominated the photographic film market for the entire 20th century, and it was Kodak first built a digital camera way back in 1975.

The management of Kodak was so focused on film's success that they missed the digital revolution opportunity and filed the bankruptcy in 2012.

It can be said that the digital camera was too early development for the market to adopt in 1975 when the entire world was focusing on film cameras.

Keeping an eye on the future is key to risk management success.

Why read risk management

Risk Management helps reduce earnings volatility

A study was made to investigate the effect of risk management on earnings volatility on shares of banks listed on the Tehran Stock Exchange.

All 20 listed banks on Tehran Stock Exchange were studied over the period 2009-2015. It was found that Risk management has a significant effect on the reducing volatility of earnings of accepted banks in

Tehran Stock Exchange.

Risk Management Adds Value to Shareholders

It has been found that those companies that follow risk management typically add around 20% to 30% more shareholders' value.

One study was made between 1990 and 1995 where the ratio of market value to book value was studied for those companies doing the hedging activities. It was found that more attractive companies were rewarded with an average increase of 20% in market value

Fewer Surprises

Organizations keeping an eye on the future regularly identify risks and develop mitigation action reduce surprises.

Better decision making

Organizations knowing that risk can disrupt the business helps them in making better business decisions. Therefore, it is strongly recommended that the decision-making should be risk-based, where every decision is based on risk identification and planning for the mitigation action.

Maximize capital utilization and profit

It has been proven in many academic works of literature that the implementation of risk management enhances the value of the organization, capital utilization, and profits.

Principles of Risk Management

The fundamental principle of risk management is a valuable addition to the organization by reducing the volatility of the outcome.

ISO 31000 has 11 risk management principles.

The eleven risk management principles are:

1. Risk management establishes and sustains value.
2. Risk management is an integral part of all organizational processes.
3. Risk management is part of decision-making.
4. Risk management explicitly addresses uncertainty.
5. Risk management is systematic, structured, and timely.
6. Risk management is based on the best available information.
7. Risk management is tailored.

8. Risk management takes human and cultural factors into account.
9. Risk management is transparent and inclusive.
10. Risk management is dynamic, iterative, and responsive to change.
11. Risk management facilitates the continual improvement of the organization.

Difference between Risk Management and Enterprise Risk Management (ERM)

As the name suggests, 'Enterprise" means companywide risk management, a risk management which starts at the top of the hierarchy at the Board level and goes to the last employee in the Company's supply chain.

Fragmented risk management does not work as risks are highly correlated and cannot be segmented and managed independently. **Correlated risk** is the simultaneous occurrence of many losses from a single event. For example, Natural disasters such as earthquakes, floods, and hurricanes produce highly **correlated** failures: many homes in the affected area are damaged and destroyed by a single event

There is also a higher cost of management of independent risk as the benefit of diversification of risks will not happen. For example, liquidity risk may arise due to the crystallization of credit risk. If you manage both the risks independently, it will be very expensive; however, if you manage just the credit risk, liquidity risk will be automatically managed.

So, there is an excellent value in enterprise risk management against silo risk management.

What is ERM

- ERM is a risk management process integrated across the Company flowing right through the top of the hierarchy with ownership of the Board running through the last employee in the ladder chain.
- In ERM, risk management is part of the daily working culture and an integral part of the decision-making process

In ERM, risk management is not done once in a while; it is a daily part of the working culture. Every activity that all employees are doing is to think like a front-line risk manager; what if thinking should be every day part of the culture. In ERM, risk management is not just the work of risk function, but everyone takes ownership of the risk management.

To progress systematically, the different ownership of risks need to be defined, employed, and executed

Under ERM, ownership of the risks is defined. Generally, the function head takes ownership of their respective risks.

A **risk owner** is an accountable point of contact for an enterprise **risk** at the senior leadership level who coordinates efforts to mitigate and manage the **risk** with various individuals who own parts of the **risk**. The responsibilities of the **risk owner** are to ensure that: ... **Risks** are clearly articulated **in risk** statements.

Broken links are a recipe for disaster

Under the ERM structure, if links are broken down, for example, underwriting and claims team within an insurance company stops talking, then the flow of information between them will be broken down. This may lead to an increase in the number of claims. Therefore, all the links within the Company must be working well.

It's like the entire body linked through the veins and blood flowing through it; if any vein is cut, there will be a severe problem within the Company, and the risk management cycle will break.

Accountability at the Top part of ERM

As mentioned above, under ERM, the Board at the top of the hierarchy have the overall responsibility of providing oversight by developing policies and procedures around the **risk** that are consistent **with** the organization's strategy and **risk** appetite. The Board also ensures that the policies approved and risk appetite set are followed and reported back to the Board regularly, often quarterly.

- One of the critical causes of the 2008 economic crisis is attributed to the failure of the different Boards to execute a proper risk assessment plan.
- Some of the questions raised in the post-2008 economic crisis analysis were
    - On Composition of the Board/Age of the members
    - Relevant experience and qualifications of independent directors
    - Infrequent meetings
    - Remuneration structure not based on performance
- For ERM to be successful, Board is to play a key role in executing the ownership of all risk management policies, oversight, action plan, etc
- Without proper Board involvement, ERM cannot be successful
- This will be based on what should be the overall Governance structure?

Role of the hierarchy, part of ERM

Hierarchical structure plays a significant role in the success of risk management

- Tone from the top at the CEO level makes a lot of difference; it has been found where the tone from the top is strong, the Company has performed well on the ERM front. A tone from the top sets the right pitch and culture for embedding risk management within the organization. Such tone from the top should be a regular feature rather than one thing.
- In a Company with sound risk management embedding, a separate Risk Management Function is required, headed by CRO, to implement the risk management policies approved by the Board across the Company. The job of the risk management function is to provide oversight of risk management and help develop the risk culture.
- The role of the CRO is the implementation of risk management policies across the Company approved by the Board. In addition, the CRO is responsible for all **risk** management strategies and operations and supervising the organization's **risk** mitigation and identification procedures.
- The role of CROs is becoming crucial at a global level as they provide independent review and challenge all the risks within the organization. A CRO needs to have a futuristic vision to challenge the business plan, products that are priced and distributed and question the Company's strategy and embedded risks within the Company strategy.
- A good CRO should have the following skills
    - Keeping up to and well-read, aware of daily events and developing risks
    - Good understanding of the industry and business
    - Understanding the needs of the business
    - Critical thinking and consulting skills
    - Good communication skills
    - Technical skills
    - Ability to influence,

Corporate Governance

Corporate governance is the way the Board runs the Company and sets and controls the processes in the best interest of stakeholders

Corporate governance is the combination of rules, processes, or laws by which businesses are operated, regulated, or controlled. The term encompasses the internal and external factors that affect the interests of a **company's** stakeholders, including shareholders, customers, suppliers, government regulators, and management.

Corporate governance is essential for the success of risk management. If the corporate governance is not strong, then risk management cannot succeed because the holes within the corporate governance will dilute the impact of risk management, or it will not let risk management apply appropriately within the organization.

A typical best practice in Corporate Governance is

1. Communication with stakeholders
2. Independence of Board
3. Board performance
4. Board Compensation arrangement

Risk Management Framework

To do risk management within an organization, the Company requires having a risk management framework. A risk management framework is a combination of all tools and techniques that will be used for risk management Purpose

The risk management framework has specific components such as risk policies, risk management process, the risk appetite of the Company, and what defense structure the Company is following, such as three lines of defense.

- Risk Policies
- Risk Management Process
- Risk Appetite
- Three Lines of Defence Model

Some companies may have a few more components within the risk management framework.

Risk Management Policies

Risk management is defined as the culture and processes for the systematic application of management policies, procedures, and practices to the tasks of establishing the context, identifying, analyzing, assessing, treating, monitoring, and communicating **risks**

Types of risk management policies will depend on the types of business because, based on the industry, the risks will change, so relevant policies are required to address that risk. For example, financial companies will have financial risks with an interest rate, equity, liquidity, etc. In contrast, the manufacturing industry will have other than financial risks such as risks of supply of raw materials, third party risk, etc. So, the two types of companies have to write different risk management policies. However, most companies will have some common policies, such as operational risk policies, because all the companies use people, processes, and systems, resulting in operational risk.

Another example in insurance key risks are mortality, interest rate, lapses, etc. however, in banking, key risks are credit risk, liquidity risk, etc.

Certain risk policies could be common such as Operational Risk, as every Company runs through its operation.

Risk Management process

The risk management process consists of **five related risk management activities, each dependent on the previous step.** The risk management process is a crucial step as it forms the risk management engine. The risk management process includes

1. Risk identification,
2. Risk measurement,
3. Risk management
4. Risk monitoring
5. Risk reporting.

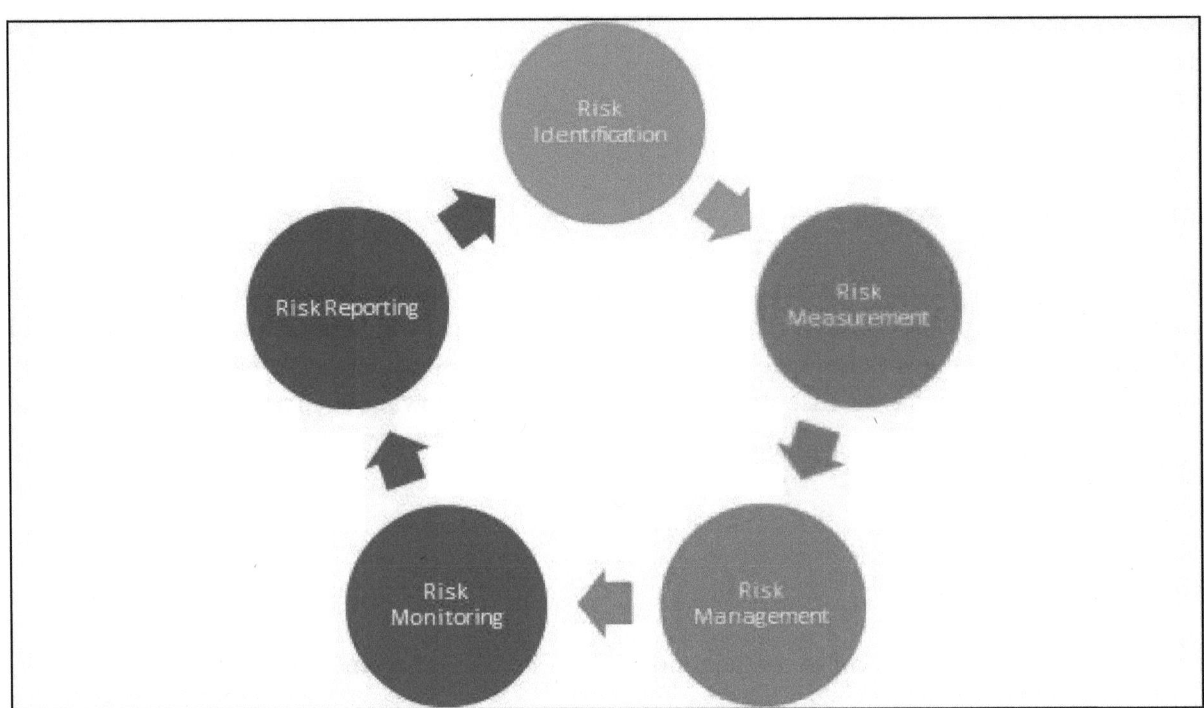

Risk Management Process

Risk Identification

Risk identification is an essential part of the risk management process. If risks are missed or not identified or inadequately identified due to any reason, then subsequent steps will not be performed.

It is just like a doctor, if you go to the doctor and tell him about your disease and your disease is not identified correctly, you will either get the wrong medicine or inadequate medicine. So, risk identification is a crucial step. When it is asked from people what risk is, they will say there is a no-risk, or it will not happen, or it has never happened. Such statements do not help in risk identification; therefore, there could be four situations

1. The first situation is "I know what I know", which means you are aware of what you know.
2. This second situation is perhaps the best (I know what I don't know); you are aware of what you know and what you do not know.
3. I don't know what I know-
4. I don't know what I don't know

The first situation is clear, in the second situation, you know what you don't know, so you will be able to find the risk. The challenge comes in situations 3 and 4 when you don't know. You have to explore the risks under the 3 and 4 categories, and this can be done by identifying the sources of risks.

Issues and Risk

In risk identification, one must be clear about the difference between **issues and risk**. The risk is futuristic and yet to happen, while an issue or problem has already occurred, so while making the risk identification, the issues or problem is to be left for auditors to handle because that has already happened. So, this clarity is essential that issues or problems are not included in the risk identification process. Instead, ask whether it has happened or will happen; if it is "will happen," then it is a risk; otherwise, it is an issue or a problem.

Cause and Effect

In risk identification, there is a strong relationship between cause-risk-effect. It is a cause that leads to an event or risk, and the event leads to effect. They occur in sequence. While doing the risk identification, one needs to be careful not to put cause or effect in the risk bucket. For example, poor wire quality leads to a fire destroying the building. So here, poor quality is a cause of the fire; fire is an event or risk, and destruction due to fire is an effect. Therefore. poor quality of wire or destruction of houses cannot be placed under the risk category. **Here the risk or event is fire**. This relation of cause-event-effect helps in risk mitigation by addressing the controls on the cause, such as better quality of wire will help prevent fire and the destruction of the building.

Sources of risk

As stated above, the cause is the driver of risk, and while doing the risk identification, the causes of risk should be addressed. This is also referred to as sources of risk. If sources of risks are known, it will help in spotting the resulting events leading to risk. So, in the quest to identify risk, one should always scan all sources of risks, such as all environments around your organization which could be internal or external.

There will be no risk to the person from an increase in urbanization as that will not change the value of retirement proceeds or a steady flow of income.

Risk Measurement

Risk measurement helps organizations in prioritizing the risks for management to take action. All risks are not material, so the quantification in terms of likelihood and severity helps decide to take actions based on the organization's risk appetite.

Both likelihood and severity are measured; the quantifiable risks, such as interest rate risks, liquidity risks, etc., are measured through statistical methods, while the non-quantifiable such as people, process, or system risks, are measured in terms of a scale of low, medium and high.

Overall, the risk is quantified as Probability * severity

Risk Management

There are four methods of management of risk in the risk management domain; they are

1. Accept the risk
2. Manage the risk
3. Transfer the risk
4. Avoid the risk

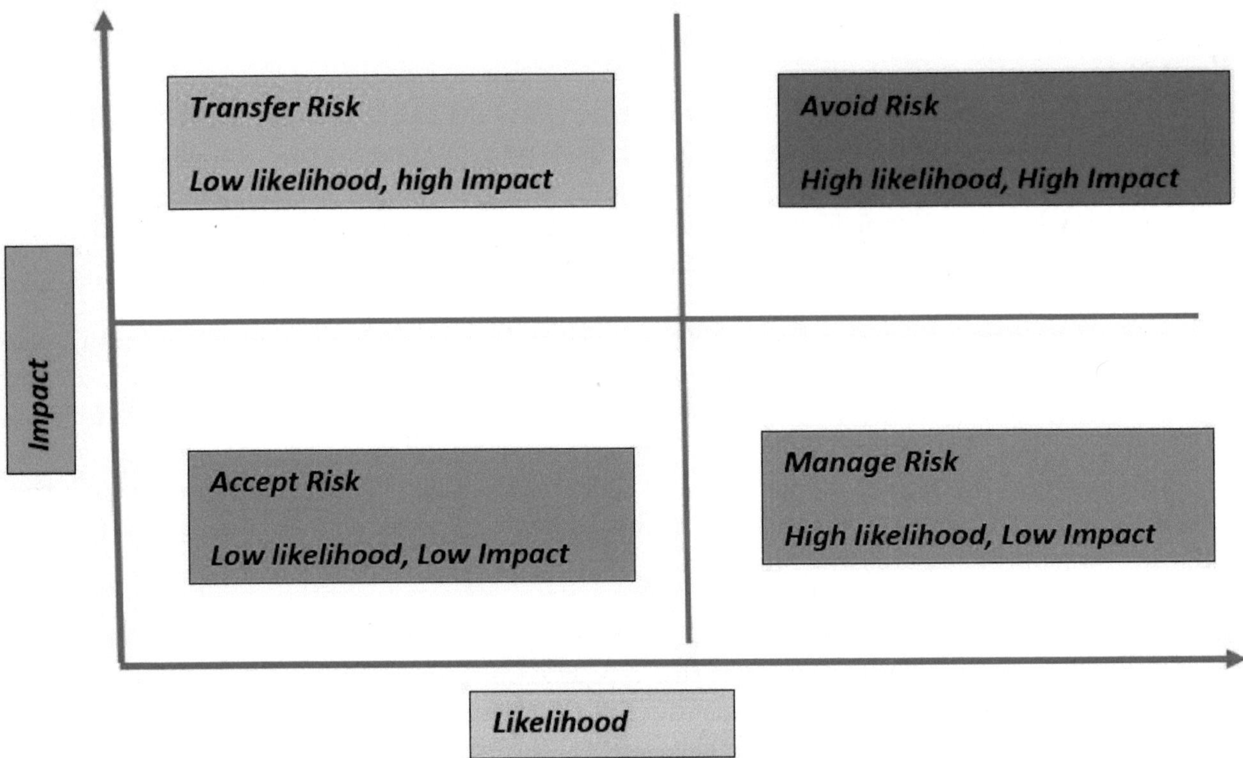

Risk Management

Acceptance of Risk:

The first option available to the risk professionals is to **accept the risk**. But every risk cannot be accepted. Therefore, only those risks are taken with low likelihood and low impact. Such risks are often within the acceptance range of the organization or within the risk appetite. Such acceptance of risks is a healthy proposal at standard premium rates in the insurance business. Similarly, customers with good credit ratings are accepted for giving loans at the standard interest rate in the banking sector.

Manage the Risk:

The second option with the risk professionals is to manage the risks. Such risks are generally high on likelihood and low on the impact scale. Certain customers are non-standard lives in the insurance business, such as customers with diabetes, hypertension, heart disease, etc. Such customers are accepted by the insurance company with an extra premium; here, the chances of making a claim are higher, so they are categorized under a separate bucket to manage the risk. Similarly, in the banking industry, those customers with poorer credit ratings are accepted for a loan with a higher interest rate to manage the risks with a higher premium. So, where an organization sees that the likelihood of a claim is high, but the impact is low, they accept and manage the risk. Another practical example of management of risk is wearing a seatbelt while driving a car or wearing a helmet while driving a two-wheeler. Having a sprinkler system is an example.

Transfer the Risk:

The third option with the risk professionals is to transfer the risk. Those risks that are low in likelihood and high in impact are transferred to a third party. Such risks under the insurance business are those risks that are either of high value (say more than USD 5 million) or very substandard life where the impact of claims will be higher. Such risks are reinsured with the reinsurance company by paying a premium to a reinsurer. So, the insurance company transfers the risk to the reinsurance company.

Avoid the Risk:

Those risks that have a high likelihood and high impact should be avoided. Those bank customers with very high default rates on repayment of the loan will be declined for a loan as Bank wants to avoid giving such a loan to the customer. Such risk is outside the appetite of the Company. We are in a lockdown situation because we want to avoid the risk of the contraction of the covid virus.

Residual Risk

Risk mitigation helps in reducing the overall risks to the Company. However, it is possible that after applying the risk mitigation, some risk remains within the Company; such risks are referred to as **residual risk**. The residual risk should be within the risk appetite of the Company.

If the residual risk is out of the appetite, the Company may have to re-work the objectives or persuade shareholders to pump more money or drop the objective. Such an example could be entering into unknown markets, trying new products, or making a hefty investment in a troubled area with many anti-social activities.

Risk Monitoring

Risk monitoring acts as a feedback loop; before risk monitoring, there are three steps: risk identification, measurement, and management; monitoring allows knowing whether the identified risk was adequate or not or if there was a need to change in the risk identification method.

Also, monitoring lets the organization know whether the risk quantification was adequate; for example, who would have thought the world economic activity would stop between December 2019 and March 2020? So, the quantification was very poor during this period.

Monitoring helps in knowing the risk mitigation plan; in certain countries, the lockdown during the peak of COVID 19 was either slow or inadequate, leading to lots of deaths, so what would you say about the management plan. It was perhaps insufficient, and a more stringent lockdown was required.

So, monitoring exercise gives time and space to look back and take stock of the situation and make the correction for the future.

Actual performance against the expected

As the future is unknown, assumptions are made about the future; that assumption is based on past experience, present data, and professional judgment; however, the reality may still be different from expected. So, monitoring allows the opportunity to make corrections in setting assumptions for the future. Such assumption setting is widespread in the life insurance business, which is long term in nature, 15 years or 20 Years or even whole life.

Early warning signals

Monitoring also allows the organization to spot a trend and identify the early warning signal. For example, if the country's GDP is regularly declining quarter after quarter, it gives a warning signal that there could be something wrong, which will help find the reason and correct the problem.

Examples of Risk Monitoring

1. Regular assessment of the development of GDP against the target and make changes if it is lagging against the target.
2. On the business front, regular progress of profit against the target helps in taking any corrective action or identifying new risks such as the emergence of a competitive product, change in customer behavior, or any change in customer financial situation due to change in economic condition.
3. It is common for insurance companies to monitor the actual claims experience against the expected to know whether actual claims are higher or lower.
4. In many financial products, certain future interest rate assumptions are made; it becomes essential to determine whether the actual interest rate rises or falls against the assumptions made. Such actual movement in interest rate

may lead to profit or loss for the Company

5. It is essential to know how brand value is doing from a marketing perspective. Such monitoring is necessary for Company's popularity, brand recall, and future product sales.
6. If there is a deviation against the expected line, the advantage of monitoring is taking corrective action and completing the risk management process cycle.

Risk Reporting

Risk reporting is the final step in the risk management process. It enables the Company to communicate the risk and other information to all relevant stakeholders. The key stakeholders are the Board of the Company, Risk management committee, Audit Committee, senior management, employees, regulators, rating agencies, securities exchange, and customers, both current and future.

Summary of the risk management process

The first step of the risk management process is risk identification, which can be performed by brainstorming, workshop method, Stress and Scenario testing, SWOT, Survey, etc. There are many more methods of risk identification that will be covered later in the chapters.

Similarly, the second step is risk measurement, where risks are measured quantitatively or qualitatively. The quantitative method is used where risks are measurable by a number, such as interest rate risk, while under in qualitative risks are not measurable by number, so they are measured on a scale of low, medium, and high or other scales.

The third step is risk management; there are four ways; accept the risk, manage the risk, transfer the risk or avoid the risk.

Risk monitoring is a feed loop and refines all the previous steps of the risk management process.

In risk reporting, communication about the risk is made to the relevant stakeholders.

The risk management process is critical and forms the engine of risk management.

Three Lines of defense

The first line of defense is the business unit, the second line of defense is the risk and compliance function, and the third line of defense is the audit function

Under the three lines of defense, the model is to identify their risks and the mitigation action; since they are subject matter experts in their areas, they are best placed to identify the risks and the mitigation action.

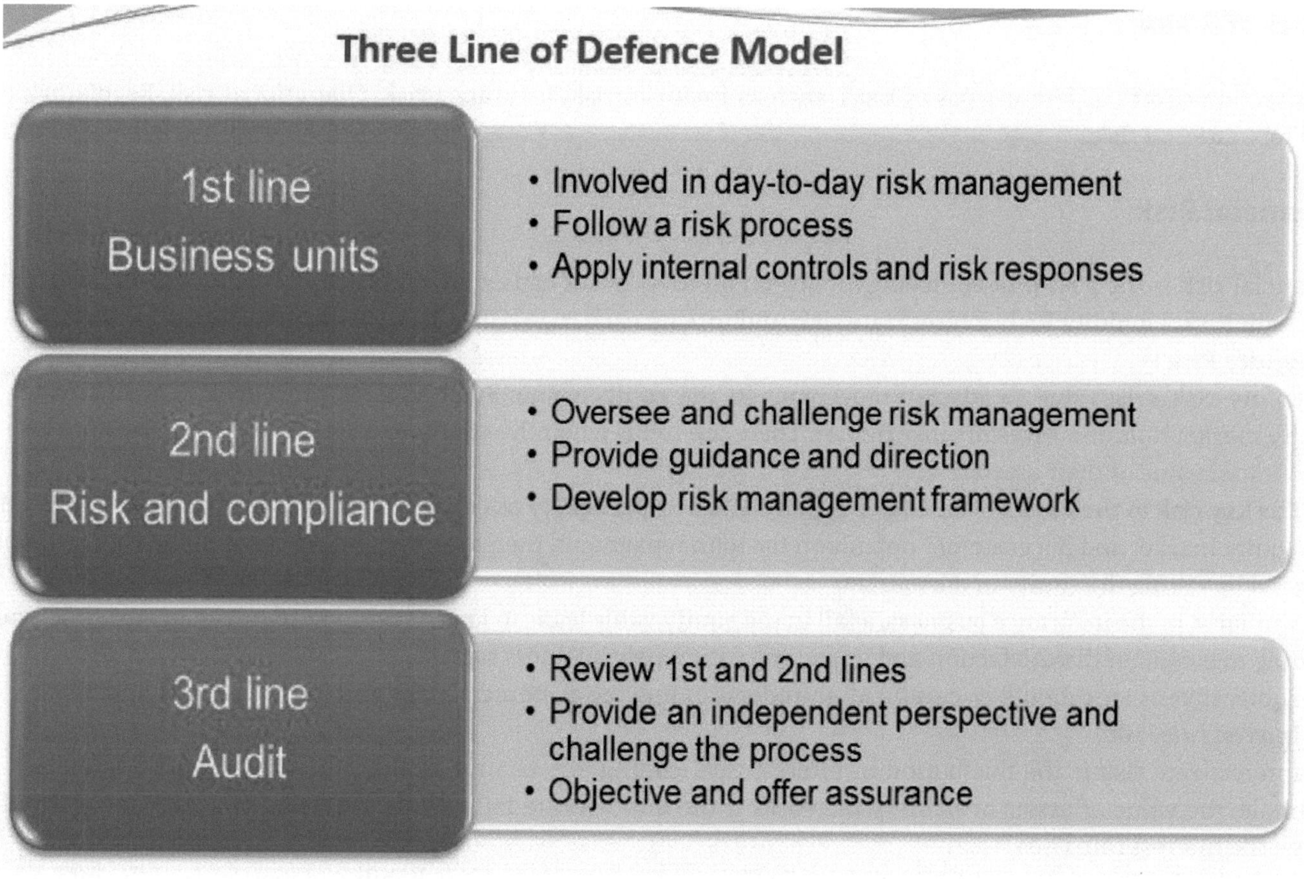

Three Line of Defence Model

1st line Business units	• Involved in day-to-day risk management • Follow a risk process • Apply internal controls and risk responses
2nd line Risk and compliance	• Oversee and challenge risk management • Provide guidance and direction • Develop risk management framework
3rd line Audit	• Review 1st and 2nd lines • Provide an independent perspective and challenge the process • Objective and offer assurance

Three LInes of Defence

The integration of enterprise risk management comes when the first line of defense act as a risk manager.

The role of the second line is to provide oversight on the risks that have been identified by the first line of defense and provide the monitoring and reporting activities. The second line is to see whether the first line has identified all the risks and their mitigation actions or if something is missed out. The second line is to challenge the first line and ask the right questions; therefore, risk managers should have interpersonal skills and consulting skills to guide the first line in mitigating risk.

The failure of the second line comes when they fail to raise adequate reviews, do not ask the right questions, and do not challenge to first-line work enough. These many times create conflict between the first and second lines.

The second line also guides on risk management matters, framing the risk management policies, taking the lead in different risk committees, and acting as an internal regulator.

The third line of defense is the Audit function; they provide independent assurance to the Board on different aspects of risk management, the effectiveness of governance, and internal controls within the Company.

Summary of Risk Management Framework

The above sections covered the following areas under the risk management framework.

1. Risk Policies
2. Risk Management Process
3. Risk Appetite
4. Three Lines of Defence Model

Types of Risks

This section covers different types of risks, such as financial risk, insurance risk, Operational risk, Regulatory risk, and reputational risk.

Financial Risk

Financial risk is the possibility of losing money on an investment caused by market movements due to factors such as Credit Risk, Liquidity Risk, interest rate risk, and foreign exchange risk.

Equity *Risk*

Equity risk arises due to adverse movement in the equity value. Such adverse movement happens when the equity market falls and investors lose money. There are times when the equity market crashes and investors lose the substantial value of their assets.

The key risk to the Banks from equity is that Bank accepts **equity** as collateral against the loan; in case of a fall in the equity market and if a customer default on the loan repayment, then the outstanding value of the loan will not be covered by selling the equity in the market.

Similarly, in the insurance business, a fall in the equity value leads to lower customer maturity or surrender value, leading to customer dissatisfaction and impacting future new business sales.

Equity investment should be careful after understanding the customers' risks and individual risk appetite.

Interest rate risk

Interest rate risk is the fluctuation in interest rate leading to a change in the value of assets and liabilities. For example, the value of assets or liability increases if the interest rate falls, while the value of assets or liability falls when the interest rate rises.

In the banking sector, assets (loan given) are of longer tenure compared to liability (deposits), so if the interest rate rises, the value of assets falls more than the value of liability leading to a mismatch between assets and liability.

In the insurance sector, liabilities (customer's payouts) are longer than assets (investments), so when the interest rate falls, the value of liability rises more than the value of assets leading to a mismatch between assets and liability, so fall in the interest rate is a risk in the insurance business.

Liquidity Risk

Liquidity risk is the risk of not being able to convert the available assets into liquid cash when needed to pay out the liability. Liquidity risk does not mean that the Company does not have money or they are insolvent; it simply means that the assets are not converting into cash. Such illiquid assets could be property; property is not easily liquidated, and it may take time to sell a property where a Company has investment to meet the payouts.

Liquidity risk arises more under the economic stress conditions when certain assets are either not liquidable or will not be getting enough market price. For example, during the COVID situation, most property prices fell. If the property is sold, there will not be enough buyers, and even if buyers are there, the property prices could attract lower value by 30% to 40%, for example.

Liquidity risk also arises when liquidity from the market dries up.

Liquidity risk arises when rating agencies downgrade the rating of certain companies, in which case the assets become illiquid- not enough buyers for low-rated assets.

Liquidity risk is one of the key risks in financial institutions.

Foreign Exchange risk

Foreign exchange risk is the risk of financial loss resulting from changes in ***foreign exchange*** rates. The Company is exposed to this risk when its financial transaction is denominated in foreign currency. Export and import business are greatly affected by the foreign exchange risk.

Insurance risk

Three key risks are mortality, expense, and lapses specific to life insurance. Along with mortality, two other risks of the same family are morbidity and longevity risks.

The mortality risk is defined as the actual number of claims higher than expected. This means that if one expects that there will be 100 deaths in a year from the policies that have been sold, if the actual death turns out to be 120, there are 20 extra deaths for which Company has not priced the risk, and they have to pay the 20 claims from their pocket, which is a loss.

Morbidity risk is related to sickness instead of death, as in the case of mortality. The definition goes similarly as higher actual sickness claims compared to expected.

Longevity risk is related to living longer than expected. This in the insurance business comes with the pension products where the life company expects that they have to pay pension for say 15 years but actual customer survives for 20 years. In this case, the Company is to pay five years of extra pension from their pocket, which is a loss.

Expense Risk

Expense risk is, in fact, common in all businesses where actual expenses turn out to be higher than expected. The situation in the life insurance business is slightly complicated as the business is long term, the premium is level for the premium paying period, and incidences of expenses are uneven with very high initial expenses leading to a problem in recovery if the future premium does not come.

Lapse *risk*

Lapse risk occurs when policyholders stop paying future premiums; this leads to loss because a certain premium volume is assumed when the product is priced. As stated above, lapse risk leads to non-recovery of expense. Lapse risk occurs when the customer is either not satisfied with the product or the product is mis-sold to him, or the customer faces a financial crisis and is unable to pay the premium. If the premium is not paid, the policy lapses, and future benefits get terminated then and there.

Operational risk

The operational risk is defined as a risk of loss resulting from inadequate or failed **internal processes**, **people**, and **systems** or from **external events.**

Operational risk is present in all businesses because all the Company has either people, process, system, or combination. Therefore, operational risk is in all companies.

The building block of operational risk is "cause" leads to the "event", and the event leads to a "consequence". The cause may be people, processes, systems, or a combination of one or all. It is important to note that one cannot control the event or the consequence because both result from the cause. So, in operational risk management, applying control on the "cause" is the only way to manage the operational risk.

For example, because of the inefficient recruitment process, the Company has recruited incompetent people, which led to a material error in the business plan, leading to the loss of millions of dollars. The event is an error in the business plan, and the consequence is a loss of million dollars, but one cannot control either the event or the consequence without addressing the cause. The cause is an ineffective recruitment process; once the recruitment process is strengthened, hire the right people with appropriate qualifications and experience to make a robust business plan.

Regulatory risk

Regulatory risk occurs when the Company breaches the regulation and commits fraud or any illegal activities that may lead to a penalty, warning, restriction in doing certain business, administrative takeover, or suspension of license to operate.

Management often has zero appetite for regulatory risk; such breach of regulation also leads to a loss in reputation.

Reputational risk

Reputational risk is a **risk** of loss resulting from damages to a firm's **reputation**, leading to a loss in revenue; increased operating capital or regulatory costs; destruction of shareholder value, etc.

As with the operational risk, where the cause is the responsible factor for the operational risk, similarly, under the reputational risk, loss of reputation may happen because of specific causes. So, loss in reputation at times is a consequence of another event. For example, consistent customer complaints on social media may lead to a loss in reputation that may impact their business adversely.

TWO

RISK MANAGEMENT AND ENTERPRISE RISK MANAGEMENT

Introduction

This chapter discusses the differences between risk management and enterprise risk management. Though the concept of risk management is very old, almost as old as the beginning of human existence the concept of ERM is new around two decades old. The importance of enterprise risk management increased over the period of time due to various crises and the emergence of risk-based capital in the banking and insurance industry. The chapter discusses the various factors necessary for the success of enterprise risk management.

What is the risk?

Risk is always about the "Future" and the future is unknown therefore uncertainties are there about the future. Risk in the simplest form may be defined as the "**effect on future uncertainties on the objectives**". The uncertainty about the future may lead to adverse outcomes. So uncertainties about the future may deter achieving the objective. It is important to note that if there is no objective, there is no risk, also if there is no future, there is no risk. So in order to have risk both the conditions of the future and the objective must be satisfied with the event to be classified as risk.

From a statistical point of view, the objective is an expected value or mean and risk is the actual deviation or dispersion from the mean value. The higher the dispersion around the mean, the higher is the risk. The dispersion is represented by the standard deviation.

What is Risk Management?

Risk management is a process through which risks are identified, their likelihood and impacts are measured, mitigation actions are planned and risks are monitored regularly and reported to the Senior Management.

Risk management is a tool and not specific to any sector; so this can be applied in any sector. Traditionally, risk management is applied more in the financial sectors such as insurance and banking. However, its application over the years has increased in many areas such as the energy sector, construction sector, environment, etc.

Benefits of Risk Management

Risk Management helps reduce earning volatility

A study was made to investigate the effect of risk management on earnings volatility on shares of banks listed on the Tehran Stock Exchange. All 20 listed banks in Tehran Stock Exchange were studied over the period 2009-2015. It was found that Risk management has a significant effect on the reducing volatility of earnings of accepted banks on the Tehran Stock Exchange.

Risk Management Adds Value to Shareholders

It has been found that those companies that follow risk management typically add around 20% to 30% more shareholders' value.

1. This happens because investment return and pricing happens that reflect underlying risks
2. In such cases, capital earns a risk-adjusted return
3. In such cases, assessment of business and individual happens in conjunction with risks that affect the objectives.

One study was made between 1990 and 1995 where the ratio of market value to book value was studied for those companies who were doing the hedging activities. It was found that more attractive companies were rewarded with an average increase of 20% in market value

Fewer Surprises

By keeping eye on the future and regularly identifying the risks and their mitigation action, there are high chances that there will be fewer surprises at the end of the year.

Better decision making

Risk management help in better decision-making as all future scenarios are explored before making the decision.

Maximize capital utilization and profit

In the academic world, it has been proved that risk management helps in maximizing profit and optimizing capital requirements.

The fundamental principle of risk management is a valuable addition to the organization, by reducing the volatility of the outcome.

Difference between Risk Management and Enterprise Risk Management (ERM)

Risk management and Enterprise Risk Management (ERM) are not the same. Risk management on the one hand is the process of risk identification and risk mitigation, ERM on the other hand is a risk management architecture that binds the risk management across the organization. It can be said that ERM is an enabler of Companywide risk management.

As the name suggests, 'Enterprise" means companywide risk management, a risk management which starts at the top of the hierarchy at the Board level and goes to the last employee in the supply chain of the Company.

Risk management on the other hand is a fragmented approach followed in silos by a few departments. Silo risk management does not work because risks are highly correlated and cannot be managed independently. **Correlated risk** refers to the simultaneous occurrence of many losses from a single event. For example, Natural disasters such as earthquakes, floods, and. hurricanes produce highly **correlated** losses: many homes in the affected area are damaged and destroyed by a single event

There is also a higher cost of management of independent risk as the benefit of diversification of risks will not happen. For example, liquidity risk may arise due to the crystallization of credit risk. If both the risks are managed independently, it will be very expensive; however, if just the credit risk is managed, liquidity risk may not result.

In ERM, risk management is not done, once in a while; it is a daily part of the working culture. In every activity that all employees are doing is to think like a front-line risk manager, what if thinking should be part of everyday culture. In ERM, risk management is not just the work of risk function, but everyone takes ownership of the risk management.

So there is a great value in enterprise risk management as against silo risk management.

Accountability at Top

Under ERM, the Board at the top of the hierarchy has the overall responsibility of providing oversight by developing policies and procedures around the risk that are consistent with the organization's strategy and risk appetite. Board also ensure that the policies approved and risk appetite set are followed and reported back to the Board at regular interval.

- One of the key causes of the 2008 economic crisis is attributed to the failure of the different Boards to execute proper risk assessment plans.
- Some of the questions raised in the post-2008 economic crisis analysis were

    - On Composition of the Board/Age of the members
    - Relevant experience and qualifications of independent directors
    - Infrequent meetings
    - Remuneration structure not based on performance

- For ERM to be successful, Board is to play a key role in executing the ownership of all risk management policies, oversight, action plan, etc
- Without proper Board involvement, ERM cannot be successful
- This will be based on what should be the overall Governance structure?

Role of the Hierarchy

Hierarchical structure plays a very important role in the success of enterprise risk management

- Tone from the top at the CEO level makes a lot of difference, it has been found that the tone from the top is strong, and the Company has performed well on the ERM front. A tone from the top set the right pitch and culture for embedding risk management within the organization. Such tone from the top should be a regular feature rather than one thing.
- In a Company with good risk management embedding, a separate Risk Management Function is required Headed by CRO to implement the risk management policies approved by the Board across the Company. The job of the risk management function is to provide oversight risk management and help develop the risk culture.
- The role of the CRO is implementation of risk management policies across the Company approved by the Board. The CRO is responsible for all **risk** management strategies and operations, as well as supervising the organization's **risk** mitigation and identification procedures.
- The role of CRO is becoming very important at a global level as they provide independent review and challenge of all the risks within the organization. A CRO need to have futuristic vision to challenge the business plan, products that are priced and distributed, challenge the strategy of the Company that what are embedded risks within the Company strategy.
- A good CRO should have following skills

    - Keeping up to and well read, aware about daily events and developing risks
    - Good understanding of the industry and business
    - Understanding the needs of the business
    - Critical thinking and consulting skills
    - Good communication skills
    - Technical skills
    - Ability to influence,

Corporate Governance

Corporate governance is the combination of rules, processes or laws by which businesses are operated, regulated or controlled. The term encompasses the internal and external factors that affect the interests of a **company's** stakeholders, including shareholders, customers, suppliers, government regulators and management.

Corporate governance is a very important in the success of risk management; if the corporate governance is not strong, then risk management cannot succeed because the holes within the corporate governance will dilute the impact of risk management or it will not let risk management apply properly within the organization.

A typical best practice in Corporate Governance are

1. Communication with stakeholders
2. Independence of board
3. Board performance
4. Board Compensation arrangement

Conclusion

ERM is a binding glue that combines the risk management in a one force across the Company and some of the factors for its success are role of the Board, tone from top, risk governance, risk culture, etc.

THREE

Twenty Years of ERM Development

This chapter is in continuation of the previous chapter showing the development of how ERM has moved.

ERM Development

ERM development is a relatively recent phenomenon that started developing around the year 2000. The COSO (Committee of Sponsoring Organization of the Treadway Commission) came up with ERM standards in 2004, while the ERM framework by ISO 31000 was first published in 2009. There is always a time lag between the standards framing up and getting into use.

The academic research in the field of ERM started around the year 2000. As per the analysis of around 400 research papers on ERM, the first paper on ERM was published in the year 2001. Below is the graph that shows the development of ERM academic research at the global level.

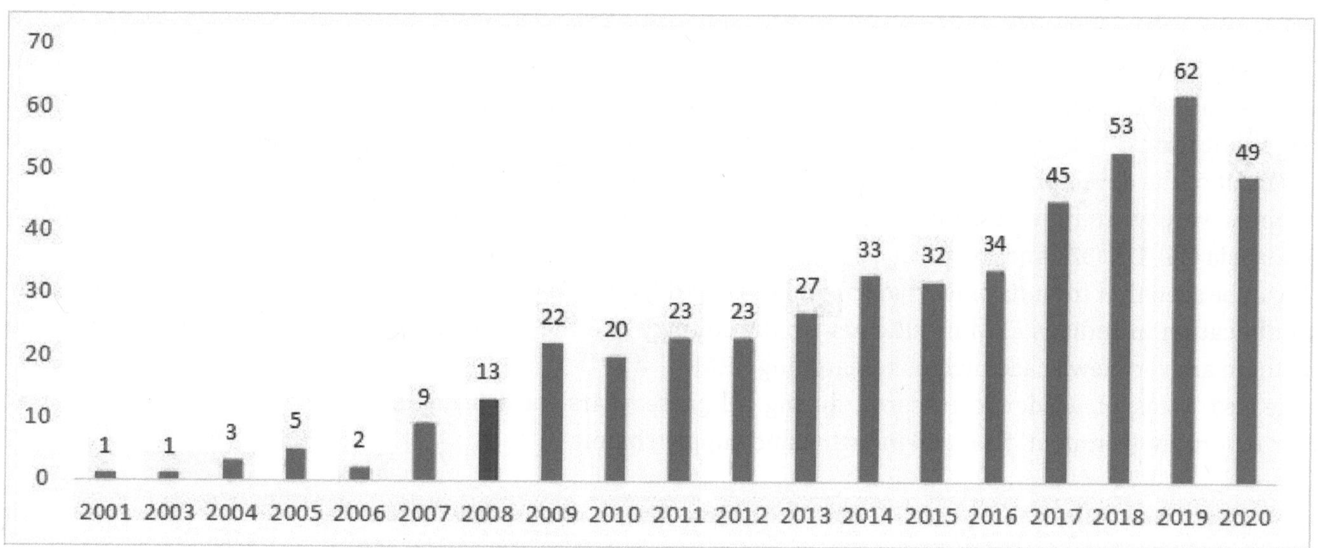

The graph shows the development of the publication of ERM research papers from the year 2001. During the initial years, few research papers were published on ERM, this is quite obvious as the ERM development was in a very initial stage. However, post the 2008 economic crisis, the focus on ERM research increased which can be seen from the increase in the number of research papers publications. During 2009, the publication almost doubled from 13 to 22 and then increased in later years. The interest in ERM increased in light of the 2008 economic crisis as well as the introduction of the risk-based capital regime both in the banking and insurance sector.

In risk-based capital, the banks or insurance Companies set aside capital based on the risk that is faced by the institution. Higher capital is required if the institution takes a higher risk, therefore, the Board of the Company is varied in this fact and focuses on ERM that helps in reduction in risk and thereby reducing the capital.

The data was also analyzed based on research on the country of the research.

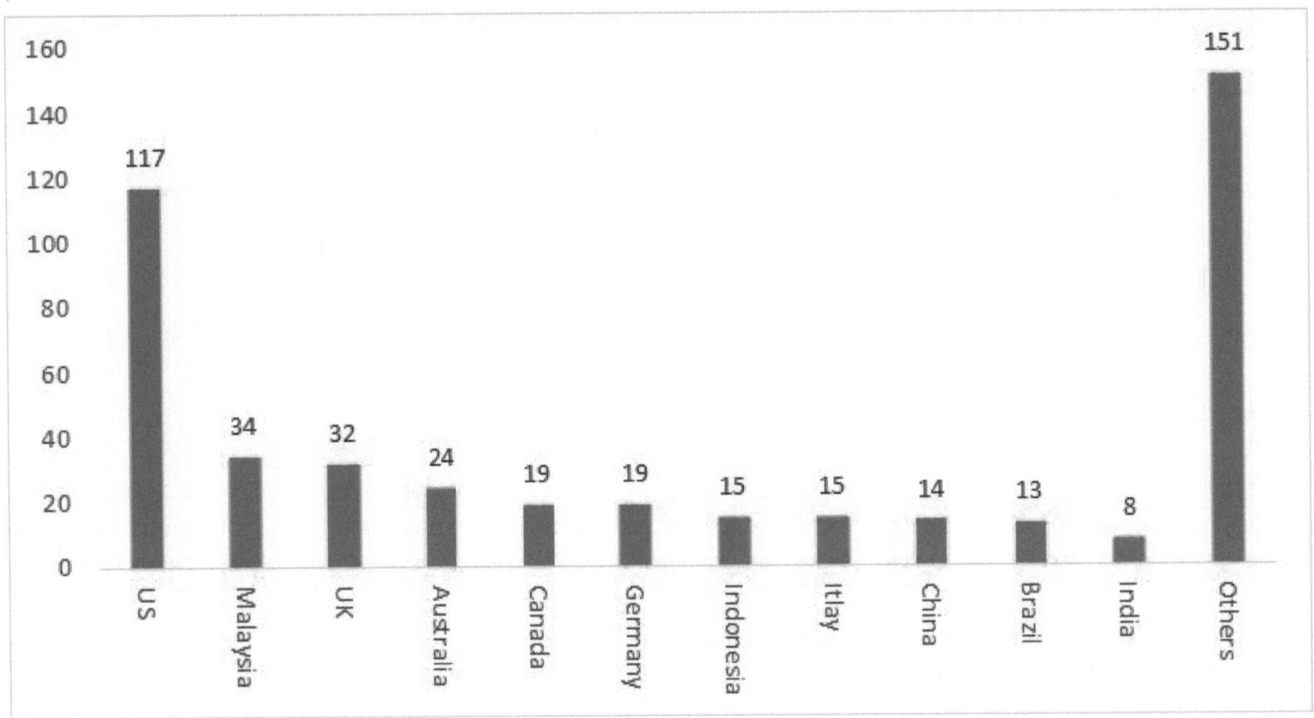

The graph shows the top 10 countries in a form of publication of research papers. There is a total of 60 countries that have published papers on ERM, therefore, the other category has such a high number. In the top 10 list of ERM paper publications, it can be seen that only two Asian countries are there, one is Malaysia and the other is Indonesia.

As most of the development in the area of risk-based capital happened in the developed market, therefore most of the papers were written in those markets. It can be seen that most of the papers were written in the US (117) followed by Malaysia (34), UK (32), and so on.

It can be seen that in India only 8 papers on ERM is published over the last two decades. One of the key reasons for low publication in India is ERM is quite new in the country and the insurance sector risk-based capital is not there. Also, there are very few academicians researching ERM.

The key areas of academic research during all these years have been in the areas of banking, insurance, construction, environment, financial industry, and supply chain.

- In banking, key countries are the UK, the US, Canada, Malaysia, and Taiwan. The key reason for the application in this country is that they have the Basel norm where the capital is a function of risk and ERM plays a very pivotal role
- The application of ERM in the Construction industry is a very welcome application where most countries in Asia such as China, Singapore, Malaysia, and Australia. It would be worth exploring the reason for the same further as this is a very non-traditional area.
- The application of ERM in the environment are in Australia, the Czech Republic, Turkey
- The study on ERM itself has happened in almost all the countries but the US and UK are leading in this field. It can be seen that the study on ERM increased over the period.

- As with the banking sector, the application of ERM in the insurance sector has mostly been in the US and the European Union. The risk-based capital has been in place in the US, however, the risk-based capital application increased during the latter half of 2010 leading to an increase in academic research on ERM in Europe.
- Similarly, the application of ERM in the Supply Chain has been in the US and Europe.

Conclusion

ERM is a relatively recent area of research where development started around the year 2000 and its pace increased post-2008 economic crisis. The prominent countries where most of the academic research has taken place are the US, UK, Malaysia, etc. The key areas of research are banking, insurance, construction, environment, financial industry, and supply chain. The application of ERM is increasing in many other areas than the traditional financial market. It has been proven in many academic pieces of research how ERM helps in increasing the shareholder's value. The wider application of ERM is a welcome sign. ERM is binding glue that combines risk management in one force across the Company.

FOUR

THE EMERGENCE OF ENTERPRISE RISK MANAGEMENT FROM THE INTRODUCTION OF RISK-BASED CAPITAL

Introduction

Though the concept of risk management is very old, almost as old as the beginning of human existence, however, enterprise risk management (ERM) is relatively new, started around the year 2000. The need for enterprise risk management increased over time due to the introduction of risk-based capital in the banking and insurance sector. In the insurance sector in the U.S., the Risk-Based Capital (RBC) was introduced in 1993, while in the banking sector, the RBC was introduced in 1999 (Basel-II), in European Union (31 countries), the Solvency-II, a similar version of RBC in the insurance sector was introduced in 2016. The preparation for the introduction of RBC in E.U. in the insurance sector started in 2002 with the recommendation of the KPMG report (on the request of the European Commission).

This chapter discusses the emergence of RBC and the introduction of ERM as they are closely related. RBC provides better protection to financial institutions; prior to the introduction of RBC, around 300 insurance companies failed or nearly missed together in U.S. and E.U. between 1975 to 2016.

Role of Capital in the Financial Sector

Capital is money that protects the solvency of the financial institution. This money belongs to the shareholders that are kept aside to be used only to protect the Company's solvency when all reserves are exhausted. Solvency capital act like a buffer or safety margin for overall reserves held by the financial institutions. There are strict regulatory investment guidelines on its investment, and therefore, the return on this money is compromised. In another way, a lower return to the shareholders on this solvency capital is a cost they pay in doing business in the financial sector over investing the same money in the stock market. So, there is a value attached to this money to shareholders; on the other hand, the regulator wants the protection of customers; therefore, they want this money to be as higher as possible. So, there is a dichotomy between shareholders and regulators on the amount of solvency capital to be kept.

Establishing Solvency Capital

Both banking and insurance institutions have been subject to failures since the early 1970s due to either economic downturn or emergence of the crisis, or other reasons. The insurance and banking regulators have worked towards strengthening the regulation to improve the financial condition of these institutions and increase the general public's trust. Therefore, the setting of the solvency capital has gone over various changes over successive decades in both the banking and insurance sectors. Risk management is another way to protect the financial institution from multiple risks; however, before 2000, risk management was limited to certain areas such as credit risk, liquidity risk, underwriting, reinsurance, assets and liability management, etc. This type of risk management is often called Silo-risk management, not taking a companywide view and is limited by specific organization departments.

In the banking sector, the Basel Committee was established in 1974 by ten central bank governors after serious issues in international currency and the banking failure of Bankhaus Herstatt in West Germany. In Latin America also, following the debt crisis in the early 1980s, there was a decrease in the capital ratios of leading international banks. Therefore, in the 1980s, the Basel committee started greater conversion towards capital adequacy with a weighted approach to the measurement of risks both on and off-balance sheet items. In 1999, the committee brought a new framework known as Basel-II based on the three-pillar approach of minimum capital requirement, supervisory review of institution's capital adequacy, and internal assessment process and disclosure to strengthen market discipline and sound banking practices. The shift in the banking supervision towards risk-based capital enhanced the focus on the management of risk that was enterprise-wide rather than focused only by a few departments. The concept of enterprise-wide risk management adoption was simple: better management of risk optimizes the capital requirement where shareholders and regulators are both interested.

Difference between Risk Management and Enterprise Risk Management

Risk management and Enterprise Risk Management are not the same. Risk management, on the one hand, is the process of risk identification and risk mitigation. ERM, on the other hand, is a risk management architecture that binds the risk management across the organization. It can be said that ERM is an enabler of Companywide risk management.

As the name suggests, 'Enterprise" means companywide risk management, a risk management which starts at the top of the hierarchy at the Board level and goes to the last employee in the supply chain of the Company.

Risk management, on the other hand, is a fragmented approach followed in silos by a few departments. Silo risk management does not work because risks are highly correlated and cannot be managed independently. Correlated risk refers to the simultaneous occurrence of many losses from a single event. For example, Natural disasters such as earthquakes, floods, and. hurricanes produce highly correlated losses: many homes in the affected area are damaged and destroyed by a single event

There is also a higher cost of management of independent risk as the benefit of diversification of risks will not happen. For example, liquidity risk may arise due to the crystallization of credit risk. If both the risks are managed independently, it will be very expensive; however, if just the credit risk is managed, liquidity risk may not result. In ERM, risk management is embedded in the daily working culture of the organization.

So, there is a great value in enterprise risk management as against silo risk management.

Insurance sector

Similar to the banking sector, insurance has also passed through turbulent times, leading to changes in regulation toward risk-based capital. As per the National Association of Insurance Commission (NAIC) [1], in the United States, risk-based capital (RBC) is an amount of money required to protect the solvency based on the size of the insurance company and the risks that the Company takes. A bigger-sized company taking a higher risk will need to hold higher capital. Before 1993 in the U.S., the **capital was set aside based on fixed capital standards** where insurance companies used to hold fixed minimum capital irrespective of financial condition, size, and risk profile. Between 1975 to 1990, 176 life and health insurance companies failed in the U.S., 80% of them came after 1982. This costed gratuity fund $515 million [2]. According to the 1992 U.S. General Accounting Office (GAO) [2] report, the average number of insolvencies between 1975 to 1982 was five insurance companies per year. **One of the key reasons identified in these insolvencies was fixed capital standards, where the capital assessment was not based on risks.** In 1993, in the U.S., RBC was implemented in life, health, property, and casualty insurance.

The key reasons for those failures were thin capital, fast growth, a small group of health and non-life companies with a high loss ratio, unprofitable products, and mismanagement and fraud. The GAO report highlighted that in the 1980s and early 1990s, the life and health insurance companies **competed aggressively against banks, mutual funds, and other financial institutions for investment-oriented customers. The products developed was interest rate-sensitive product with thin margins. To draw a high return on these products, insurers were investing in high-yielding risky assets.** But taking the high risk was not warranting higher capital as per the insurance regulation prevailing at that time.

U.S. led the introduction of RBC in the insurance sector earlier than other countries; in Europe, the European Commission presented a paper in 1999 on "The Review of the Overall Financial Position of an Insurance Undertaking" that started the discussion on modernization of insurance supervision [3]. In European Union (E.U.), the RBC version of solvency capital in the form of Solvency-II started in 2002 with the recommendation of the KPMG report (on the request of the European Commission) on the adoption of a three-pillars approach similar to the banking sector Basel-II [4]. The report recommended the first pillar as a quantitative requirement, the second pillar as supervisory activities, and the third pillar as reporting and public disclosure [5]. As per the paper [5], the Sharma report, named after the chairman of the Conference of Insurance Supervisory Services working group, Paul Sharma, studied the failure or near misses of insurance companies in E.U. **The report identified that most of the firms failed primarily due to under-pricing and mispricing, and many of them were small insurance companies.**

Further, European Insurance and Occupational Pensions Authority (EIOPA) analyzed in their report [6] the failure and near misses of 180 insurance companies in 31 countries in European Union between 1996 to 2016. The report observed that the most common causes of this failure and near misses were **lack of risk management skills, lack of experience or professional qualities of staff, inadequate or failed systems of corporate governance, and overall control.**

A few common reasons for various failures in the banking and insurance sector were inadequate capital, capital not based on risk, under-pricing and mispricing, excessive risk-taking, silo-based risk assessment, competencies issues, market competition, governance issues, etc. A direct relationship was observed between adequacy of capital, level of risks taken either based on size or amount of risk and companywide risk management practices.

The RBC was finally introduced in E.U. in 2016. The introduction of RBC in the U.S., E.U. and the rest of the world (Singapore, 2004) led to the development of ERM. In the ERM development, both the practicing and academic communities participated in their respective areas.

Integration of Enterprise Risk Management

In the practicing risk management world, the COSO (Committee of Sponsoring Organization of the Treadway Commission) came up with ERM standards in 2004, while the ERM framework by ISO 31000 was first published in 2009, indicating the correspondence with the development of RBC

The academic research in the field of ERM started around the year 2000. The analysis of 400 research papers published in ERM areas has below distribution by year of publication. Nevertheless, a clear relationship can be seen between the development of RBC across the world and the development of ERM. Y-axis is the number of papers published in a particular year.

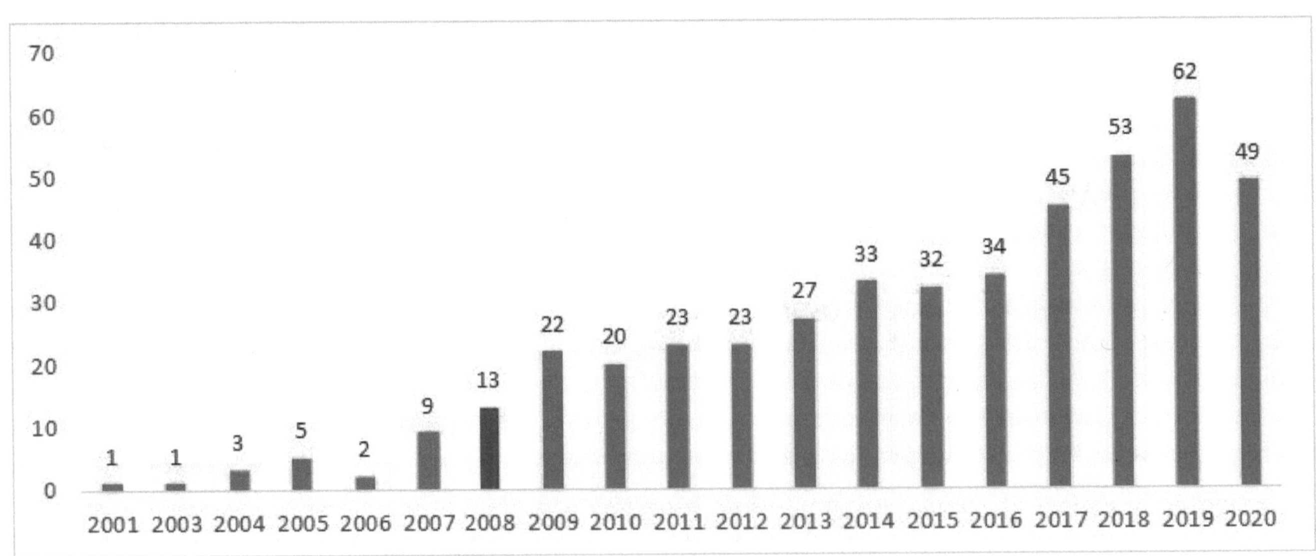

Growth of research paper publication on ERM

The graph shows the development of the publication of ERM research papers from the year 2001. During the initial years, few research papers were published on ERM; this is quite obvious as the ERM development was in a very initial stage. However, post the 2008 economic crisis, the focus on ERM research increased, which can be seen from the increase in the number of research papers publications. During 2009, the publication almost doubled from 13 to 22 and then increased in later years steeply.

A closer analysis by country of publication of these papers indicates a close relationship between the RBC development and ERM development in the U.S. and in E.U. from the graph below. The other countries include South Africa, Taiwan, Switzerland, Singapore, Denmark, the Middle East, and others.

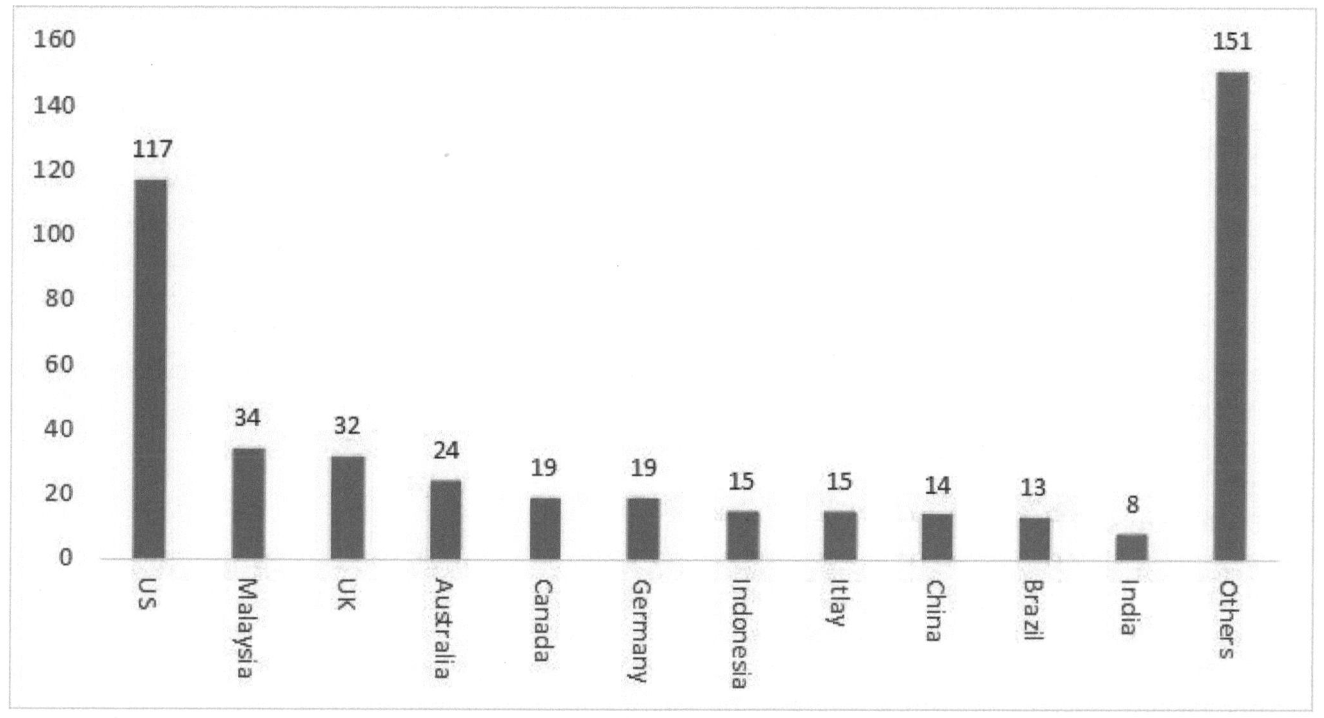

Country-wise ERM Research papers written

Further, these papers are primarily written in the banking and insurance sector. However, the application of ERM also spread in other areas like supply chain, construction industry, information technology, environment, and other financial sectors. The papers analyzed above also include these areas.

Conclusion

Financial institutions have been subject to failures over the last five decades, and regulators worldwide moved more toward risk-based supervision where risk is in the center, either in setting capital or its management. Risk-based capital has triggered the development of ERM across the world.

References

1. https://content.naic.org/cipr-topics/risk-based-capital
2. https://www.gao.gov/assets/ggd-92-44.pdf
3. https://www.eiopa.europa.eu/browse/solvency-ii/solvency-ii-background_en
4. https://www.insuranceerm.com/guides/solvency-ii-timeline.html
5. Eling M, Schmeiser H, Schmit JT. The Solvency II process: Overview and critical analysis. Risk management and insurance review. 2007 Mar;10(1):69-85. https://register.eiopa.europa.eu/Publications/Reports/EIOPA_Failures_and_near_misses_FINAL%20(1).pdf

FIVE

RISK MANAGEMENT FRAMEWORK

Introduction

This chapter covers details of COSO frameworks that came out in 2004 and 2017; this also covers ISO 31000 that came out in 2009 and 2018. The chapter discusses similarities and differences between these frameworks to help understand the fabrics of enterprise risk management. The chapter further explains the concepts of risk appetite, three lines of defense, and risk management policies.

These topics are fundamental to enterprise risk management, which a good risk management professional must know. The examples given are based on my practical working experience in the life insurance sector for over two decades in actuarial and risk management.

Risk Management Framework

In this chapter, we shall cover the risk management framework. We briefly covered the risk management framework in chapter 1, where we covered risk management policies, risk management process, risk appetite, and three lines of defense model. We shall go deeper into the risk management framework here. First, we shall start with the COSO framework, ISO, risk appetite, three lines of defense model, and risk management policies.

Overview of Risk Management Standards

Let's first look at how the development of risk management standards started; the first risk management standard was developed in Australia in 1995. Subsequently, the standards were developed in the US, UK, Japan, Canada, etc. Finally, some high-profile scandals, such as Enron, led to the development of SOX law. The overall approach of different standards is similar, and we shall see many of these standards are developed by re-arranging many topics that we have already covered. Still, we must know what is there in each of the standards.

Among the different standards, the organization should select the most suitable standard for their organization; for example, many organizations develop their risk management framework that suits their needs. Institute of Risk Management (IRM) also published its first standard in 2002. It is said that the IRM standard is suitable for non-risk management specialists. The COSO ERM Standard was first published in 2004 and revised in 2017. The COSO ERM standard covers both internal control and ERM framework, whereas ISO 31000 covers only the ERM.

The ISO 31000 standard was first published in 2009 and later revised in 2018.

COSO Standard 2004(ERM Advantage)

COSO 2004 standard has stated certain advantages of ERM, which are covered below.

Aligning risk appetite and strategy

Enhancing risk response decisions – Enterprise risk management provides the rigor to identify and select among alternative risk responses – risk avoidance, reduction, sharing, and acceptance. This we have considered under Accept, Manage, Transfer, and Avoid.

Reducing operational surprises and losses

Identifying and managing multiple and cross-enterprise risks–It must be noticed in a recent example of Uber Eats that the ride-hailing firm's delivery service made more money than its core cab business during the second quarter of FY 20. Uber Eats revenue increased by 103% compared to last year's same period, whereas Uber Cab service revenue dropped by 67%. Of course, this is due to Coronavirus, but this is how different events interact. This is another example of the integration of strategy and ERM.

Improving deployment of capital – Obtaining robust risk information allows management to assess overall capital needs and enhance capital allocation effectively.

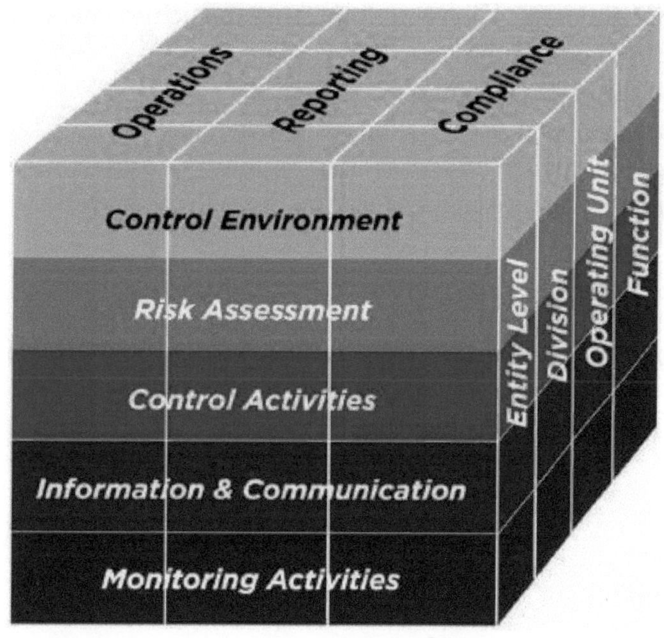

COSO Cube

COSO Cube- One Side

It discussed the definition of risk in the first chapter as an impediment to achieving objectives. It was also covered during the strategy chapter 3 as an objective is one of the key components of achieving the business plan to meet the strategy to achieve the mission. COSO covers strategy in four categories:

- *Strategy* – high-level goals supporting the mission
- *Operations* – effective and efficient application of resources
- *Reporting – reliability of reports*
- *Compliance – compliance with laws and regulations.*

These categories are distinct but overlapping categories – a particular objective can fall into more than one category addressing different entity needs and may be the direct responsibility of different individuals within the organization

As objectives related to **reporting and compliance** are related to adherence to laws and regulations which are under the control of the Company and enterprise risk management should provide reasonable assurance of achieving those objectives.

On the other hand, **strategic and operations objectives are** exposed to **external events** not always within the control of the Company, so enterprise risk management can provide reasonable assurance that management and its Board are providing oversight roles toward the achievement of the objectives.

COSO Cube- Second Side

As per COSO, ERM consists of eight components

1. *Internal Environment* – Under the internal environment, COSO talks about the tone of an organization and how risk is viewed and addressed.
2. *Objective Setting* – COSO talks about the objective setting, and even in the previous part, the objective setting was discussed. So setting an objective and managing it is a key part of risk management.
3. *Event Identification* – Internal and external events impacting the achievement of objectives must be identified, distinguishing between risks and opportunities.
4. *Risk Assessment* – Analysis on the basis of likelihood and impact,
5. *Risk Response* – Risk responses are Avoid, accept, transfer manage
6. *Control Activities* – Policies and procedures to address risk responses are effectively carried out.
7. *Information and Communication* –Effective communication through the leadership
8. *Monitoring*

The Third Side of the Cube

ERM Consider activities at all levels of the organization

- **Enterprise Level**
- **Division**
- **Business Unit Level**
- **Subsidiary level**

Limitation of Risk Management

COSO has also very well written about the limitation of ERM, which was noticed during the time of COVID.

My following text was quoted in Strategic Risk Website in Europe:

" Barring in the countries where Covid-19 reached in January and February, the world was waiting to spread the fire further, and it did," commented Sonjai Kumar, CMIRM, Global Ambassador, IRM India. "Why don't our risk management frameworks have buttons which prompt taking immediate actions rather than leaving the actions for the decision-makers?"

"It's like having an immediate sprinkler system as soon as a fire is visible or smoke is there. Suppose we need to protect the world from the next disaster that may come anytime in the presence of global warming. In that case, we need to tighten up the risk management framework that everyone must agree to as a part of the national constitution. The losses to human life and economic cost are enormous, we have to have a sprinkler system, and decision making cannot be left to choice."

So COSO correctly identified the limitation in the risk management framework.

COSO 2017 Framework

The new COSO 2017 version, *Enterprise Risk Management—Integrating with Strategy and Performance*, highlights the importance of strategy-setting and performance.

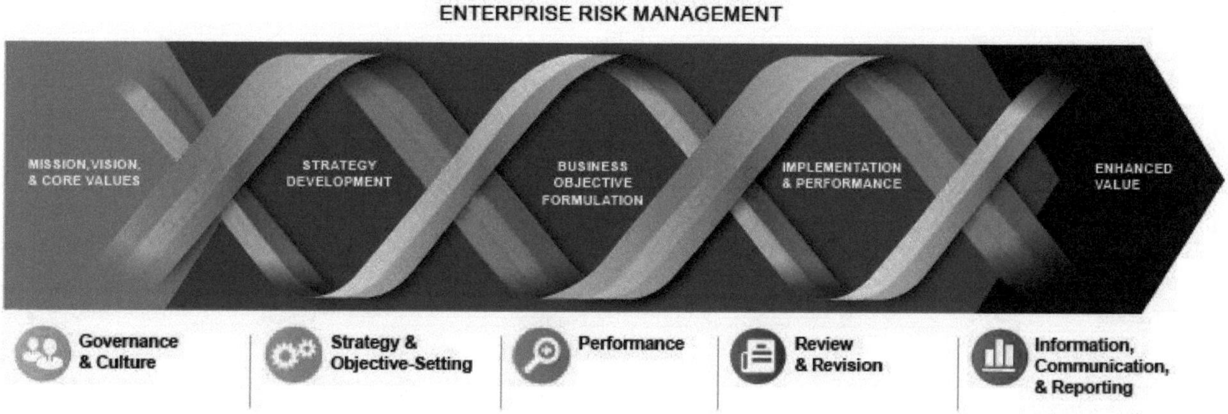

The COSO has five pillars as below:

1. **Governance and Culture**: Governance sets the **tone of the organization**, reinforcing the importance of and establishing **oversight** responsibilities for enterprise risk management. **Culture** defines ethical values, behaviors, and understanding of risk in the entity.

   In 2004 Cube, this principle was covered under the Internal Environment.

1. **Strategy and Objective Setting**: Enterprise risk management, strategy, and objective work in tandem.

   In 2004, this principle was covered under Objective Setting

3. **Performance**: Risks that impact the achievement of strategy and business objectives **should be identified and assessed.** Risks are **prioritized by severity** in the context of risk appetite. The organization then **selects risk responses** and takes a portfolio view of the amount of risk it has assumed. The results of this process are reported to key risk stakeholders.

   In 2004, this principle was covered under two heads, Event Identification, and Risk Assessment

4. **Review and Revision**: By reviewing entity performance, an organization can consider how well the enterprise risk management components are functioning over time and in light of substantial changes and what revisions are needed.

   This principle in 2004 Cube was covered under Risk Response and Control Activities

5. **Information, Communication, and Reporting**: Enterprise risk management requires a continual process of obtaining and sharing necessary information from both internal and external sources, which flows up, down, and across the organization.

This principle is a combination of Event identification where it talked about internal and external sources of risks and Information and Communication in 2004 Cube

The five components in the Framework are split into manageable 20 principles. Most of these principles are derived from the descriptions given above. Adhering to these principles can provide management and the Board with a reasonable expectation that the organization will be able to manage the risks associated with its strategy and business objectives.

1. Exercises Board Risk Oversight
2. Establishes Operating Structures
3. Defines Desired Culture
4. Demonstrates Commitment to Core Values
5. Attracts, Develops, and Retains Capable Individuals

Strategy & Objective-Setting

6. Analyzes Business Context
7. Defines Risk Appetite
8. Evaluates Alternative Strategies
9. Formulates Business Objectives

Performance

10. Identifies Risk
11. Assesses Severity of Risk
12. Prioritizes Risks
13. Implements Risk Responses
14. Develops Portfolio View

Review & Revision

15. Assesses Substantial Change
16. Reviews Risk and Performance
17. Pursues Improvement in Enterprise Risk Management

18. Leverages Information and Technology
19. Communicates Risk Information
20. Reports on Risk, Culture, and Performance

ISO 31000 2018
https://www.iso.org/obp/ui/#iso:std:iso:31000:ed-2:v1:en
ISO 31000 2009
https://www.iso.org/obp/ui/#iso:std:iso:31000:ed-1:v1:en
https://pecb.com/whitepaper/iso-31000-risk-management--principles-and-guidelines
https://risk-engineering.org/ISO-31000-risk-management/

ISO 31000 (2009)

Risk is defined as the effect of uncertainty on the organization's Objective. This definition comes from ISO 31000: "The effect this uncertainty has on an organization's objectives is "risk."

ISO 31000 risk management framework guides performing the risk management effectively and efficiently. As stated earlier, these are different sets of ways to manage the risk within an organization.

ISO 31000 can be used by any industry. Therefore, this Standard is not specific to any industry or sector.

This Standard can be applied during any stage of life cycle like strategies decisions, operations, processes, functions, projects, products, services, and assets.

There are three key building blocks of ISO 31000 standards: Principles, Framework, and Process, similar to COSO cube or newer structure. Let's first look at the principles

ISO 31000 Components

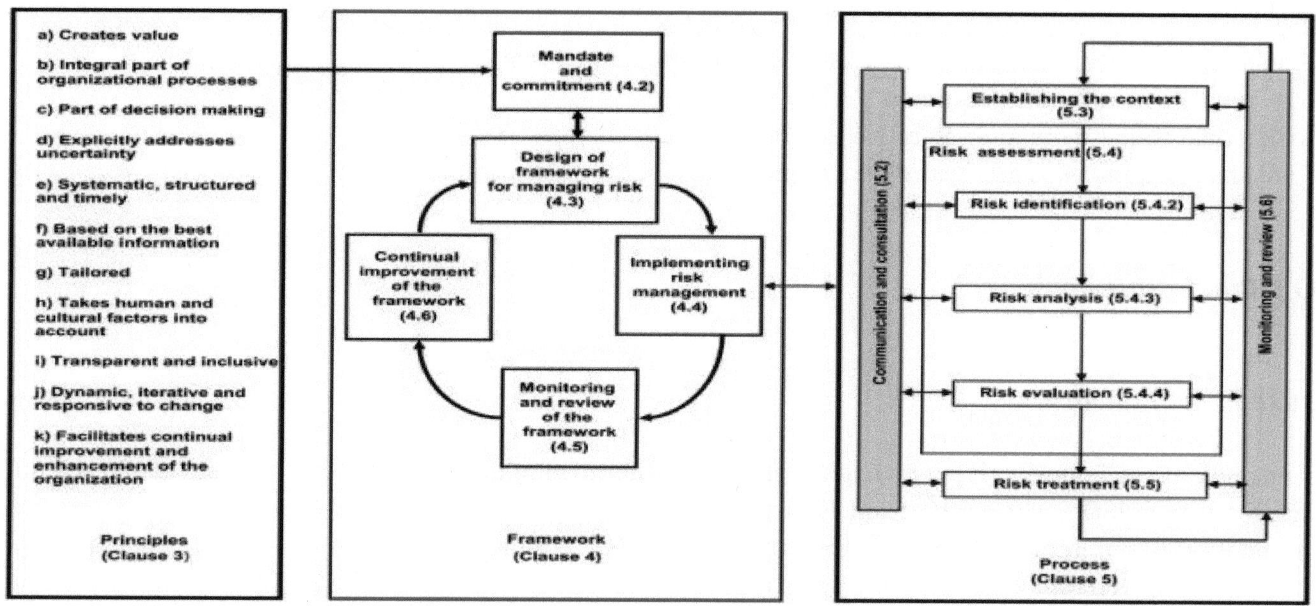

The **three building blocks of ISO 31000 risk management standard** are ***Principles, Framework, and Process***: There are some similarities and differences between the structure of COSO and ISO. Both are addressing the same issue of risk management. In the practical world, different organizations prefer any of the two standards. Different risk management professionals prefer one over another.

Briefly, let's look at the details of each of the three buckets.

ISO 31000 Principles

Clause 1: Principles of risk management

To have adequate risk management, an organization has to comply with these 11 principles:

1. Risk management creates and protects value; the opposite of this, it can be said that if risk management is not done, it destroys the value, and so far, it has been seen so many examples of Jet Airways, Cafe Coffee Day, and Nokia, etc.
2. Risk management is integrated part of organizational processes; This is fundamental to Enterprise Risk Management. And three lines of defense are one of the outcomes of the integration
3. Risk management is part of decision-making; the organization must go through the entire risk management process. For example, if Company is entering into a new distribution channel, the Company must identify all the risks and its mitigation if any of the risks materialize. However, this area is still under development in many Indian organizations.
4. Risk management explicitly addresses uncertainty; this is quite obvious.
5. Risk management is systematic, structured, and timely
6. Risk management is applied using the best available information for company to use; yes, one can identify the risks based on whatever is available. Often, all the information is not available to fully conclude; therefore, a disclaimer must be written about how the conclusion about risk is drawn so that the reader/management is aware of the details and authenticity of the data. Many times, getting data is a challenge.

7. Risk management is tailored; Risk management needs to be tailored based on the entire spectrum of the organization.
8. Risk management should take human and cultural factors into account;
9. Risk management is transparent:
10. Risk management is dynamic, iterative, and responsive to change;
11. Risk management helps in the continual improvement of the organization.

ISO 31000 Framework

Clause 2: Framework

Second, look at the Framework for managing risk and its iterative manner. There are five components within the Framework under ISO 31000 2009 version. First is

Mandate and commitment: The Framework's first component tells the organization to give a mandate for adopting and implementing risk management within the organization. One can say that is the first step in the direction, and once this direction is given, there should be a commitment to facilitate the process through defining risk management policy and objectives, ensuring legal and regulatory compliance, ensuring necessary resources are allocated to risk management, communicating the benefits of risk management to all stakeholders. This is like saying, yes, we have a will to move in the direction of risk management.

The second component of the Framework is

Design of Framework for managing risk: Next step is designing the Framework for the Company to manage the risk; the Company needs to ensure that the Company understands the risk, sets up risk management policies, sets accountability, integrates risk management with Company's process, identify resources and allocate, create communication structure with stakeholders, etc.

The third component of the Framework is

Implementing risk management: where the Company is to implement the risk management process by adopting the risk management process discussed in the next part under process.

The fourth component of the Framework is

Monitoring and review of the Framework: where the Company needs to ensure the effectiveness of the risk management within the organization by reviewing whether the risk management framework, policy, and plan are still appropriate. This is a mechanism to create monitoring performance to perform the feedback look.

The fifth component of the Framework is

Continual improvement of the Framework: to complete the feedback loop of the monitoring exercise.

ISO 31000 Process

Clause 5: Process

Under the third bucket of ISO 31000, the risk management framework is the risk management process that has already been covered under risk identification, measurement, management, Monitoring, and reporting. Here, the terminology is different with identification, analysis, evaluation, and treatment, and on the side is Monitoring and communication.

Under Establishing the context: the organization articulates its objectives, defines the external and internal parameters to be considered when managing risk, and sets the scope and risk criteria for the remaining process.

ISO 31000 2018-Principles

The definition of risk remains the same "effect of uncertainty on objectives."
The main changes compared to the 2009 version are the following:

1. Some of the principles of risk management have been changed; while many are retained, few are tucked into other categories. There is now a total of 8 principles, and one principle of creating and protecting value has come to the center.

   ISO 2009 Principles Changed to Red One

1. Risk management creates and protects value; Centre
2. Risk management is an integral part of all organizational processes;
3. Risk management is part of decision-making;
4. Risk management explicitly addresses uncertainty;
5. Risk management is systematic, structured, and timely; Tweaked to Structured and Comprehensive
6. Risk management is based on the best available information;
7. Risk management is tailored; - Renamed as Customised
8. Risk management takes human and cultural factors into account;
9. Risk management is transparent and inclusive;
10. Risk management is dynamic, iterative, and responsive to change;
11. Risk management facilitates the continual improvement of the organization.

ISO 31000 2018-Principles

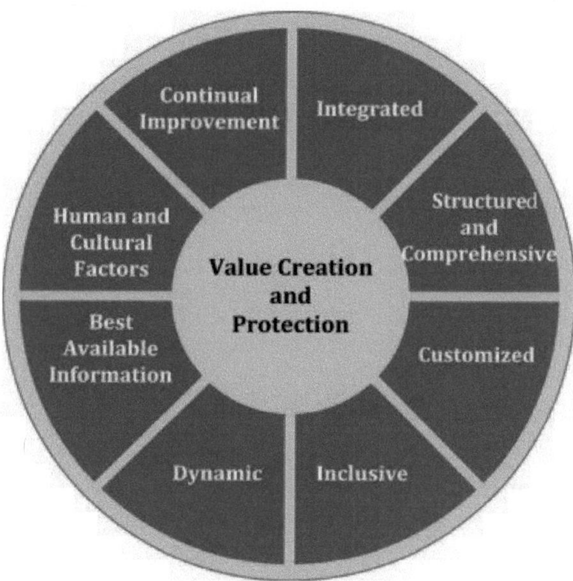

One can notice that Value creation and protection have come to the center; integration is next, followed by Structured and Comprehensive this is made systematic, structured, and timely. Customized is reworded from tailored. Rest, inclusive, dynamic, best available information, human and cultural factor, and continual improvement are the same.

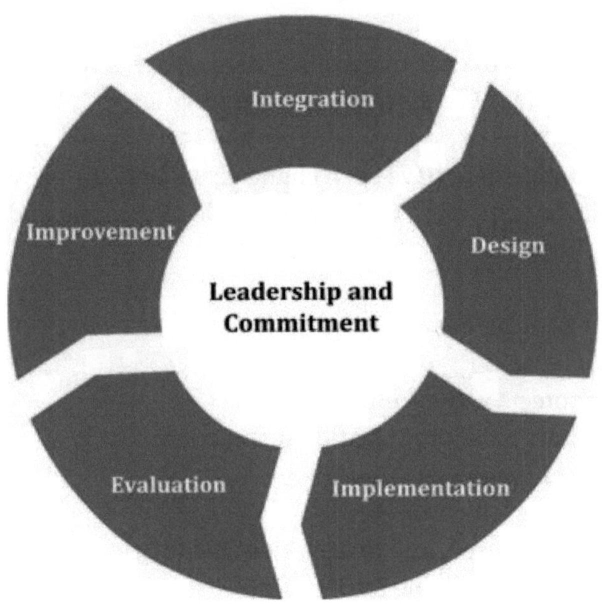

ISO 31000 2018-Framework

Leadership and Commitment

In ISO 31000 2009, the Framework started with Mandate and Commitment. In 2018, this is changed to Leadership and Commitment. This is a significant change as it needs to ensure that the management takes the buy-in on the development of risk management. As discussed in the previous lessons, the tone from the top is key to success and sending the right message to all down. This acceptance of risk management by the leadership automatically develops the risk culture, which is one important change the ISO made in 2018, though during 2009,

1. *Integration*

   It has been discussed that integrating risk management within the organization is a necessary condition for ERM.

2. *Design*

   In 2009, this was the design of the risk management framework, in 2018; this item is divided into five parts as

1. Understanding the organization and its context
2. Articulating risk management commitment
3. Assigning organizational roles, authorities, responsibilities, and accountabilities
4. Allocating resources
5. Establishing communication and consultation

3. *Implementation*

   This is the same as in 2009 regarding the implementation of risk management

4. *Evaluation &*
5. *Improvement*

In 2009 this was under one category of review and monitor. Here this also includes continual improvement.

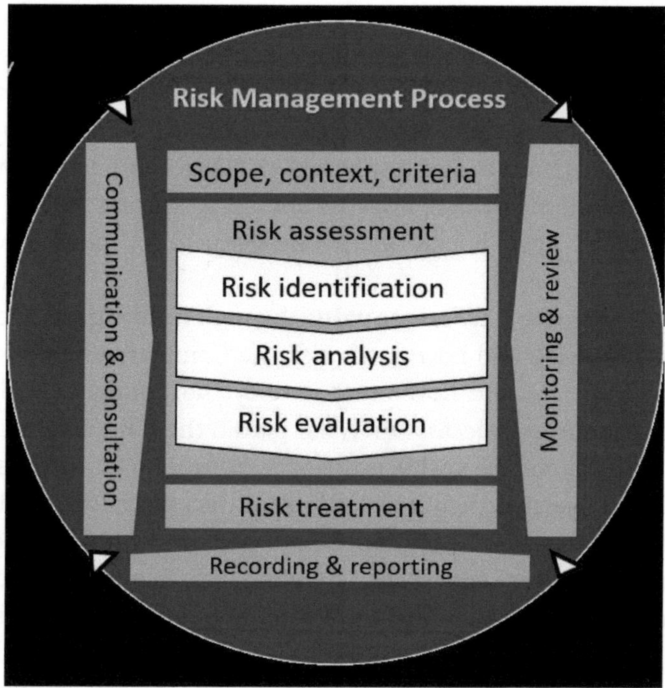

ISO 31000 2018-Process

Over the last many years, the risk management process has remained the same except for the nomenclature difference; only recording and reporting are explicitly added, which was inherently assumed under communication.

Risk appetite

Risk Appetite is a most important concept in successfully laying down the ERM methodology and, at times, not very well understood.

Risk appetite in the Context of Business

The COSO defines risk appetite as:

"The types and amount of risk, at a broad level, an organization is willing to accept in pursuit of value."

In order to do business, one has to take the risk; the question is how much to take the risk to achieve the business objective is the risk appetite. This is related to how much risk to take to innovate and which strategy to follow to achieve the vision. There could be various strategies to achieve the vision, and different path may require different risk appetite; the key question is which strategy to follow that optimizes the return on capital and deliver output.

The risk appetite should be framed in such as way that it has the flexibility to adjust based on emerging conditions; for example, the Company at a bad time, such as Coronavirus, may have to take more risk to achieve the same Objective than compared to a good time. If risk appetite is defined in terms of capital, the Company may have to shell out more capital to achieve the same Objective in a bad time compared to a good time. Many insurance companies across the world have kept additional money to meet the challenges of corona virus-related additional claims.

How to Set Risk appetite

There are various ways to set the risk appetite, and this has been mentioned in different documents that are available on the public platform, but not many of them talk about a systematic approach to set the risk appetite. However, ***COSO has come out with a Thought Leadership paper on risk appetite entitled 'Risk Appetite- Critical to Success," talking about an approach to risk appetite in a very systematic way, and anyone who wants to get a grip on risk appetite is a must-read paper***. The paper has taken details to discuss the risk appetite approach below.

It starts with a fundamental question, how risk appetite should be set and whether it should be **Objective**-based or **risk-based** once it has been decided bigger bucket where one wants to set appetite, whether Objective-based which is at a higher level of the risk level.

For example, if the Company's objective is to **"create value through innovation"**, then risk appetite is to be created around how the innovation will be made and how much risk the Company will take. What resources it will apply, what it will do and what it will not do, and how much money the Company will keep aside for research and development. What if the innovation is not successful? What plan B the Company will follow. How much loss is the Company ready to bear if it fails, of course, the upside is the opportunity. So it can be seen when the Company tries to create the risk appetite around the Objective, then it has to look at the macro-level of risks.

On the other hand, the Company may set the risk appetite based on the risks. For example, in a **volatile market, the risk is Company's profit may swing very adversely**. Therefore, the Company may create the boundaries and plan that it should not have profit lower than last year and work around the processes and strategies such that the overall resulting annual profit is not less than last year's numbers. So it can be said that a risk-focused risk appetite is a bottom-up approach while the objective focus is a top-down approach. The key point is that it provides the right way of approaching and knowing what the Company is doing.

The **third alternative could be a combination of objective focus and risk focus** which will have a combination of both upper boundaries of objectives and lower boundaries at the risk level. This will depend on what suits the Company and what best results give to them.

Choice of Setting Risk appetite

COSO has discussed five ways the Board and management can apply the risk appetite; they are

1. To adopt an approach of objective-focused or a, risk-based or combined
2. The focus is on monitoring performance and decision-making.
3. The focus is not only on risks the organization wishes to avoid but also on those it wishes to take on to enhance value.
4. The extent of natural tensions needed for appetite to add depth in discussions on analysis in support of decisions.
5. Stakeholder views of the organization will incorporate into the appetite.

Decision-making or Monitoring

Let's look into the detail of the monitoring and decision-making approach

Monitoring Based

One way to set the risk appetite is by creating various boundaries around the parameters such as profitability, capital, and customer satisfaction score and monitoring them against the appetite as time rolls by and see whether the Company is not breaching those boundaries. This may be looked at backward-looking risk appetite.

Decision-Making Approach

Another approach is to set the risk appetite, which is more futuristic, and use it in decision making. For example, the Company will not launch any new product if it does not meet the profit criteria and customer satisfaction score.

One may notice that both approach have the same example of profit and customer satisfaction scores. The difference is in the monitoring approach; the Company monitors its actual profit and customer satisfaction score to take a call on what to do if they breach risk appetite. This is backward-looking. While in the second example, before the product launch, one identifies the expected profit and customer satisfaction score. If both criteria are not met based on an initial estimation of the future, the decision to launch will not be taken.

From a common-sense perspective, the monitoring approach will always be backward-looking as it is compared against the benchmark. However, at the same time, decision-making will always be futuristic as it is about the future. Ideally, the Company should adopt both.

Enhancing Value, Natural Tension

Focus on Enhancing Values

The third approach the COSO has recommended is developing the appetite not only for downside risk but also for upside risk to enhance the value.

Natural Tension

COSO has defined Natural tension in risk appetitein such a situation where one appetite statement appears to support a decision while conflicting with another statement. For example, if a company is willing to accept more risk to grow its customer base but wants to keep the same gross margin while maintaining the current amount of risk to its profit margin. In this scenario, a marketing incentive to attract new customers through deep discounts creates a natural tension between these two aims.

This is a common situation in business where one decision has a slightly negative effect on another Objective, but that may be catering to a more significant aspect of the vision. So the message here is when different objectives have the opposite effect. The Company may have to see the overall impact of risk appetite rather than just the sum of the two individual risk appetites.

Stakeholders

Stakeholder's View

This is an important point as these talks about considering risk appetite in the context of different stakeholders such as shareholders, customers, regulators, environment, health hazards, etc. However, only considering the risk appetite from a shareholder's point of view may create long-term problems.

For example, in pursuing industrial development, the Companies may have added shareholder value but destroyed the environmental value. Therefore, in the coming time, the environment may become one of the key factors in corporate development to set appetite.

Similarly, slowly, the customer is taking center in every business, and the Companies must define how much risk they can take on the customer front, or they may shift to competitor's products.

Nokia did not consider entry into the smartphone when they were on top of the market during the middle of 2000 and, therefore, did not take any risk to enter into that line of business; the rest is history. Innovation has a high cost, but it may change the path of the Company.

Validating Risk Appetite

COSO has discussed validating appetite, and they have suggested the following approaches

1. Backtesting the assumptions
2. Compared with peer companies and industries, data
3. Looking at the emerging trend
4. What-if analysis

Back Testing Assumption

This approach is similar to the approach that is used in actuarial to test the assumptions taken in pricing or setting assumptions for new products. To draw that comparison, risk appetite is how much risk a company will take to fulfill its objectives. And this can be extended to how much deviation one can bear from the central assumption. This means if one is setting an assumption for a product that one wants to price using a long-term interest rate assumption (say 15 years) of 6%, then what is the risk appetite that the Company can bear if the interest rate is to move away from 6%. This could be, say 0.75% up or down. When the company price the product, they test the sensitivity of the profit margin using an interest rate is to be 6.75% or 5.25% and see whether the margin is still within the profit margin appetite or not. If not, then re-design the product.

The next question is how one sets interest rate assumptions. If the current interest rate is 7%, what should be the assumption for the next 15 years. The Company is to see what is the risk; the risk could be a fall in interest rate, so one will set 15 years interest rate assumption lower than 7%, but how much lower, one can draw this conclusion from past experience about the volatility in the actual interest rate over last many but the relevant time period and this volatility could be somewhere between 0.5% to1% and one apply judgment about the future and may conclude as a margin of prudence, one may choose 6% as the assumption of an interest rate for next 15 year to price a product. In **actuarial terminology, this is called the best estimate assumption.** But risk appetite is over and above 6%, which is taken in the above example as 0.75%. That is, if the actual interest rate in the future goes below 5.25%, the Company will withdraw the product. **This is one example of back-testing the assumption.**

Scanty Data, Emerging Trend, and What if Analysis

If a company does not have its own experience entering a new market, it can look at the industry data or data of those companies that already have similar products. They must adjust the assumption based on their experience, shareholders' expectations, and other factors and use them in the new product. Industry data is also used to compare experience against the peer group to assess how the Company stays in the market.

Looking at the emerging trend is very important because past data may or may not be relevant, so in the actuarial world, a credibility factor is used to give the amount of weightage to current and past data. Initially, more weight is assigned to the past data, and the reliance on emerging experience increases as new information starts coming and updating the assumption. As risk is all about the future and uncertainty, life insurance, in particular, is a long-term business, and lots of risk management techniques are used in setting different assumptions. To price a product, one needs interest rate, mortality, expense, lapses, taxes assumptions, etc., so it can be seen that in pricing one product, how many risk factors are to consider. And one is to monitor all the assumptions as time rolls by to assess the emerging experience.

What if

What if is another strong risk management tool to check whether the Company can stay within risk appetite or not. For example, taking the above interest rate assumption forward, the Company wants to test how much the interest rate to fall so that their margin will turn out to be zero. And say this interest rate comes out to be 4.5%; that is at a 4.5% interest rate, Company's profit margin will be 0%.

In this case, for the next 15 years' time, with today's interest rate at 7% and the product is priced at 6% while 0% margin will be at a 4.5% interest rate, then the Company knows when to take a decision on this product, and such decisions are generally withdrawing the product from the market if interest rate starts falling.

In Japan, there have been so many examples, and many insurance companies lost billions of dollars when the interest rate fell to a record low.

So all the methods listed in COSO are already used as an actuarial tools in the long financial analysis.

Risk Tolerance

Risk appetite is a broad-based description of the desired level of **risk** that an entity will take in pursuit of its mission. **Risk tolerance** is about acceptable variation in outcomes related to specific performance measures linked to objectives the entity seeks to achieve.

Risk tolerance is the level of risk that an organization can accept **at an individual risk level**, whereas risk appetite is the **total risk that the organization can bear in a given risk profile**, usually expressed in aggregate. Risk appetite statements are often translated into a detailed set of risk tolerance limits across the enterprise.

For example, a company will take a risk up to the risk appetite of Rs.200 Cr, say for five risks; however, for each risk, the tolerance range is plus and minus 10%, but the overall risk should remain within Rs.200 Cr. For example, if the respective capital allocated for each of the five risks is Rs.40 Cr, the tolerance range is within Rs. 36 Cr to 44 Cr; however, the total should not breach the overall limit of Rs.200 Cr.

Three Lines of Defense

The goal of any organization is to achieve its business objectives. These objectives involve taking opportunities, pursuing growth, taking risks, and managing those risks. Failure to take the appropriate risks and properly manage and control risks can prevent an organization from accomplishing its business objectives. Therefore, there is a need to create the right structure to facilitate taking appropriate risks and managing them. Such structure is the three lines of defense model.

The three lines of defense model help segregate the roles and responsibilities of risk management and control within the Company.

Three lines of defense help in effective operation, reduce gaps, and avoid unnecessary duplication of effort. This helps the Board of directors receive unbiased information about the organization's most significant risks and how management is responding to those risks.

Three Lines of Defense Structure

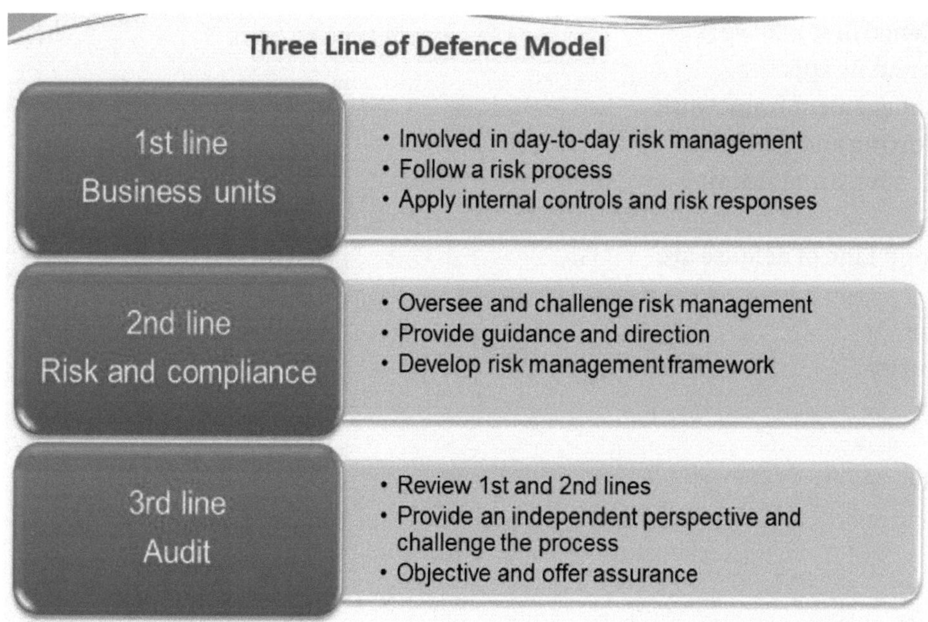

In the Three Lines of Defense model, front line management is the first line of defense, risk management, and compliance functions are the second line of defense, and Audit and independent assurance is the third line.

Neither governing bodies nor senior management is part of three "lines" of defense. Instead, governing bodies and senior management are the primary stakeholders served by the three lines.

First Line of Defense

1. The first line of defense is the business and process owners who facilitate the achievement of business objectives by managing risks. This includes taking the right risks. The first line owns the risk, design, and execution of the organization's controls to respond to those risks. The first line is responsible for

    a. Day-to-day risk management decision making
    b. Risk identification, assessment, mitigation, monitoring, and management
    c. Effective implementation of the risk management framework
    d. The first line of defense examples are Sales, Marketing, Finance, Operations, Investments, Strategy, HR, etc.

Second Line of Defense

2. The second line of defense is the risk and compliance function

    a. The second line of defense functions are separate from the first line of defense but are still under the control and direction of senior management
    b. The second line is essentially an oversight function that owns many aspects of the management of risk.

    The typical role of the second line of defense are:

- Review and challenge first-line work
- Oversight of risk and its appetite
- Develop a risk management framework
- Independent reporting and escalation
- Provide specialist advice and training

Examples of Second Line of defense are

- Risk Management
- Information Security
- Physical Security
- Quality
- Health and Safety
- Compliance etc

Third Line of Defense

3. The third line of defense assures senior management and the Board over both the first and second lines' efforts

    a. The third line of defense is to provide assurance to the Board

    The role of the third line is

- Independent assurance that risk management framework has complied with operating effectiveness
- Review appropriateness, effectiveness, and adequacy of the risk management framework.

The audit team is in the Third Line of Defense.

Role of Senior Management and Board of Directors

Senior management and the Board have an important role to play. Senior management is responsible for the selection, development, and evaluation of the system of internal control with oversight given by the Board of directors.

Senior management and the Board is not a part of one of the three lines of defense. Instead, they are collectively responsible for setting the organization's objectives, defining high-level strategies to achieve those objectives, and creating governance structures to best manage risk.

Senior management to support governance, risk management, and control. In addition, they are responsible for the activities of the first and second lines of defense. Therefore, their engagement is critical for the success of the overall Model.

Risk Management Policies

Importance of Risk Management Policies

Reactive mindset: In many organizations, risk management is a reactive exercise process where the Company acts when a crisis happens and then start formulating risk management practices followed by developing policies and procedure. Such a mindset is not proactive, leads to many losses, and tarnishes the reputation because it is unprepared for uncertainties.

Policies are not useful: Such a mindset could result from the fact that the Company believes that policies and procedures are merely for documentation purposes and is not able to realize the true value of policies and following them.

Defining policies: Risk Management Policies are high-level documents that define principles and objectives on what is covered under the given document; for example, if it is a market risk policy, it determines what is covered or not. Define different risks such as under-market risk, covering interest rate, equity, exchange rate, commodity risk, etc. It defines the roles and responsibilities of the members etc. Such policies set the direction and tone for managing the risk. This helps greatly as it sets out the clear principles in advance on how to deal with risk on a proactive basis.

An extreme example of Coronavirus caught the world on the wrong foot as no one was prepared to deal with such a situation. Therefore, different countries took different routes to handle it but followed each other in some way. Consequently, it has been said from the beginning that if you fail to identify the risk, you fail to manage it.

Importance of Risk Management Policies-2

One of the key advantages of framing risk management policies is giving direction to the Company on how to handle each of the risks that the Company may face. On the risk management front, at an overall level is the "Risk

Management Framework Policy," which defines the overall way to manage the risk. It sets out high-level guidance at the concept level. Individual policies follow this, and this is based upon the line of business the Company is doing. For the financial sector, manufacturing sector, garment industry, or any other industry, the risk management policies will vary according to the products that the Company is selling, and risk will change for each Company.

For the manufacturing sector, the key risk could be ancillary industries that supply the different parts to manufacture the product. For warehousing companies, the key risk could be how goods are kept in storage, while for the mutual fund industry, risk could be the fluctuation of the prices of different assets. So different companies will frame different risk policies to manage them.

Once the policies are approved by the Board and key activities are written down in the policy, it becomes easy to communicate with all the stakeholders and implement different risk management activities. For example, suppose it is written down in the policy that risk assessment and mitigation are mandatory in all decision-making. In that case, it leaves little choice for everyone not to do this activity. It has been seen that such documentation helps in implementing different risk management processes.

As it is covered in the previous chapters and mentioned that the risk assessment is not performed in many Indian companies during the business plan or in the strategy development, one of the reasons for such absence is that the policy is not carefully drafted.

The policy may contain to-do items in some organizations, but its implementation is weak due to the poor risk culture.

So, in summary, risk management policies are not just a piece of paper; they have their importance in the success of the business. It can be said that risk policies and their implementation are two sides of the same coin.

A Big Picture

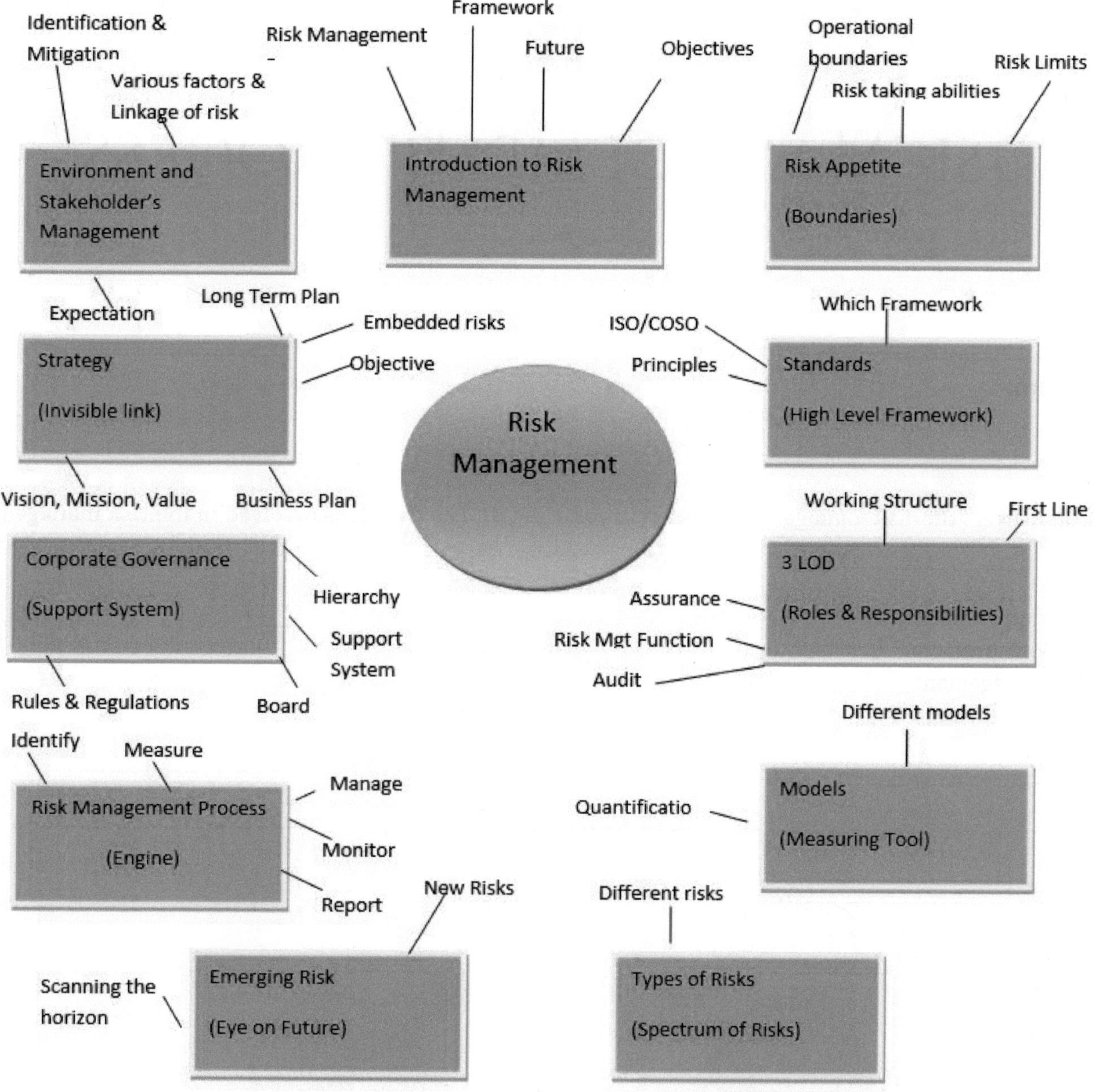
Risk Management
Environment and Stakeholder's Management
Identification & Mitigation
Various factors & Linkage of risk
Expectation
Introduction to Risk Management
Risk Management
Framework
Future
Objectives
Risk Appetite
(Boundaries)
Operational boundaries
Risk taking abilities
Risk Limits
Strategy
(Invisible link)
Long Term Plan
Embedded risks
Objective
Vision, Mission, Value
Business Plan
Standards
(High Level Framework)
Which Framework
ISO/COSO
Principles
Corporate Governance
(Support System)
Hierarchy
Support System
Rules & Regulations
Board
3 LOD
(Roles & Responsibilities)
Working Structure
First Line
Assurance
Risk Mgt Function
Audit
Risk Management Process
(Engine)
Identify
Measure
Manage
Monitor
Report
Models
(Measuring Tool)
Different models
Quantificatio
Emerging Risk
(Eye on Future)
New Risks
Scanning the horizon
Types of Risks
(Spectrum of Risks)
Different risks

SIX

Risk Management Process

Introduction

This chapter covers the risk management process in some detail. The five steps involved in the risk management process are

1. Risk Identification
2. Risk Measurement
3. Risk Management
4. Risk Monitoring
5. Risk Review

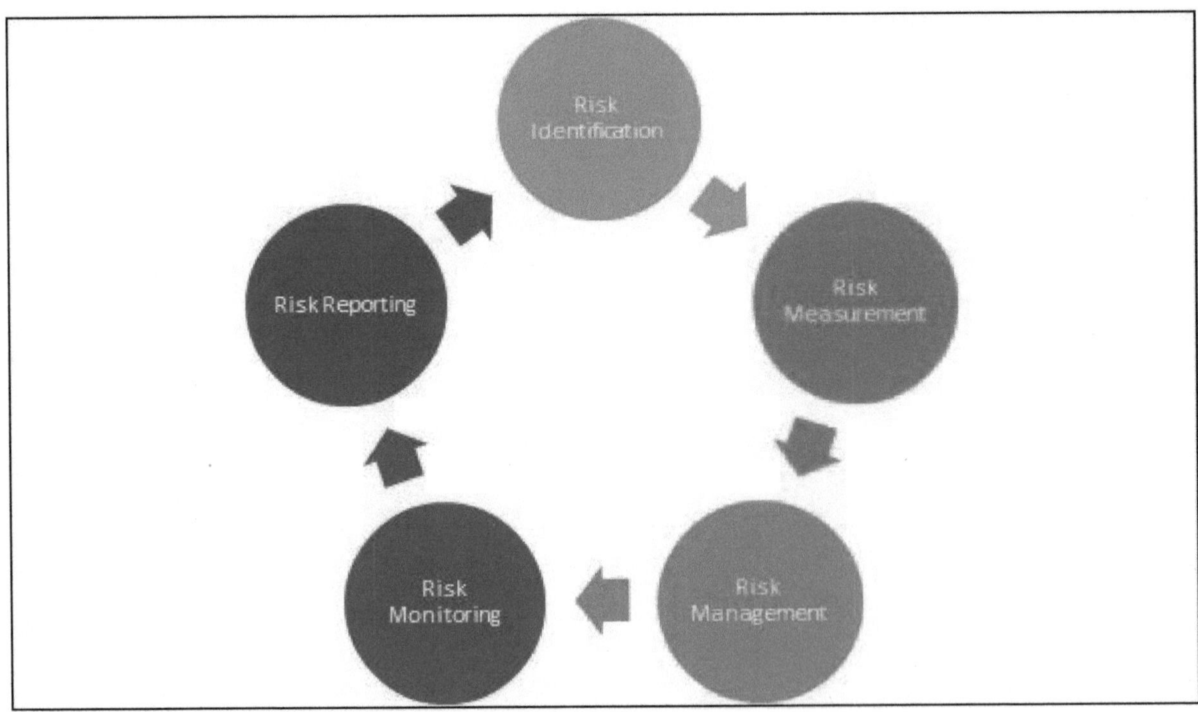

Risk Management Process

This chapter is the heart of risk management or the engine of risk management. Without this chapter, risk management is incomplete. This chapter was briefly introduced in Chapter 1 with risk identification, risk measurement, risk management, risk monitoring, and risk reporting. It has been seen that the same has been described with different names in different risk management standards such as COSO or ISO 31000.

Risk identification

Risk identification is the first and most important step and without the identification of risk, the engine of risk management cannot start. There are many risk identification methods such as

- Documentation Reviews
- Brainstorming
- Delphi Technique
- Interviewing
- Root Cause Analysis
- Swot Analysis (STRENGTH, Weakness, Opportunities, And Threats) ...
- Checklist Analysis

Documentation review of risk identification method is the review of previous reports like annual reports, review of reports of the similar industry which can give an idea about the prevalent types of risks, review of previous audit report, previous minutes of the meeting, etc. Such a review of the report can be a good starting point for risk identification purposes.

The brainstorming method is jotting down all the ideas that come in respect of related risks. It is not necessary that all the points are relevant, idea is to list down all the possible points

Delphi Technique is a refined method of questionnaire method that will be discussed.

Interviewing method is taking firsthand information from the relevant people; this can be the Head of the function, CEO, CXOs, etc. Discussion with subject matter experts can also help in risk identification.

Root cause analysis is another way for risk identification. This is about cause finding mission which has led to the crystallization of risks in the past. The idea is to fill those gaps so that such risks do not occur in the future.

The SWOT analysis identifies any opportunities that arise from organizational strengths, and any threats arising from organizational weaknesses. The technique is particularly useful for identifying internally-generated risks arising from within the organization

The checklist method is an exhaustive list of risks to cross-check that any of the risks are not left out.

Brainstorming Method

Brainstorming sessions are made with respect to generating random points with respect to the risks under consideration. The objective of the session is to be clearly understood by the participants. This session draws on the creativity of the participants that can be used to generate a list of risks.

Such sessions are to be facilitated; the participants collaborate together to identify the risks that may be known by some participants in the group.

In such a session, risks that are known unknowns may emerge, and perhaps even some risks that were previously unknown unknowns may become known.

Facilitating a brainstorming session takes special leadership skills, and, in some organizations, members of the internal audit and ERM staff have been trained and certified to conduct risk brainstorming sessions. In addition to well-trained facilitators, the participants need to understand the ERM framework and how the brainstorming session fits into the ERM process.

The participants may very well be required to do some preparation prior to the session. Using a cross-functional team of employees greatly increases the value of the process because it throws light on how risks and objectives are correlated and how they can impact business units differently.

The brainstorming session helps in risk identification bottom-up, where the micro-level of risks is identified. Risk Control Self Assessment is one such example of brainstorming where different teams sit with the risk function members to identify the area say, finance, sales, marketing, etc. This method is more useful when there are groups of people or maybe when the company is identifying the risks for the first time.

Flowchart Method

The flowchart method is a systematic demonstration of various linkages between the processes and different risks which would otherwise be difficult to spot. The visual presentation allows for thinking more widely and establishing relationships. In this method, there are fewer chances to miss out on risks as it is like a mind map.

The Flowchart Method is used to graphically and sequentially depict the activities of an operation or process to identify exposures.

This method can be used for different purposes such as risk identification in products, dependency analysis, decision analysis, and critical path analysis.

These methods can illustrate interdependency within your organization; they can easily pinpoint bottlenecks and can determine a critical path.

A very useful method in analytical thinking.

SWOT Analysis Method

SWOT (Strengths-Weaknesses-Opportunities-Threats) analysis is a technique often used in the formulation of strategy.

The strengths and weaknesses are internal to the company and include the company's culture, structure, and financial and human resources.

The major strengths of the company combine to form the core competencies that provide the basis for the company to achieve a competitive advantage.

The opportunities and threats consist of variables outside the company and typically are not under the control of senior management in the short run, such as the broad spectrum of political, societal, environmental, and industry risks.

For SWOT analysis to be effective in risk identification, the appropriate time and effort must be spent on thinking seriously about the organization's weaknesses and threats.

The tendency is to devote more time to strengths and opportunities and give the discussion of weaknesses and threats short shrift.

Risk Questionnaire and Risk Survey

A risk questionnaire that includes a series of questions on both internal and external events can also be used effectively to identify risks.

For the external area, questions might be directed at political and social risk, regulatory risk, industry risk, economic risk, environmental risk, competition risk, and so forth.

Questions on the internal perspective might address risk relating to customers, creditors/investors, suppliers, operations, products, production processes, facilities, information systems, and so on.

Questionnaires are valuable because they can help a company think through its own risks by providing a list of questions about certain risks.

Whether using a questionnaire or survey, the consolidated information can be used in conjunction with a facilitated workshop. In that session, the risks are discussed and defined further.

Delphi Technique

The **Delphi Technique** refers to the systematic forecasting method used to gather opinions of the panel of experts on the problem being encountered, through the questionnaires, often sent through the mail. In other words, a set of opinions pertaining to a specific problem, obtained in writing usually through questionnaires from several experts in the specific field is called a Delphi technique.

In a Delphi technique, the group facilitator aggregates all the anonymous opinions received through the questionnaires and sent them two or three times to the same set of experts. The experts are required to give justification for the answers given in the first questionnaire and on the basis of it, the revised questionnaire is prepared and is again sent to the same group of experts.

The experts can modify their answers in accordance with the replies given by other panel members. The objective of a Delphi technique is to reach the most accurate answer by decreasing the number of solutions each time the questionnaire is sent to the group of experts. The experts are required to give their opinion every time the questionnaire is received, and this process continues until the issues are narrowed, responses are focused, and the consensus is reached.

The Delphi Method is useful in 2 scenarios.

1. When there are many experts involved, the consensus is not likely to happen quickly.
2. When the experts are geographically spread out, it is difficult to get them into a room to discuss, brainstorm and come up with the best strategy.

When there are many experts, they all generally postulate their own theory, and it is often difficult to come to a common solution or a consensus.

Experts tend to stick to their own views and are not prepared to accept other theories in favor of their own theory. Their ego often comes in between. And we can't afford to hurt the experts or their egos... we really need their expertise.

Importance of Risk Identification-through "What if" mindset

COVID 19 has reinforced the business attention toward the risk and its management. Some of the risk that could have slipped earlier (pre-COVID era) through the business leader's mind is now in the priority list. Even people have become risk-conscious evident from the increase in the take-up rate of term insurance and health insurance.

The 2008 economic crisis also had a huge economic impact that improved corporate governance and enterprise risk management.

This section discusses the fundamental factor important in the management of risk. This fundamental factor is 'Risk Identification". Unless or until risks are not identified, the risk mitigation process cannot take off. Because of a lack of risk identification, most of the risks fall through the cracks. There are innumerable instances where the weak signals are available but not read properly leading up to the crisis.

Recall the early days in December 2019, when COVID had just hit China's Wuhan city, most people used to discuss this event over a cup of coffee rather than planning for mitigation action if that hit their shores. Similarly, another classic example is Nokia which could not sense the change in the market dynamics towards the smartphone, Kodak did the same thing with the digital camera despite they were the first to bring the same. What is common in all the above examples, risks could not be identified at the right time and the rest is history.

So, what is the most important factor for risk identification? Governance, risk culture, etc. comes very late in the list, the most important factor is the "What if" mindset. "What if" mindset is an important factor for risk identification.

"What if" Mindset

At the core, the "what if" mindset is a personal perception of risk. Because risk identification is human-driven, there are a lot of personal elements associated. People are often in a "denial mode" about the crystallization of risk with thinking driven by the opinion that "a certain event will not occur". Such thinking is not based on hard facts or data but rather just a gut feeling. When such a gut feel is included in the professional risk judgment, risks fall through the cracks.

During the early period of COVID, it was assumed in the life insurance industry that a reduction in accident-related claims due to lockdown may offset the increase in COVID-related claims. However, the reality today is that every insurance company has lost millions of rupees in paying COVID-related claims so much so that in 2020 most of the reinsurance rates were increased by 30% to 40% ultimately passed to customers by life companies. Many of the players have stopped writing the Group Term plan in 2021 due to adverse COVID claims.

Again, risks were missed here, not in 2020, but much before when the term insurance price war was going on over the last two decades.

What "what if" mindset does, it helps in spotting and smelling the weak signals present. Keeping additional capital for adverse scenarios may not work all the time, also it costs the shareholders. The future will require more proactive risk identification rather than reactive or in a "denial mode".

There is a difference between a pessimist and a careful approach. A pro-risk identification mindset may term it a pessimist but such identification should be based on signals rather than opinion. Such identifications should be based on rationale and logic.

Having such recent massive experience on missing some of the key risks, this is a time to have a what-if mindset to improve the risk identification.

Development of "What if" mindset

A personal predisposition to risk recognizes the core element of the "what if" mindset of the individual. This is more from genetic makeup. Other elements that determine such a mindset are an Individual's background, cautious nature, education, etc. Also, all living and breathing organisms in this world are born risk managers. Antibodies that help fight diseases are natural risk neutralizers. The environment corrects itself to a large extent. A newborn baby holds the mother's cloth even if the baby is held tightly. Even a dog crossing the road looks on both sides. So, there is an element of risk awareness in all living and breathing organisms. There is only a need to convert some part of this natural risk-aware behavior into a professional application.

Apart from human natural risk-aware behavior, historic learning from the past enriches the experience of individuals and community in developing further "what if" mindset. The entire subject of probability and statistics is based on using past data that guide the future is well established. Such historic analysis may help in converting some of the weak signals into a more meaningful conclusion. Experience of using past data or information makes an individual "experienced" and their judgment becomes more important. The use of past data helps in better-identifying risks.

Herd mentality does not allow logical thinking and may result in missing risk. This is also related to human behavior, where there is a tendency to follow the masses. This does not make one a good risk manager. The decision should be based on an individual's judgment rather than blindly following others. There are many examples where people lost money due to following the masses' act. Herd behavior has been seen in the stock market investment when the market is on the rise, during the boom period of the property market in India between 2005 to 2014 many investments have been made then, now either have lower than purchase value or money is stuck in semi-constructed buildings. Only a few people realized during this period that it was a bubble and made a judicious judgment.

Risk culture depends on values, beliefs, knowledge, attitudes, and understanding of risk. Risk culture is a natural extension of personal disposition to risk that implies the ability to spot risks. Apart from natural ability, human has immense power of adaptability, and therefore there is a great value in risk training within the organization and making understand employees the value of a "what if" mindset. Some of the elements that help in enhancing the risk culture are tone from the top including dealing with bad news, governance, risk-based decision and rewards, and enhancing competency. Other ways could be incentives to learn and apply risk management, it has been seen that when the incentives are given on learning and applying risk management, the risk culture has improved many folds. A classic example comes from learning incentives given to actuarial folks on passing each of their examinations and their growth is phenomenal in the insurance sector.

Another related area to improve the "What if" mindset is to focus on emerging risks because emerging risk gives an idea about what risk is brewing. For example, in today's environmental context, environmental risk is an emerging risk and this should raise a lot of "what if" questions in every sector of the economy. Leaving this risk smoldering may engulf the world in the next couple of decades. According to Swiss Re, the impact of climate change could be close to 10% of total economic value by mid-century if at the currently-anticipated trajectory, and the Paris Agreement and 2050 net-zero emissions targets are not met. The adverse impact of COVID gives a very good idea about what if the environment is left at the current stage unattended.

Risk training helps in developing the mindset about risk awareness and start thinking about how risk can crystalize. Due to the lack of formal risk management education in the course curriculum at any level, despite humans being natural risk managers, the personal risk management instinct is not converted into a professional application. Therefore, risk training remains the most effective source of risk management dissemination information systems. With more awareness about risks in the future, many courses may be developed at a formal education level but till that time risk training can fill the gap.

To assess the impact of risk in the future, a very good tool is stress testing which provides quantification of risk. This tool is in application in many financial institutions such as banks and insurance companies. However, the challenge is it is at a different level of application in different countries based on their development of risk management. In some financial institutions stress testing is only of academic importance where mitigation actions are not planned for the stressed scenario. This need to be changed to have a mitigation plan for all plausible stress scenarios.

At times, the single emerging risk may not look very daunting but their accumulating impact could be devastating. Alternatively, a chain reaction of risks could also be considered as some of the second and third-order risks may become more prominent than the original risk. So "what if" mindset should also cover the area of correlation effect of different risks and create scenarios accordingly. COVID and the 2008 economic crisis demonstrated a chain reaction of impact in different sectors which otherwise could not have been thought through. So, history provides a good guide to shape our thinking.

Conclusion

So, at a very fundamental building block level of the risk management process, developing a "what if" mindset is the need of the hour. Every effort should be made to change the current mindset helping in averting future crises and saving the planet earth.

Risk Measurement

There are two methods of risk measurement, the Qualitative and the Quantitative method.

The purpose of risk quantification is to know the level of risks and plan for appropriate action. In the list of 100 risks, all risks may not be equally important, so the most severe risk will be dealt with first.

Risk measurement is always based on two scales, likelihood and impact. The likelihood is about the chances of happening of an event (that is probability of materialization of risk), whereas severity is the amount of loss that can happen. The multiplication of the two is the expected loss that can take place.

Qualitative risk assessment is more suitable where likelihood and impact are not possible to define numerically such as assessment of the failure of an IT system. In such cases, both are defined on a scale of 1 to 5 or any other chosen scale such as low medium-high. So, qualitative risk analysis tends to be more subjective in nature.

Quantitative risk analysis, on the other hand, is objective in nature, where probability and impact can be numerically calculated such as the likelihood of a fall in the stock market and the impact of a fall in the stock market.

Methods of Risk Quantification

There are various methods of quantification of risks, however, some of the common methods used in the financial sector are the following.

- Standard deviation
- Value at risk
- Stress testing
- Scenario analysis

These methods have their advantages and disadvantages and also the limitation. Both should be known to make the best use of both methods.

Standard deviation

Standard deviation measures the dispersion of data from its expected value. The standard deviation is used in making an investment decision to measure the amount of historical volatility associated with an investment relative to its annual rate of return. It indicates how much the current return is deviating from its expected historical normal returns. For example, a stock that has high standard deviation experiences higher volatility, and therefore, a higher level of risk is associated with the stock.

For example, suppose a stock achieves the annual rates of return over five years period are 4%, 6%, 8.5%, 2%, and 4%. Suppose that the mean value or average of annual return is 5% and the standard deviation is 2.5%.

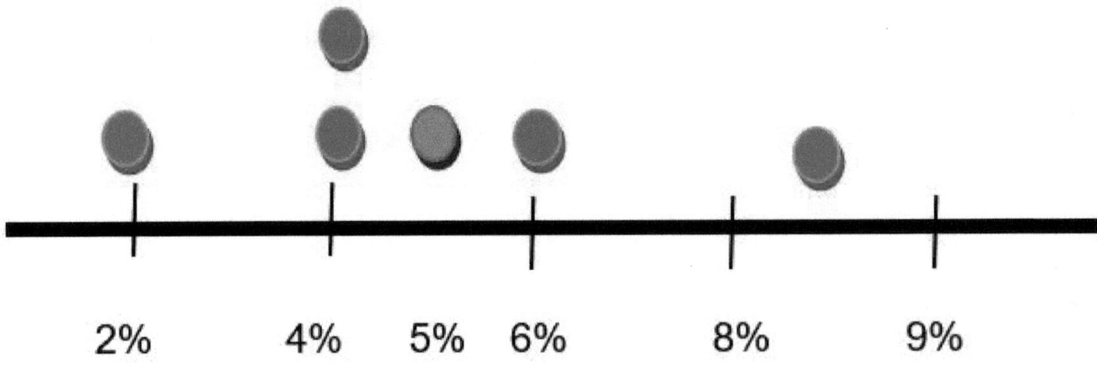

Standard Deviation

This means that on average one will get a 5% return each year and each individual yearly value is on an average of 2.5% away from the mean. This standard deviation indicates the variability in the annual return and is a measure of risk. If suppose, the standard deviation would have been 1%, then the actual return would have been more closely packed indicating that there is less variability in the annual returns. Less variable return means that the stock is performing consistently and when one invests the money in the stock market, his risk from the mean will be 1%. So those people who are risk-averse, that is, not like to take the risk, would prefer the stock with a lower standard deviation so that their actual return is close to average. On the other hand, those who are risk-takers, may prefer the stock which is more volatile, that is, have a large standard deviation so that they can gain the money, though the chances of losing the money could be equally high and ready to take the risk.

Standard Deviation Advantage/Disadvantage

So standard deviation is the simplest measure of risk. The advantage of standard deviation is, that it is very easy and simple to calculate and simple to explain. This can be applied to many different financial risks. It is also easy to aggregate the standard deviations of a group of stocks but that requires the relationship between the stock referred to as correlation.

The disadvantage of this measure is

This measure works well, when the distribution is symmetrical, that is if the data points are symmetrically distributed to the left and right of the mean. However, if the data points are too skewed either towards the left of the mean or towards the right of then, the standard deviation will make less useful. This is because, if most of the data points are to the left of the mean, then the standard deviation value may show a less variable but those data points which are on the right of mean will not be correctly represented. Therefore, standard deviation should be used carefully knowing the dispersion of data points. For distributions that are either negatively or positively distributed, other than standard deviations measures are used.

Value at Risk (VaR)

Value at Risk (VaR) is defined in the simplest form as the maximum loss that a financial institution can suffer within a given time frame and within a certain confidence level. VaR uses statistical distribution to calculate the loss within a given confidence level such as 95% or 99% over a required time horizon often a month or year. VaR is a very useful technique used to calculate the capital requirement within the banking system or in the insurance business. Such calculation of capital required is referred to as Risk-Based Capital.

Historically in 1989, JP Morgan Chairman, Dennis Weatherstone used to have a "4.15 PM Report" every day. The report used to combine the entire firm's data on market risk in one place, the intention was to collect the information sufficient to answer the question: "How much could the bank loss if tomorrow turns out to be a relatively bad day". If the bank keeps the amount equivalent to the amount of loss that the bank may suffer in one day it can sustain the business.

Risk-based capital uses exactly the same technique for each of the risks and is then aggregated.

Value at Risk (VaR)- Advantage and Disadvantage

The advantages of using the VaR are

1. Statistically, it gives a good result with all the current use of calculation of risk-based capital
2. This measure is measured in money terms so the decision-maker exactly knows how much money he is to keep aside. For example, a bank may require Rs.500 Cr of risk-based capital.
3. The VaR can be calculated for each of the quantifiable risks and then aggregated

4. Such individual calculation of risk capital allows risk diversification because of the correlation effect. For example, mortality and longevity have a negative correlation, so those companies selling pure insurance products and annuity products will have to keep relatively lower capital compared to those who are selling only protection businesses.

The disadvantages of using the VaR are

1. VaR is a good measure to quantify loss amount that occurs with relatively high frequency up to a defined level of probability; however, it is relatively poor in capturing the amount of loss beyond the defined level of probability which can be catastrophic in nature for the Company. To assess such losses, Stress testing is used in the banking and insurance industry.
2. Var is very sensitive to the choice of data and assumption, so it can give very different values if there is a problem in data or assumptions are not chosen correctly. Therefore, the developed market using Risk-Based CApital are taking special care of data and there is a proper data governance mechanism.

Stress Testing

As stated above, VaR is a good measure to quantify loss amount that occurs with relatively high frequency up to a defined level of probability; however, it is relatively poor in capturing the amount of loss beyond the defined level of probability which can be catastrophic in nature for the Company. To assess such losses, Stress testing is used in the banking and insurance industry. Stress testing is developing into a very strong tool as a part of risk management in financial sectors.

In Stress testing, assumptions are stressed to such an extent that it can give loss that can happen beyond the defined level of probability used in VaR.

The purpose of SST is to measure the impact of potential adverse scenarios that may arise on the institution helping them to devise an action plan for responding to and managing the risks identified in the stress testing exercise. This helps in assessing the risks facing the Company and keeping adequate capital to absorb the losses should such a large shock occur in the future. SST helps Board and senior management understand the Company's risk profile to an identified level of stress. It allows them to make a better-informed decision about the risk tolerance capacity appropriate for them.

The success of SST comes from a right understanding of SST results on the part of senior management and the Board and thereby helping the development of appropriate scenarios. The management action plan devised to mitigate the risk should be practical and achievable. If the action plan is superficial, then the purpose of SST will be defeated and the Company will fail to withstand the crisis situation.

Scenario Analysis

Scenario analysis is a process of analyzing future events by considering alternative possible outcomes. Thus, scenario analysis, which is one of the main forms of projection, does not try to show one exact picture of the future. Instead, it presents several alternative future developments

A scenario is all possible future outcomes at a point in time or over a period of time. A scenario may be generated through one or more events or changes in circumstances through the identification or simulation of several risk factors over a period of time. Scenario testing is useful to generate many possible outcomes for management to study and take appropriate action.

The Management is to decide whether the scenarios are standalone or correlated and interpret the results and create management action accordingly.

World Economic Forum identified various scenarios of economic recovery during this time of coronavirus impacts such as Z-shape recovery, V-Shape recovery, U-Shape recovery, and L and W shape recovery. Each of the shapes of the recovery tells the audience about the expected time that the world may take to come back to its normal growth position.

As the future is unknown, scenario analysis provides possible future position and prepare for the same.

Sometimes loosely, stress testing, sensitivity testing, and scenario analysis are interchanged, however, there are small differences between the three.

Risks in Life Insurance

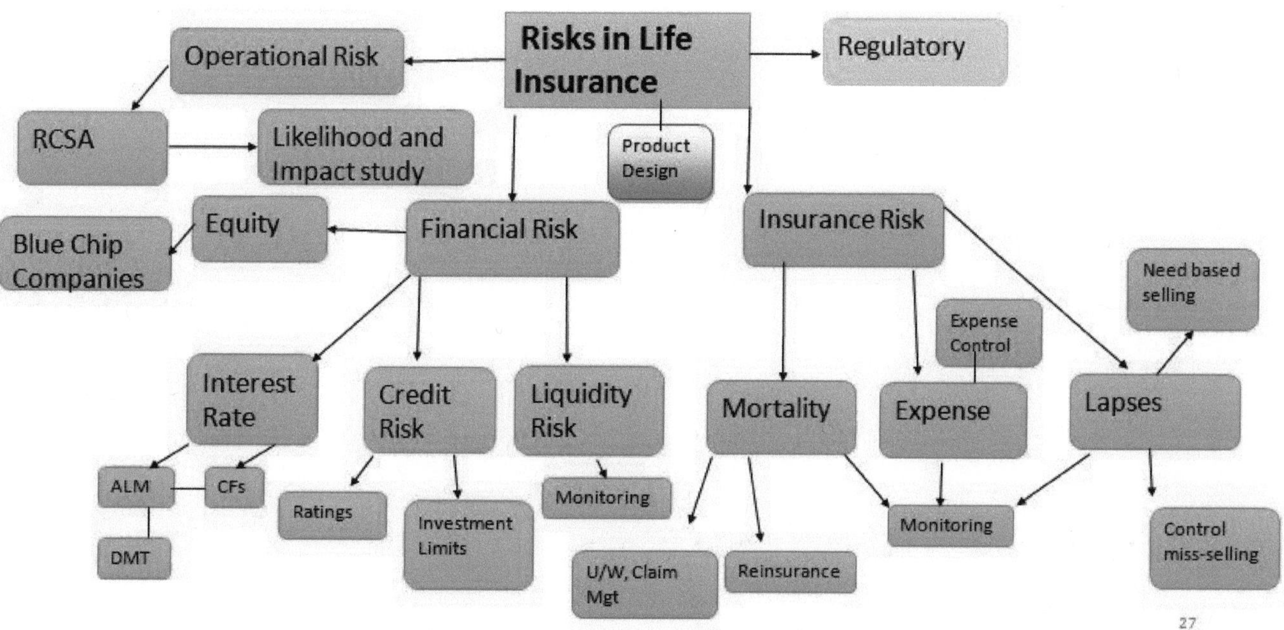

The above flowchart shows a snapshot of life insurance risks categorized into Insurance risks, financial risks, operational risks, and regulatory risks. There could be many other risks within the life insurance Company, but the above list is for quantification of risk point of view using Value at Risk, such risks are insurance risk, financial risk, and operational risk. It can be noted that under the insurance and financial risks, there are sub-categories of risks such as interest rate risk, credit risk, equity risk, and liquidity risk while in insurance risk, sub-category is mortality risk, lapse risk, and expense risk. Except for liquidity risks, separate risk-based capital is calculated for each of the risks within the insurance and financial risks. Regulatory risk is non-quantifiable. Similarly, for other businesses such as banks, the insurance risk is not there, but expense risk will be there. Mitigation techniques are also given in small boxes below the risk each risk.

Such a risk-based capital regime is not applicable in the Indian insurance industry and they are using a fixed factor approach to arrive at solvency capital.

Risks Based Capital

	RBC/Economic Capital in INR C
Insurance Risk	
Mortality Risk	200
Lapse Risk	300
Expense Risk	150
Sub Total	650
Financial risk	
Interest Rate Risk	400
Equity Risk	100
Concentration Risk	300
Sub Total	800
Total RBC/EC w/o Diversification	1450
Diversification	-200
Total RBC/EC	1250

Risk-Based Capital Numbers in INR Crore, 1 Crore = 10^7

The above table shows the individual risk capital required for each of the insurance and financial risk. This is the capital requirement in one financial year. That is if the Company keeps Rs.200 Cr of money for the mortality risks, then this money will be sufficient if the mortality experience turns out to be bad for the next year with a 99.5% confidence level. This is exactly what the JP Morgan example shows how much money to keep if tomorrow turns out to be a bad day.

Similarly, for the other two insurance risks, the individual risk capital is calculated as Rs.300 Cr for lapse risk and 150 Cr for expense risk. The total insurance risk capital is sum of the all the three individual risk capital to Rs.650 Cr.

Similarly, under the financial risk, individual risk capitals for interest rate risk Rs.400 Cr, Equity Rs.100 Cr, and concentration Rs.300 Cr. The total financial risk is Rs.800 Cr. The sum of insurance and financial risk capital is Rs.1450 Cr. That is to write the insurance business, an insurance company is to keep aside Rs.1450 Cr in one year.

As stated, the risks are correlated, so there will be a diversification advantage which is of Rs.200 Cr, so from the total of Rs.1450 Cr, Rs 200 Cr will reduce and the actual, the Company is to keep Rs.1250 Cr for a year.

As operational risks are not possible to quantify, so operational risk capital is calculated as a factor of other risks

Correlation effect

	Interest rate	equity	property	spread	currency	concen-tration
interest rate	1					
equity	0	1				
property	0.5	0.75	1			
spread	0.25	0.25	0.25	1		
currency	0.25	0.25	0.25	0.25	1	
concentration	0	0	0	0	0	1

Financial Correlation

	mortality	longevity	disability	lapse	expenses	revision	CAT
mortality	1						
longevity	-0.25	1					
disability	0.5	0	1				
lapse	0	0.25	0	1			
expenses	0.25	0.25	0.5	0.5	1		
revision	0	0.25	0	0	0.25	1	
CAT	0	0	0	0	0	0	1

Insurance Correlation

In the above two matrices; one matrix is for financial risk and the second one is for insurance risk. The correlation range is between 0 to 1. The correlation measures the linearity between the two variables. If the correlation value is 0, then there is no linear relationship between the two variables and if the correlation is 1, then there is a perfect linear relationship between the two variables. The perfect linear relationship could be negative when the correlation is -1.

Under the financial risk, the correlation between currency and equity is 0.25, this means that if currency value will increase by 1 unit, then the equity value will increase by 0.25.

Similarly, under the insurance risk, the correlation between longevity and mortality is -0.25, this means that if longevity increases by 1 year, then mortality is reduced by 0.25.

Such correlation helps in reducing the overall risks of the Company. The advantage of using risk-based capital is that the company can select the business in such a way that can reduce the overall capital requirement.

For example, if the company writes more interest rate guarantee business, then interest rate risk capital will increase and if they write more protection business, then your mortality risk capital will increase. It is for Board to decide, where they want to focus their business and which line of business will be suitable for them.

Qualitative risk assessment

A qualitative risk analysis prioritizes the identified risks using a pre-defined rating scale. Risks will be scored based on their probability or likelihood of occurring and the impact on project objectives should they occur.

Probability/likelihood is commonly ranked on a zero to one scale (for example, .3 equating to a 30% probability of the risk event occurring).

The impact scale is (for example, a one to five scales, with five being the highest impact

Likelihood assessment

For example, the likelihood can be classified under four categories **unlikely, possible, likely, and almost certain.** One can use different terminologies and different numbers of scales. These scales are generally created based on the experience of experts, some past data, use of judgment, and discussion with Senior Management.

For example, the **unlikely probability** is least likely to happen and could be **2 to 3 times in 10 years' time.** Based on experience such unlikely may be defined on a different scale such as once in a year if the time horizon of assessment is small say one year.

As the company moves from **unlikely to Almost certain**, the occurrence is increasing over the period of 10 years. The time horizon could be one year, 5 years, 15 years,s or 100 years. Therefore the quantification in qualitative risk assessment is subjective in nature.

Impact assessment

Similarly, the impact scale is also subjective in nature, where impacts are defined as **Small, Moderate, Severe, and Catastrophe.** This is just one of the examples and the company can create its own scale. Under the above categories, small represents a very small impact, while moderate is more than the small category, the severe impact has a higher impact and catastrophe is the highest scale.

Such qualitative risk assessments are very common in **operational risk assessments** where numeric value assignment is not possible. Risk Control Self Assessment is one such exercise very common in operational risk where both likelihood and impact on the scale are taken on similar scales.

Risk Matrix

Security Risk Management Aide-Mémoire
www.srmam.com

Likelihood			Consequence →				
			1	2	3	4	5
			$10,000	$100,000	$1,000,000	$10,000,000	$100,000,000
↑	A	90%	M	H	H	VH	VH
	B	75%	L	M	H	H	VH
	C	50%	L	L	M	H	H
	D	25%	VL	L	L	M	H
	E	10%	VL	VL	L	L	M

Very High (VH	Immediate action required by the Executive with detailed planning, allocation of resources and regular monitoring
High (H)	High risk, senior management attention needed
Medium (M)	Management responsibility must be specified
Low (L)	Monitor and manage by routine procedures
Very Low (VL	Managed by routine procedures

Risk Matrix

Under the operational risk, all the risk items are placed on this risk matrix which on the y-axis is the likelihood, and on the x-axis is the consequence or impact. It can be seen that on the x-axis, the scales are written in dollar terms, such impact scales are created by the management team. Above the dollar, the term can be noticed on a scale of 1 to 5. Similarly, on the y-axis, the scale is from 10% to 90% with grading A to E.

All the operational risk items such as different processes, events, and systems can be placed in this matrix and it will give a companywide snap short of various risks within the Company.

It can be noticed that on the left bottom the risks are classified as Very Low, which can be managed by regular routine process. Certain risks are written as Low which is shown as green and can be managed by monitoring while other risks are Medium depicted as Yellow, under such risk management responsibility must be assigned. High risks shown as Amber need immediate attention of senior management and the one which is very high under the red category require immediate action.

The distribution of each of these risks is based on likely frequency and likely impact based on the judgment of the first and second line.

Risk Management

Once risks are identified and measured, the next step is the management of the risk. This step is very important to treat the risk so that risk may not destroy the business value. There are four ways to treat the risk, Accept, Manage, Transfer and Avoid. The key question is how to make a decision as to which treatment will be applied.

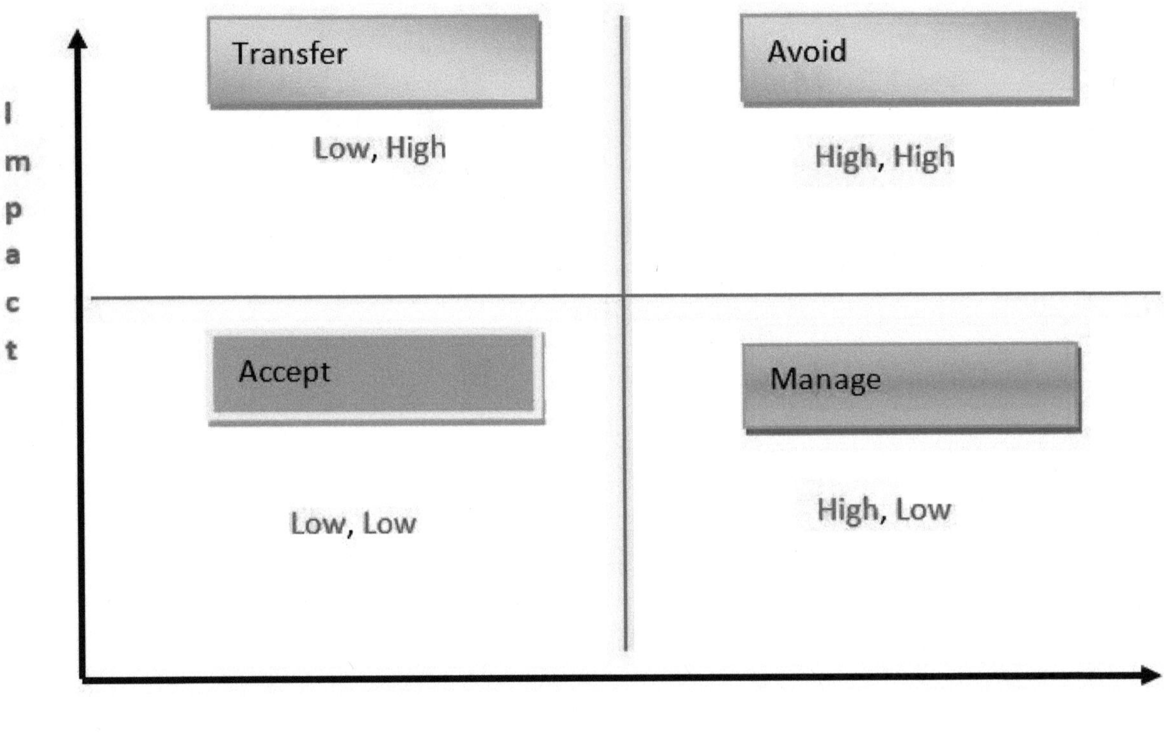

The 2x2 matrix is shown on the likelihood and impact scale, likelihood on the x-axis, and impact on the y-axis. In the first quadrant bottom left, the likelihood and impact both are on a low scale and as we move to the right, the likelihood increases to high, and the impact remain low; similarly, as we move to the upper left corner, the likelihood remains low while the impact is high. On the right upper corner, the likelihood and impact both are high.

The decision to manage risk can be accessed from the fact that which risk is on a higher scale as a low scale can be addressed. So the one where likelihood and impact both are low, the company will accept the risk. These are the standard risks such as standard lives proposing for insurance, good credit rating customers proposing for a loan, and such risks the business accepts.

When the likelihood of the risk is high but the impact is low, the company would like to manage the risk by addressing the likelihood. If there could be customers with relatively poor credit ratings applying for loans, the bank may increase the interest rate to compensate for the likely default by customers and accept the business. Other examples are in the insurance business many lives outside the standard lives limit, such business insurance companies accept by applying either extra premium or applying other condition. Under both the examples above, if someone is with a very poor credit rating or a very sub-standard life, then their risk treatment would be something different because that will start impacting the impact as well.

When the impact is high, but the likelihood is low, business houses would not like to accept the risk in full because if the risk occurs the impact will be very high, and often such risks are transferred to the third party. In insurance such an example is reinsurance, to manage the interest rate risk, companies use interest rate derivatives. If a risk transfer mechanism is not there, the company may not accept the risk. Pandemic is one such example, where cover for a pandemic is not easily available.

High likelihood, as well as high impact, could be catastrophic in nature, so businesses avoid such risks and often are outside their risk appetite.

Risk Monitoring

1. Why monitor this risk?

Risk monitoring acts as a feedback loop before risk monitoring there are three steps, risk identification, measurement, and management; monitoring gives us an opportunity to know whether the risk that was identified was adequate or not or if there is a need to change in the method of risk identification.

Also, monitoring helps us know whether risk quantification was adequate or not.

1. To test the effectiveness of the risk management plan

Monitoring helps us in knowing how was the mitigation plan, in certain countries, the lockdown during the peak of COVID 19 was either slow or inadequate leading to lots of deaths, so what would say about the management plan. It was perhaps inadequate and a more stringent lockdown was required.

So monitoring exercise gives us time and space to look back and take stock of the situation and make corrections for the future.

3. To see the actual performance against the expected

As the future is unknown, certain assumptions are made about the future, that assumption is based on past experience, present data, and judgment, however, the reality may still turn out to be different than expected. So monitoring allows us the opportunity to make corrections in setting our assumptions for the future. Such assumption setting is very common in the life insurance business which is long-term in nature. So actuaries are to make assumptions for 15 years or 20 Years to price a product.

4. To find Early warning signals

Monitoring also allows us to spot trends and identify the early warning signal. For example, if the profit is regularly declining quarter after quarter, it gives you a warning signal that there could be something wrong, which will help in finding the reason and correct the problem.

Risk Reporting

Risk reporting is the final step in the risk management process. It enables the Company to communicate the risk and other information to all relevant stakeholders. The key stakeholders are the Board of the Company, Risk management committee, Audit Committee, senior management, employees, regulators, rating agencies, securities exchange, and customers both current and future.

Under the Risk-Based capital regime, it is a regulatory requirement to disclose all the financials and risks on the Company's website so that such information is publically available to everyone.

SEVEN

Risk Appetite: A Risk Management Tool

Introduction

This chapter discusses in detail the risk appetite, setting the risk appetite, statistical ways of representation of risk appetite, and factors important for risk appetite. The chapter also describes the spread of risk appetite across a 2x2 matrix and from there how risk appetite can be set.

What is Risk Appetite

Let's address this from a very common-sense point of view, look at the two pictures below, who can eat more food? Of course, the one with a big belly.

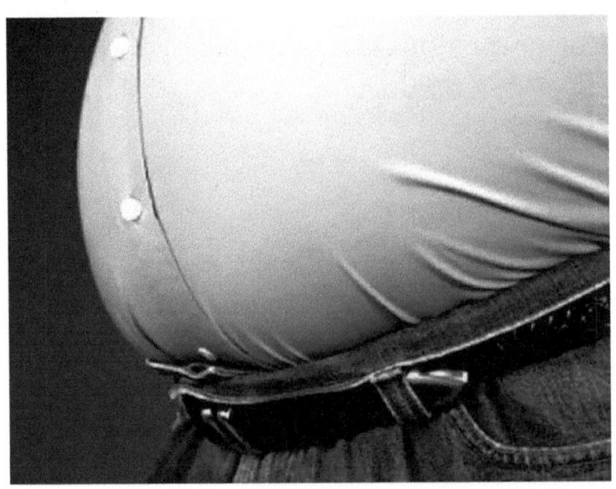

In a simple terms, a bigger belly is associated with a higher food appetite. The size of the belly and food appetite is a function of many factors such as wealth, care for physical fitness, hereditary, and many more.

The way food appetite is linked to the maximum food that an individual can eat, similarly, in the financial world, ***risk appetite is the maximum risk that a Company can take to achieve its objective.***

Risk appetite makes more sense when linked to the performance of the organization because organizations take the risk to achieve business objectives. It is just like how much gas is required in a car to reach the destination. Here gas is a risk appetite and reaching a destination is meeting the performance of the organization. In financial terms, the future is uncertain, with the roll of the financial year, the external and internal environment will bring risks, but the Company is to meet the financial objectives irrespective of what may happen. So more the uncertain environment, there is a high likelihood that the Company may breach the risk appetite limits that they set for themselves at the start of the financial year.

A risk appetite is a risk management tool that helps the Company in defining the outer limit of the maximum risk the owners are ready to take in the company within a financial year. This also helps the Company in venturing out where they are interested in doing the business and where not, which risks they are ready to take and which risks are not ready to take. It clearly defines the dos and don'ts. The Company may identify certain geographical locations where they will not do business, which risks they will take, and which risks they will not take. The Company doesn't need to be everywhere. They may decide that if they do not have experience in writing certain businesses say annuity business in the life insurance or banking sector giving a loan to certain individuals, or writing a new risk covering new disease (Ebola or Pandemic, etc), they may decide as to their risk preference. Risk preference is very much part of the risk appetite setting strategy, this helps in reducing the burn of the capital where the Company does not have expertise either in pricing risks or managing risks.

This is very similar to food appetite, which food you want to eat, which food you do not want, from where you want to eat, and from where you do not want to eat. There are no universal norms, if one has a food appetite, one can venture out to eat the food from the streets, whereas another person may not have such a food appetite. It all depends on how much is the ability of risk-taking based on experience, personal preference, and changing likely future.

In the financial world, risk appetite is often defined in money terms (but not always necessary) which is easy to quantify, and relates to a business's profit and losses. However, all the risks are not quantifiable, so for those risks, qualitative statements are made.

There are many operational risks, reputational risks, regulatory risks, etc are qualitative, for such risks, statements are created as risk appetite as zero tolerance for regulatory and reputational risks. For the operational risks, a tolerance may be defined as the customer complaints should not be more than the industry benchmark, or the claim repudiation rate cannot be more than regulatory prescribed limits. Such qualitative risk appetite helps the Company in creating additional boundaries which cannot be covered in profit and capital terms because doing the business requires many compliances requirements set by Company law, regulatory requirements, ethics, Shareholder's way of functioning, etc.

For quantitative elements, risk appetite may be defined as certain percentages of capital employed, for example, the Company may set the risk appetite limit as the actual ratio of capital to new business during the planning period not to exceed what is approved during the business plan. This appetite will ensure that any additional capital employed by the shareholders given a similar return is approved during the plan period. This will also ensure optimum utilization of capital for writing new business.

Statistical Meaning of Risk Appetite

Risk is defined as future uncertainty that may impede the achievement of objectives of the business.

Here uncertainty is due to the unknown future where the outcome may not be as per expectation. The outcome may fall on the expected line (Mean) or far from the mean creating variation. The objective here is the mean value on which the expected outcome is supposed to fall.

Extending the concept of risk, risk appetite is the maximum variation that a business house may expect. This variation can be one standard deviation from the mean, two standard deviations, or three standard deviations. This will depend on how deep the pockets of the business owners are.

Therefore, the risk appetite can be defined in terms of standard deviation as boundaries between the two limits.

(Mean-n*Standard deviation, Mean+ n*Standard deviation),

'n' will depend upon the ability of the business houses to withstand shocks.

Assuming a Standard Normal distribution If n = 2.807, then the confidence interval will be 99.5%. The probability within the confidence interval (Mean-2.807*Standard deviation, mean+ 2.807*Standard deviation) would represent that the business can bear 99.5% shock and stay solvent in the business. This means that the maximum risk that the Company will take is mean+ 2.807*Standard deviation which is within the 99.5% confidence level. The Company can convert this limit in a money term.

A further discussion is made later in the section.

Here Value at Risk (VaR) concept can be introduced which is defined as the maximum loss that a financial institution can suffer within a given time frame and a certain confidence level. VaR uses statistical distribution to calculate losses (Capital Requirement) within a confidence level (say 99.5%) over a required period (a month or a year).

Setting Risk Appetite

Risk appetite may not be the same for every organization, some organizations may define risk appetite in a form of risk and others may define it in a form of performance. For example, some organizations may define risk appetite in a form of risk while others may define it in a form of either profit or shareholder's value or others. This choice would depend upon the nature of business and what role risk plays in the nature of business.

For some organizations such as banks and other financial services, risk appetite is a driver where risk is at the center of the decision-making. In such an organization, financial performance is a function of risk management.

In other organizations, where risk is not a driver of the business but because of strategy, tactic, operations, and compliance that the business undertakes. In such an organization, the risk is the output of the business operation. Here risk appetite will not be a driver of business.

In further other organizations, risk appetite is a constraint that is placed on the staff of organizations in terms of authorization levels, expenditure limits, etc.

For the above three types of organizations, risk appetite will be defined differently.

Process of Setting risk appetite

The first step towards setting the risk appetite is for the organization to know all risks, that is, the organization must identify all the risks. Any of the key risks should not have been missed at this stage else will not be a part of the risk assessment. To rank the risk in the order of priority, the second step is a measurement of risk in terms of the probability or likelihood and its impact.

The best point to start the process of setting risk appetite is at the time of the business plan before the start of the financial year. During the business plan time, the Chief Risk Officer (CRO) should play an active role in performing the review and challenging the business plan from the point of view of risk. Some of the tools that may be used in assessing the quantum of risk are sensitivity testing, stress testing, and scenario testing. This will help in throwing out the key scenarios where the business plan may fail to achieve the plan objectives. This will help in identifying the risks and the difference between the two stress tests could be the additional resources required for a business to meet the plan.

Therefore, there is great importance of the involvement of CROs at the time of business planning. This therefore also means that there is a direct relationship between the risk culture of the Company and the process of setting the risk appetite.

Suppose during the business planning process, the Company identified 100 risks along with their likelihood and impact. The Company can calculate the likelihood and impact based on Company-specific historic data for each risk. If the Company does not have Company-specific data, may use industry-specific data but may require adjustment for the Company's purpose. Such adjustment may be based on the future forecast, judgment, and experience of experts, etc. More personal judgments are required in qualitative data. Such adjustment of industry-specific data or country-specific data for the use of the Company is quite common in actuarial in the insurance sector due to the long-term nature of the business.

All the 100 identified risks can be arranged in a 2x2 matrix on a likelihood and impact scale as shown below. Based on the likelihood and impact scale, the 100 risks will spread over the matrix, with some risks lying in the low likelihood and low impact region, and others may lie in the low likelihood and high impact region, etc. Now the company is to decide what is their acceptable level of risk appetite they can bear.

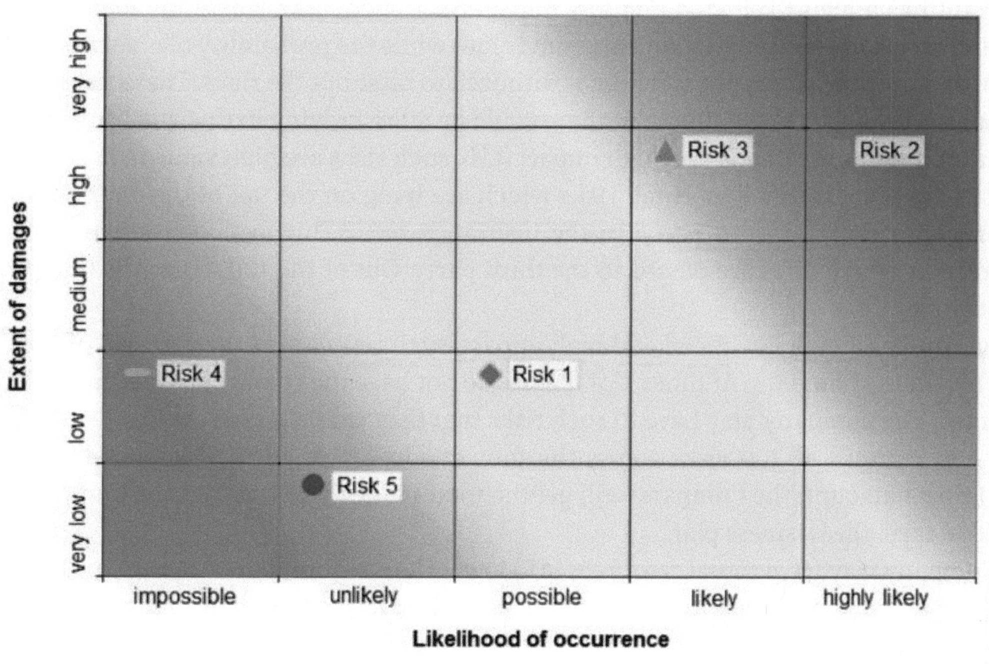

The above 100 risks plotted on a 2x2 matrix on the likelihood on the x-axis scale and impact on the y-axis scale can be represented in the below graph with four quadrants. The first quadrant has low likelihood and low impact

(LL), such risks are easily acceptable by the organization. Such risks are like standard loans that banks easily accept without any additional risk assessment or standard lives in the life insurance Company. There may be some say 30 odd risks that the Company can tolerate.

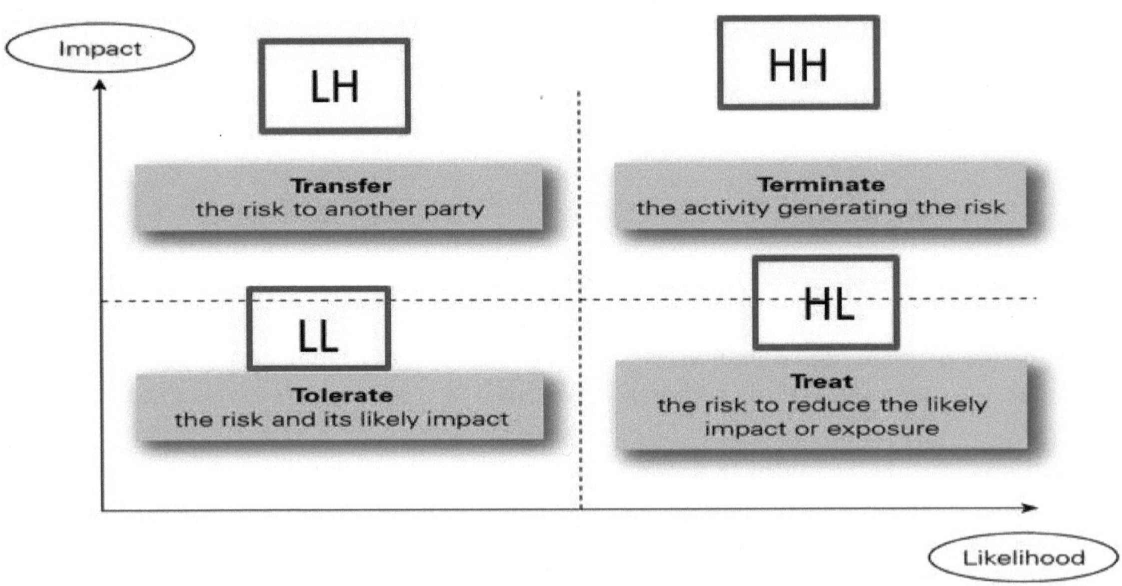

The next quadrant has a high likelihood and low impact (HL), such risks where the loan value in the banking sector is low or in the insurance sector, the claim amount is low, while the probability of claims is high. Such risks are generally underwritten or their papers are carefully scrutinized to filter out the risks. These risks are either managed or treated with underwriting. Out of the 100 risks, there could be 40 risks lying in this quadrant as an example.

The third quadrant has low likelihood and high impact (LH), such risks are high value in nature but the likelihood are small, such risks are often referred to as tail risks which are lying on the tail of the distribution. The Company prefers to transfer such risks to a third party. In the insurance sector, high-value risks are reinsured. Similarly, derivatives are contracts where risks are passed to the third party. Out of the 100, risks, the Company may have 20 such risks as an example.

The fourth quadrant has a high likelihood and high impact, such risks are at the very tail of the distribution and could be catastrophic for the Company. At times, Companies do not have the resources to accept such risks. Therefore, such risks are avoided. The Company may have 10 such risks that they would like to avoid.

The Company has a spread of 100 risks across the four quadrants. If all the likelihood of respective risks is multiplied by the impact amount, the Company will get the total money amount that the Company will require the total resources (TR) to meet the business plan.

In reality, the Company may have actual resources (AR) lower than required total resources (TR), that is AR < TR

So, the Company is to find the combination of likelihood and impact, so that their total money is equal to AR.

The Company may draw a curvature line passing through the four quadrants so that the total likelihood and impact are equal to AR. This curvature line is the risk appetite line where resources to the left of the curvature are equal to AR.

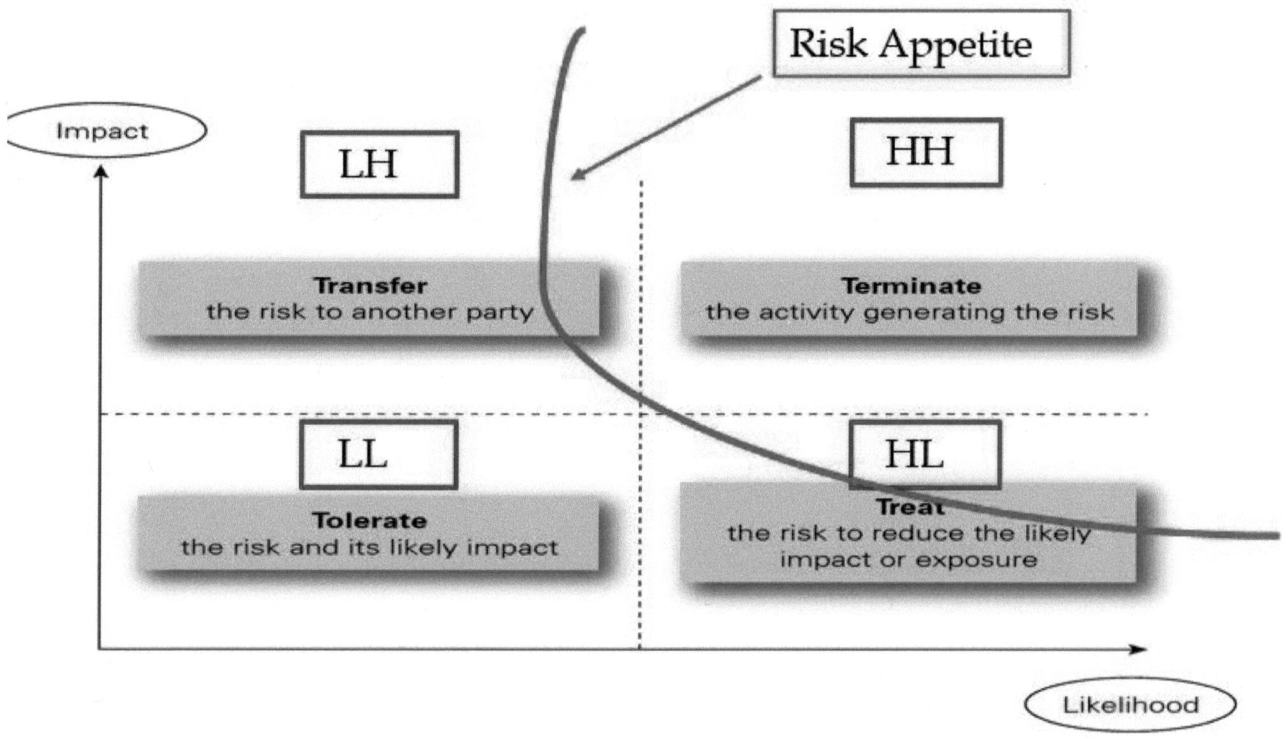

This can be explained as likelihood and impact multiplication is the expected loss in rupee terms. The expected loss in area LL will be easily met through the resources that the Company has. Most of the risks falling in this area will be regular risks like smaller credit risks with low exposure, smaller interest rate risk, etc.

Tolerance Limits

Using the same above graph, the upper and lower bounds of the risk appetite can be drawn to have working limits. Such limits also act as an early warning signal, as and when the lower limit is reached, remedial actions can be planned. The company set the upper limit as the maximum stretchable limit.

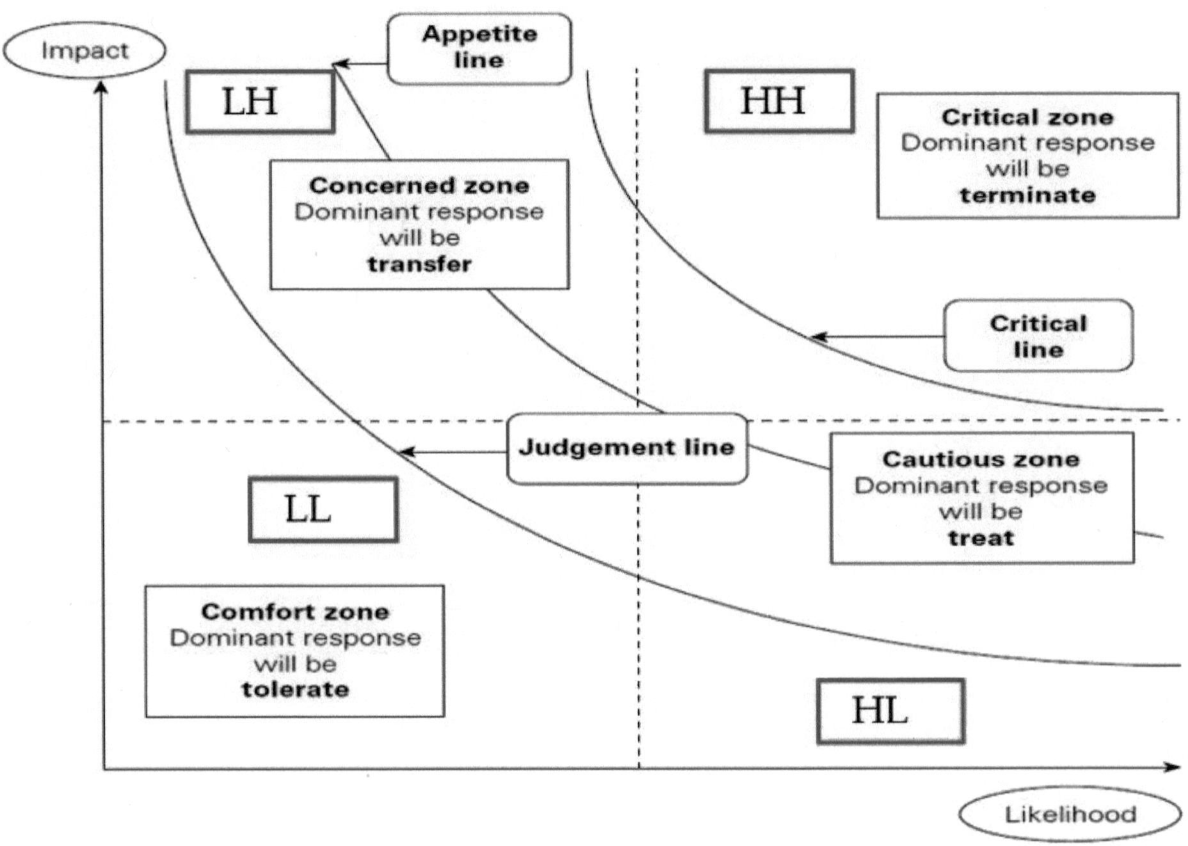

Statistical Distribution

Now suppose. The likelihood and impact scale are reversed and the data of the same 100 risks are now presented with impact on the x-axis and frequency on the y-axis. This will give a frequency distribution that could be similar to the distribution shown below in the graph.

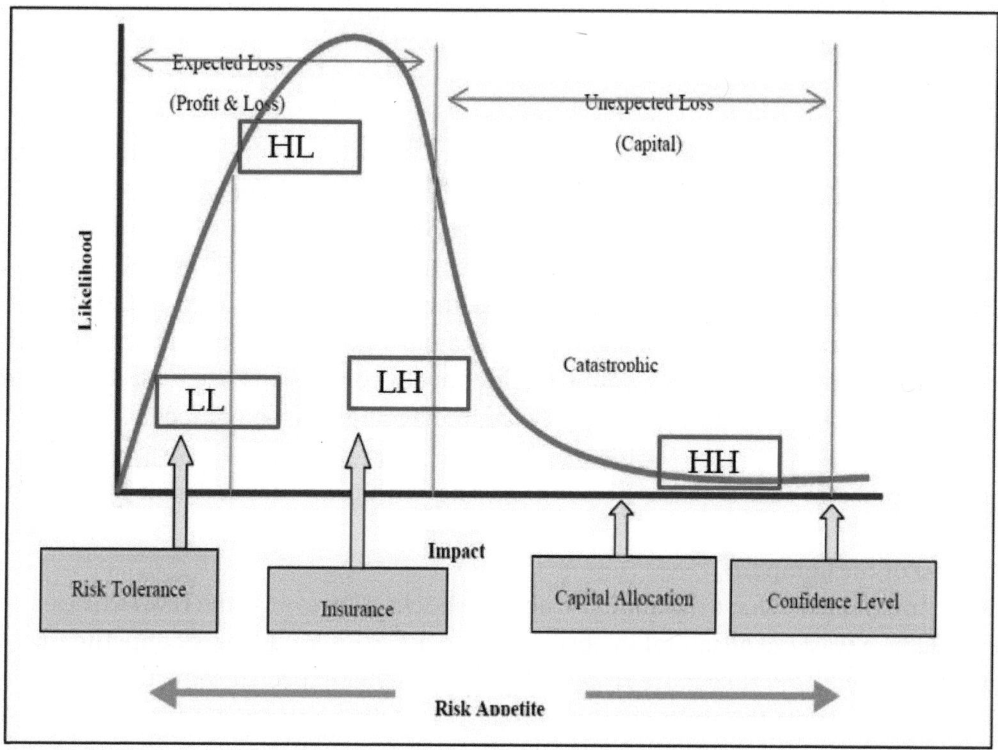

"Please note that the representation of say "LH" on the same as x and y-axis are shown in the previous section and not based on the distribution above."

It can be seen that the same 100 risks are now presented in a frequency representation. The area under the graph close to the start of the x-axis has a lower impact amount and also a lower likelihood, which is represented as the first quadrant in the above chart shown as LL.

After LL, the likelihood increases on the y-axis but the impact is still lower represented as HL. Further to the right on the x-axis, the impact amount increases, and the likelihood is lower indicating the events that are required to be passed the risk to a third party as LH. On the tail of the distribution is the high-impact area for which capital is required.

The above frequency distribution can also be analyzed as areas falling under LL, LH, and HL as the expected losses. *This means that when shareholder starts the business operation, they expect some losses to occur as a normal business process and some losses that will occur which is unexpected. The same is represented in the distribution. The business will require additional capital for the unexpected losses which are on the tail of the distribution. The vertical line marked as confidence level could be the statistical level of significance up to which an organization can bear the risk. The same concept was discussed in the above section under the statistical meaning of risk appetite. This confidence level will be different for a different company based on their risk appetite dependent on capital position and risk-taking ability.*

Factors on which risk appetite depends

There are a couple of factors on which risk appetite depends, they are

- Risk culture of the organization
- Capital Position of the Company
- Regulatory regime

- Business environment

Risk culture of the organization

Risk culture within an organization will depend on how the risk management is embedded within the Company which in turn will depend on whether the Company defines its risk appetite and use it for decision making.

It is important that when a decision is taken place, the management of the Company must re-calculate its risk appetite and see whether the resultant risk appetite is well within its defined limits or not. If the decision results in a breach of risk appetite, resultant risks must be managed so that post-decision risks remain within the appetite.

A less developed risk culture may either not define its risk appetite or may not use it for decision-making purposes.

Application of risk appetite is most effective where risk management is well embedded within the three lines of defense.

The advantage of the use of risk appetite helps in staying within the defined risk limits and avoiding future surprises.

The capital position of the Company

A well-capitalized Company will have the ability to absorb shocks. However, if the risk management is not properly embedded, there could be a wastage of capital in absorbing shocks. So, a broader risk appetite may be defined by the Company that has more capital and take more risks and hence a higher expected return.

A constraint in capital restricts the ability of the Company to define a narrow limit of risk appetite. This in turn limits the Company's ability to expand further and experiment. The capital, therefore, should be judiciously used.

Regulatory regime

The regulatory push in implementing risk management has a large say in the implementation of risk appetite. In the countries where regulators have implemented risk-based capital, enterprise risk management is more embedded within the organization. In such places, risk appetite is used for decision-making. However, where the regulator has not pushed the implementation of risk management, risk-based decision-making is superficial.

Business environment

It is important to understand what the competition is doing; it becomes a norm to follow the competitor due to the business efforts. If all the Competitors are using risk management in their business or are pushed by the regulator, there is no point remaining out of the action.

Also, if the competition is not using risk management as a tool, some businesses house may still use it as a differentiator and pass the ultimate benefits to the customers.

What to do with risk appetite

The risk appetite is used to define risk limits beyond which the business should not go; it is used as a management tool that helps in creating a forewarning signal whether the risk is going beyond limits. The risk appetite is generally set at the start of the year at the time of business planning based on the expected new business the Company is planning to do during the year. The business should monitor its actual risk against the plan regularly and take corrective action in case of a breach. This helps in saving the unnecessary burn of the Company's capital and resources.

The risk appetite should also be used for decision-making such that the overall risk remains within the appetite post any decision. Such an application of risk appetite helps in avoiding future surprises that may arise.

Summary

An overall risk appetite is a tool that helps an organization in taking the risk based on its capacity. There are different ways through which risk appetite can be measured, however, Value at Risk is one of the methods through which risk appetite can be measured. Risk appetite depends on the Risk culture of the organization, Capital Position of the Company, Regulatory regime, and Business environment. Risk appetite is a very good tool for management and helps in making risk-based decisions.

EIGHT

STRATEGY AND CORPORATE GOVERNANCE

Introduction

This sixth chapter focuses on the importance of strategy and corporate governance. Both play a very crucial role in the success of risk management. Most companies in the past have failed due to either poor strategies or not finding enough risks within their strategy. The classic examples are Kodak and Nokia, they could not see the emerging risk to change the strategy based on the emerging business model. Strategic risks are long-term in nature impacting the business model.

Similarly, risk management on its own cannot perform and be successful without solid corporate governance; risk management will just slip through the cracks of poor corporate governance. Brief cases of Yes Bank, Jet Airways, and Café Coffee Day are discussed to reinforce the importance of corporate governance. For example, when a bank disburses loans through the discussion across the table, then risk assessment cannot work. Similarly, when all the decisions are taken through a central place, the role risk managers are very limited.

A company can survive without risk management but cannot survive without proper corporate governance. Therefore, good corporate governance is a necessary condition for risk management to be successful.

Strategy

First, it will cover the strategy; the idea is to introduce what is strategy, what are the components of strategy, why strategy is essential from a risk management point of view, and some details about strategic risk management.

There is a need to look into the strategic side of the risks because of changing business realities. The business challenges are:

1. The constantly changing business landscape
2. Limited Resources
3. Return to investors
4. Changing regulation
5. Social, Technical, and digital changes
6. How to manage the business

Risk management is about spotting risks and working toward its management, while strategy is a long-term sequence of actions intended to take a company from its present position to its future state.

Strategy is about determining the direction and scope of the organization and creating competitive advantage through cost leadership; strategy is exposed to internal and external risks. External risks are macroeconomic factors, general business environment, industry, competitive environment, etc., while internal risks are policies, culture, political dynamics, leadership, etc.

Integration of strategy and risk management is important because they meet together. Unfortunately, a significant failure has happened due to missing the strategy.

Competitive and Corporate Strategy

Competitive strategy is about a single business unit, while corporate strategy refers to the overall strategy of an organization that is made up of multiple business units operating in multiple markets. It determines how the corporation as whole support and enhances the value of the business units within it; and it answers the question, "How to structure the overall business so that all of its parts create more value together than they would individually

Every organization embarking on the journey of business first identify the vision of the Company, that is, what they ultimately want to achieve through the guiding light of mission. So, vision and mission are two important statements that help them take forward on the business journey.

A vision statement provides the organization with a destination, a big picture that the organization wants to attain.

The following statement is the guiding light to reach the destination, it is a general statement to achieve the vision, and this is a **mission** statement.

Along with vision and mission, there are the **core values**; this is about how to behave while on the path to the attainment of the vision. Core values define the Company in terms of the principles and values the Senior Management will follow in carrying out the events of the organization.

Statements of vision and mission are important for everyone's involvement, including outside stakeholders, to understand what the organization will accomplish and how it will be achieved.

Vision and mission are closely related. As the vision statement is a static mental picture of what you want to achieve, the mission statement is a dynamic process of how the vision will be accomplished.

Vision Mission Value

Once the Company has created statements of vision and mission, and possibly core values, it can then develop the strategies, goals, objectives, and action plans needed to activate the mission and achieve its vision.

Strategies – A strategy is a statement of how the Company will achieve something. More specifically, a strategy is a unique approach to how the Company will use its mission to achieve its vision. Strategies are critical to the success of an organization because this is where the Company begins outlining a plan for doing something.

Goals – A goal is a general statement of what you want to achieve. More specifically, a goal is a milestone(s) in implementing a strategy. Examples of business goals are:

- *Increase in New Business of the Company*
- *Increase profit margin*
- *Increase efficiency*
- *Capture a more significant market share*

Be sure the goals are focused on the important aspects of implementing the strategy.

Objectives – An objective turns a goal's general statement of what is to be accomplished into a specific, quantifiable, time-sensitive statement of what is going to be achieved and when it will be achieved. Examples of business objectives are:

- *Increase new business by Rs.200 Cr*

Earn 15% profit after tax

- *Increase market share by 10 percent over the next three years.*

• Lower operating costs by 15 percent over the next two years through improvement in the efficiency of the manufacturing process.

Action Plans – Action plans are statements of specific actions or activities that will be used to achieve a goal within the constraints of the objective.

Example

- The sales team will recruit 500 front-line salespeople to increase new business
- The finance team will work towards cost reduction.

Corporate Governance

Corporate governance is the way the Board runs the Company and sets and controls the processes in the best interest of stakeholders

Corporate governance is very important in the success of risk management; if the corporate governance is not strong, then risk management cannot succeed because the holes within the corporate governance will dilute the impact of risk management, or it will not let risk management apply properly within the organization. There are many peripheral things along with risk management itself which is required for its success.

Why Corporate Governance

The case study of the Enron Scandal throws light on the need of having good corporate governance. This is the story of the rising and fall of Enron is a reflection of how poor corporate governance can bring a downfall of a mighty company. The fall of the Company adversely affected thousands of employees and shook Wall Street. It can be thought that how such a powerful business can disintegrate almost overnight. It is also difficult to imagine how its leadership managed to fool regulators for so long with fake holdings and off-the-books accounting.

Arthur Andersen was an auditor with a high reputation and quality risk management.

Despite Enron's poor accounting practices, Arthur Andersen provided signing off on the corporate reports. Arthur Andersen was found guilty of destroying Enron's financial documents to conceal facts from them by the US Security Exchange Commission.

Many of Enron's executives were framed for conspiracy, insider trading, and fraud.

New Governance

In July 2002, US President signed a new Sarbanes-Oxley Act (SOX) law. The Financial Accounting Standards Board increased its levels of ethical conduct and made company boards of directors more responsible. These new measures were important mechanisms to spot and close loopholes that companies have used to avoid accountability.

Enron's collapse was the largest corporate scandal ever to hit the financial world. The shareholders lost $74 billion in the four years leading up to its bankruptcy, and its employees lost billions in pension benefits. As a result, regulation and oversight were increased to help prevent corporate scandals of Enron's magnitude.

Role of Board

The key to corporate governance is how Board controls the Company, Board sits in the Company's driver's seat, and any accident resulting in the corporate landscape is attributed to the Board. Corporate governance is like a traffic rule on how the corporate bus will be driven. For example, the Enron accident resulted from faulty rules and regulations, which the SOX law corrected.

Board is overall responsible for the success of the Company and therefore has the responsibility of identifying and managing all the risks. One of the primary roles of the Board is to set the risk appetite of the Company and operate within that limit.

At the top of the ladder, the Board is to consider the companywide risk that can threaten its existence. The responsibility of the Board is to set the Company's direction, structure, and culture and allocate human and financial resources to optimize the return. Culture plays a crucial role in the success of risk management which is developed over a period of time using tone from the top.

The role of the Board is also to develop the leadership and how risk management is placed in the order of importance. The example of Enron and Yes Bank suggests that the Board at the top of the ladder failed. Many volumes of papers have been written on the failure of the Board in the 2008 global economic crisis. So, setting the priority of risk management within the scheme of operation is for Board to appoint.

The Board is to set the code of conduct and ethics for employees and leaders of the Company. In addition, the Board is to develop how the risk management will be integrated within the Company, and the performance evaluation process will be made on the risk management front. An element of risk management implementation and success in the annual business plan for all employees in developing a positive risk management culture.

So, the importance of the Board is clear from the implementation of corporate governance point of view and that plays a key role in the success of risk management.

Development of Corporate governance and code of conduct.

Several codes of conduct have been developed globally by different regulatory bodies, such as the Central Bank, Insurance regulators, and the stock exchange, after the number of failures worldwide led to significant losses.

These codes of conduct have been developed to strengthen risk management and internal control, so companies operate on sound principles.

Some of these controls are holding correct, adequate, and accurate data. In many financial institutions, the CEO is to ensure and certify that the data provided to the concerned department are valid and correct.

The companies must prevent fraud and safeguard the Company's assets; therefore, the Company must have fraud prevention departments.

The Company must ensure that the financials that are provided are correct and accurate; therefore, there is a need in many jurisdictions to disclose the financials of the Company on their website for public scrutiny.

The Company must ensure proper risk management and compliance with the law and supervisory guidelines. Internal control and risk management should be developed, keeping in mind the risks of the Company.

Corporate Governance in the UK

Corporate governance in the UK started in 1993 with the Cadbury Code of Best practices to improve people's confidence in the financial sector. Some of the main recommendations of the committee were

1. There should be a full Board meeting at a regular interval
2. The Board should be aware of the all-key activities
3. Non-executive directors were given the responsibilities of specific control and monitoring function
4. Shareholder's approval was required for Directors to continue beyond three years
5. The remuneration committee should approve directors' remuneration made up of mainly non-executive directors

Corporate Governance in India

Corporate governance in India started in 1998 through the efforts of several committees appointed by the Ministry of Corporate Affairs (MCA) and SEBI. It sets guidelines and standards for the Board of directors, financial and non-financial disclosures, and information to be shared by the management with stakeholders and the wider public. The Confederation of Indian Industry (CII) is privileged to have been a part of this movement. The Confederation of Indian Industry (CII) set up a task force in 1995 under the Chairman of Bajaj Group, Rahul Bajaj

Enhancements in the corporate governance framework were made on 01 April 2019, when the SEBI regulation was amended in 2018, which had the recommendations made by the Kotak Committee – a panel formed under the chairmanship of Uday Kotak to improve corporate governance standards in India.

For the financial institutions in India, the corporate governance guidelines are issued by SEBI, RBI, and IRDA for their respective jurisdictions under their control. In addition, the companies must comply with other corporate governance guidelines issued by different ministries and governing bodies.

Kotak Committee Recommendation

The committee recommended

Composition of the Board

- Minimum six directors
- At least one independent woman director
- Maximum number of directorships capped to 8
- Role of Chairperson and managing director to be separated
- Competencies/expertise of directors to be disclosed
- Independence of directors - Promoter/relatives not to be independent directors in each other's companies

Accounting and disclosure

- Disclosure of consolidated financial results mandatory for all the listed entities every quarter
- Disclosure of cash flow statement on a half-yearly basis mandatory for all listed entities
- Limited review/audit of at least 80% of financial information of the group
- Mandatory disclosures of quantification of audit qualifications
- Disclose the list of all credit ratings obtained along with any revisions in the corporate governance section of its annual report
- Disclose specific critical financial ratios in the section of management, discussion, and analysis in the annual report

Best Practices in Corporate Governance

Some of the best practices in corporate governances are

1. **Communication with Stakeholders**- Board has the responsibility of disclosing certain types of information to stakeholders in the annual report to have transparency. All the listed companies on the London Stock exchange must disclose compliance with the code of conduct to investors. This helps in accessing information to the investors. In India, Board oversees the process of disclosure and communication; Board is to ensure that all the

required disclosure are given on time to the stock exchange. Auditors have a responsibility to audit the financials and report the fraud.

2. **Independence of Board**- To maintain independence and provide oversight, the Board should not be involved in the Company's day-to-day functioning to provide better oversight. Instead, the Company's daily functioning is rested with the Managing Directors and Key Management Personnel (KMP), such as the CFO and Company Secretary, under the guidance of the Board.

   Some of the best practices are

1. The Board should have the optimum combination of executive directors and non-executive directors. The majority of the Board members should be independent directors; that is, the Company does not employ them
2. Where Chairperson is Non-Executive Director or not a promoter, the Board should comprise one-third of independent directors; otherwise, half of the Board should have independent directors.
3. Some of the sub-committees, such as remuneration, audit, risk management, etc., should have non-executive and independent directors

3. **Appointment of Management**- The Board appoints the Director and KMP. In certain appointments in the Banks and Insurance industries, clearance from the regulator is mandatory. This ensures that the appointee has the required qualifications, experience, and background checks.

4. **Compensation arrangement**- The Board should set the objectives for the CEO and regularly appraise the performance. The remuneration committee sets the criteria for determining the remuneration of Directors and KMP and ensures that the total remuneration is a combination of fixed pay and variable incentives to align with the long-term objectives of the Company

Risk Committees

Under Company law 2013, the report from the Board of Directors to Shareholders should include a statement indicating the development and implementation of a Risk Management Policy.

SEBI's guideline for listed companies requires the Company to lay down a procedure to inform Board Members about Risk Assessment. In 2014, SEBIs were prescribed constituting a Risk Management Committee in each of the top 100 companies by market capitalization.

The overall responsibility of the Company's risk management rests with the Board but is delegated to Risk Management sub-committee. The majority of members of the committee consist of directors. The Chairperson of the Risk management committee shall be a member of the Board of directors. The risk management sub-committee has a term of reference based on which they operate. The terms of reference define the committee's roles and responsibilities, composition, frequency of the meeting, etc.

Audit Committee

The Audit Committee provides 'independent' assurance to the Board through its oversight and monitoring role. The audit committee is one of the main pillars of the corporate governance system in Indian public companies.

The Audit Committee to have **a minimum of 3 directors** with **independent directors forming a majority.**

Powers of Audit Committee:

- To ask for the comments of the auditors about internal control systems, the scope of the audit, including the observations of the auditors and review of financial statements before their submission to the Board
- To discuss any related issues with the internal and statutory auditors and the management of the Company.
- To investigate any matter about the items or referred to it by the Board
- To obtain professional advice from external sources
- To have full access to the information contained in the records of the Company.

Compliance Function

The role of the compliance function is to ensure that the Company follows all the rules and regulations laid down under different operating regulations. Compliance requires a good knowledge of regulations to comply. Companies that are quoted in the stock exchange need to ensure that they comply with the market standards set by the authority. Failing to observe the rules and regulation attracts penalties from the regulator.

In 2012, HSBC Holdings was pulled up by regulators of three jurisdictions for Anti-Money Laundering (AML)/Combating Financial Terrorism (CFT) violations in transferring money illegally through its subsidiaries. Several lapses were identified in HSBC's AML compliance which included ignoring internal warnings on the inadequacy of internal monitoring systems, miscategorization of Mexico as a 'low risk' country, leading to transactions being exempt from detailed monitoring, etc. As a result, a fine of US$ 1.9 billion was imposed on HSBC Holdings.

On the Indian front, non-compliance with the regulatory and internal rules has also resulted in a rise in bank fraud. For example, in July 2014, RBI imposed penalties on 12 banks for their non-compliance with regulatory guidelines in the conduct of the loan and current accounts of Deccan Chronicle Holdings.

The purpose of the compliance function is to assist institutions in managing their compliance risk, which is defined as the risk of legal or regulatory sanctions, financial loss, or loss to the reputation that an institution may suffer due to its failure to comply.

The Basel Committee in its guidance issued in April 2005, states 'the compliance function is an independent function that identifies, assesses, advises, monitors and reports on the bank's compliance risk,

In 2007, RBI issued guidelines to banks on the compliance function based on the Basel Committee guidance. The guidelines articulated the minimum requirements for implementing an effective compliance function in banks.

Compliance assessment is an integral part of supervisory oversight in the financial institution.

After the economic crisis, considerable progress has been made in enhancing and refining regulatory/supervisory standards; an important aspect of the reform measures is a greater focus on ensuring compliance with the standards across jurisdictions on a sustained basis. The compliance function is where all this comes together - ensuring that all applicable rules, regulations, and standards are adhered to and implemented coherently, consistently, and in the right spirit.

To ensure the financial system's integrity and to guard against its misuse for illegal purposes, compliance with Anti-Money Laundering (AML) and Combating Financial Terrorism rules has assumed great significance globally.

Risk Function

A Chief Risk Officer heads the risk management function, supported by specialist team members such as operational risk, financial risk, IT risk, market risk, etc. The risk management function generally does not manage risk. Under the three lines of defense model, the risks are managed by the first line of defense and supported by the second line of defense, which provide oversight.

The risk team provides a review and challenging role on the risks identified by the first line of defense; this includes asking questions on risks identified and mitigation action found.

The success of the risk team lies in highlighting whether the Company has missed any risk during its identification process and the practicality of mitigation action. There are times when the first line cannot identify the risk; in that case, the risk management team helps the first line in the risk identification. Because the first line does not have the expertise to risk identification, it is quite a challenge for the first line to perform the role of the risk manager in many markets. Three lines of defense are slowly embedding.

The role of the risk function is to advise the Board on different aspect of risks within the Company, including giving independent advice on key risks faced by the Company, including opinion o mitigation action.

Risk function helps bring out the entire spectrum of risk in front of the risk management committee, including their opinion.

The risk function also helps set the Company's risk appetite, monitor the risks against the risk identified, and raise the alarm when the risk is about to breach the appetite.

The role of the risk function is to set the risk management policies with the help of the Board and regularly update them based on the emerging environment.

Support management and business units in implementing the approved Risk Management Policies and processes and ensure they are integrated into the business operations and with Internal Control and compliance processes;

Keep the Board and management informed of the latest development in international standards and practices in Risk Management

Providing risk management training and developing the risk culture is one of the primary roles of the risk function. As stated above, the first line is not accustomed to risk management, so the risk function plays a key role in helping in risk identification methodology.

Provide analytical support to the executive-level risk committees in formulating risk management strategies and making functional risk decisions;

The risk management department is ultimately accountable to the Risk Management Committee for coordinating the effective and efficient running of the Risk Management Process, which encompasses identifying, assessing, controlling, and reporting risks.

The risk function fails if risk goes unnoticed.

Risk Culture

Risk culture is a behavioral approach of the employees taken towards risk management within its business to make it successful by proactively identifying the risks and planning the mitigation action in every act and decision. Such behavior is linked to how leadership considers risk management within their organization. Such behavior is often driven by tone from the top (Board) through the CEO.

There needs to be effective implementation of risk frameworks and processes; people need to be willing and able to use the appropriate behaviors to support risk-related activities. These behaviors will create the desired risk management culture over time. Therefore, it can be said that human behavior and capability are key to effective ERM.

Developing Risk Behavior

There could be three ways to improve the risk behavior

A culture may be developed where the mindset is not about eliminating the risk but taking the risk that the organization can take and manage. A classic example is the insurance regulator in India has proposed to insurance companies to develop a product that can protect the customers from the health hazard of the corona. So here, insurance companies are taking the risks that they can manage. This is the positive development of risk culture and sends the right message to customers.

Supporting this is a second core concept that people need to feel confident to speak up about in this risk management context. This may involve a full and frank discussion of the risks being considered, whether they are minor process issues in a call center or risks associated with a potential acquisition. It also means people feel confident to communicate bad news promptly when things go wrong without fear of retaliation. This requires managers to provide an encouraging environment at all levels.

It has been stated in the first chapter that there is a tendency for people to hide the risk, thinking that mentioning risk will create impediment; this happens when risk culture within the Company is not developed. More, there is an open talk about the risk, better the risk culture helping in developing the business. Risk management means removing roadblocks.

A third way to develop the risk culture is by developing the skills, capability, and empowerment to undertake the behaviors necessary to manage risk situations.

How to improve risk culture

1. There is a need to develop a common language through which everyone in the organization communicates. For this, the Company can impart risk training to develop core competencies, evaluation criteria, and talent assessment
2. The organization can create an environment around the development of their ERM framework that facilitates better integration of the management of upside and downside risks, where opportunities are also explored.
3. To develop a positive risk culture, the Company can introduce a reward structure related to risk management. Care should be taken when constructing incentive programs that include a component aimed at improving risk management practices or extracting value through better risk management

Bias

The meaning of bias is inclination or prejudice for or against someone or something. It is a strong inclination of mind or opinion about something. Bias can be intentional or unintentional.

Unintentional bias happens due to missing the risks or not being highlighted due to a lack of data to draw a meaningful conclusion. Still, no intention is built-in while not reporting. This also happens if a risk assessment is taken up in the very end and many risks are missed out in a hurry. Sometimes, unintentional bias also happens due to overconfidence which often leads to missing out on the risk.

Unintentional bias often happens with emerging risks when initial information has come out. People tend to use personal opinion to accept or reject its further emergence and often go out of the radar. It is questionable whether the emergence of Covid-19 during the early days, how seriously it was taken?

In the hierarchy structure, bias is often driven by the opinion of the seniors often, where open and frank discussion does not occur.

Intentional biases are deliberate when risks or decisions are not revealed due to protecting themselves or managing the short-term gain. Excessive optimism is also part of intentional bias as the decision-maker knows it is impossible, but optimism is shown to meet the interest.

It has also been found that when there is a homogenous group in the discussion, then the decision goes in one direction, which can be just opposite to reality.

The Company should try to avoid both intentional and unintentional bias and develop a culture of open and frank discussion; otherwise, the entire business and risk management process will go for a toss.

Culture should be developed to have an open mindset and non-linear thinking and may be rewarded accordingly.

Human Behavior and Risk Management

It is discussed above about bias where things are driven by personal thought processes when interpreting the risk and deciding what to do with it. A similar topic is how human behavior comes into play when the risk management team interacts with the rest of the function.

Role of Risk professional

The role of a risk management professional from the second line of defense is to ask the right questions and challenge the first line's work. For example, if the products team has developed a new design of the product, that has come to the risk team for review. Then the role of the risk team will look into the following questions; whether the product will be marketable or not, what could be the price range, what competitors are selling, what is the unique feature of the product, and why the product is brought to the market, what is the target market for the product, what will be the price range, whether the Company has done any market research before developing the new design, whether the sales feedback is taken or not, is the design meets all the regulatory guidelines, how much will be the margin for the Company so on and so forth.

Human Psychology

Asking a question is difficult as humans are not tuned to be asked questions. In addition, individual behavior depends on many factors such as upbringing, personal relationships, professional development, and tone from the top, buy-in of risk management by function heads.

The real challenge with the risk team comes when they raise questions and challenges because human tends to refute questions raised unless the Company culture is developed in that fashion. One of the important factors to the success of the risk function is how they communicate and create personal relationships with their respective stakeholders. Any friction here can create an operational challenge, so the risk team must be cautious when and how they raise questions. Whether they are raising direct or indirect questions, a direct question means asking a straight reason for the context, and an indirect question is suggestive; both can have a very different effect on the reader of the question. So risk team needs to be very careful about their language and tone. At times there are sensitive questions; therefore, for the risk professionals, written and verbal communication skill is very important. Every question needs to be backed up by reasoning.

The role of risk professionals is complicated and full of challenges as they have to act as part of the Company simultaneously; they have to act independently and raise the right risks to meet the Company's objectives. It is not always easy to balance this act, as the first line's objective is growth while the risk team's objective is to find risks that contradict and create friction with the first line.

If the risk team is raising too many risks, there could be an issue about the impediment. If the risk is not rising enough risks, they are not doing their job properly, and any risk in the future that is identified and not reported, risk people will be pulled up.

It is important to understand human behavior because one often has to undergo a challenging situation where technical skills are less useful than interpersonal skills. Therefore, the risk professionals should be good negotiators to communicate the message in difficult matters.

Sometimes the CEO is dominant; it could be challenging to challenge the CEO and report to the CEO. People sometimes lose their job if a fine balance is not created.

Case Study- Can you help this Head of Operational Risk with an ethical dilemma?

This Case Study was developed by Mr. Manoj Kulwal, CRO of Risk Spotlight. He has been allowed to use the case study

This is a brief case study inspired by some recent operational risk events. It highlights an ethical dilemma faced by a Head of Operational Risk. Below are some topics which provide context to the case study.

- James is the Head of the Operational Risk team at a large national bank.
- He has 8 team members in his Group OpRisk team (2nd line). The bank has 4,000 employees.

- James joined the bank 12 months ago. Over the last 12 months, James has noticed various unethical practices widespread across the organization, such as sales team members opening fictitious customer accounts without customer consent, the financial advisory team charging fees to customers without delivering any services, and intentional mis-selling of insurance policies to customers.
- James shared his concerns about the unethical practices with the internal audit team and Chief Risk Officer (CRO) 6 months ago. However, the CRO and internal audit team have not escalated these significantly to the risk committee and board members. The practices have been included in the reports submitted to the risk committee and board members but only as a low priority concern which is not aligned with the scale of the actual issue.
- Last week James raised this with the CRO and was shocked by the response he received. The CRO shared that the bank is under tremendous financial pressure and hence generating revenues/profits is the top priority for the Board and senior executive team at the moment. The bank may need to file for bankruptcy in 12 months if the revenue/profit performance does not improve. So it is a matter of life and death for the bank, and in light of the crisis, the Board and senior executives are not interested in investing their focus on the unethical practices.
- The CRO also shared that the regulator is aware of the unethical practices but has decided not to pursue these rigorously in the short term as the bank's bankruptcy will significantly impact the overall financial system.
- James is dissatisfied with the current situation and has contacted recruitment agencies to explore whether senior operational risk roles are available with other banks. Unfortunately, there are no current suitable opportunities available for James. New job opportunities in senior operational risk roles don't open very frequently. So it may take 6-12 months for a suitable opportunity to be available with another bank. He does not want to end up in a situation where he is not employed, as he needs to financially support his 25-year-old daughter, who is undergoing cancer treatment.

So, what is your recommendation to James?

1. Stay in your current job and become indifferent about the unethical practices. After all, if the Board, senior executive, CRO, the internal audit team, and regulator do not care about the unethical practices, then why he should be worried about these?
2. Leave the job and wait for a better opportunity, even if this takes 6-12 months and may delay the completion of his daughter's cancer treatment.
3. Contact a news media outlet and share the details of the unethical practices with them with the hope that this may generate pressure on the bank to address the unethical practices. Of course, he will most likely lose his job in this scenario, but at least he will have the satisfaction that he did something to address the issue.
4. Any other alternatives you may recommend to James

Failure of Corporate Governance- Yes Bank

The Reserve Bank of India took control of YES Bank in March 2020. The style of working of former Managing Director and CEO Rana Kapoor was to agree to disburse loans to corporate borrowers who other banks rejected. The bank used to charge a large upfront fee, and most borrowers were defaulters at will.

Kapoor held a 26 percent stake in Yes Bank; it has been seen that most promoter-driven organizations have failed in recent times, and it seems that such organizations may need special regulatory focus and corporate governance.

Other private banks need to note that focusing on technology and chasing high growth in relying on corporate banking and wholesale deposits to boost balance sheets won't work. The golden rule of prudential lending and high corporate governance is vital for any bank's survival.

Distress signals started coming from Yes Bank from 2016-to 17. Its loan book jumped from Rs 55,000 crore in 2014 to Rs 2.41 lakh crore in 2019, despite the slowdown in the economy post-demonetization. The annual scrutiny of banks by the regulator should have rightfully raised questions and prompted early action. However, most of Yes Bank's exposure was to companies that have gone bankrupt or are going down.

Failure of Corporate Governance- Jet Airways

Jet Airways failed because of poor governance. There are two points to note in the context of the governance of promoter-controlled companies.

First, promoters with skin in the game protect and create their wealth. The second is that the promoter understands the business better than independent directors; therefore, the Board of directors cannot contribute to operating and financing decisions.

For every Company, Board is critical; Naresh Goyal, the founder of Jet Airways, decided to become a one-person army for Jet Airways and did not hire a sound management committee to assist him in running the airline. Insiders often talk about his poor financial acumen. He relied on a single management team to handle all the operations related to Jet. Understanding that specialized teams are needed to run different departments is no rocket science. And when you acquire one more airline (Sahara), you can't rely on your existing management board that's already burdened to take up additional responsibilities!

Failure of Corporate Governance- Café Coffee Day

The Last Letter

The letter says: "I have failed to create a suitable, profitable business model despite my best efforts. However, I want to say I gave it my all. I am very sorry to let down everyone who put their trust in me. I fought for a long time, but today I gave up as I could not take any more pressure.

"I could not take any more pressure from one of the private equity partners forcing me to buy back shares, a transaction I had partially completed six months ago by borrowing a large sum of money from a friend. Unfortunately, tremendous pressure from other lenders leads to me succumbing to the situation. In addition, there was a lot of harassment from the previous DG income tax in the form of attaching our shares on two separate occasions to block our Mindtree deal and then taking the position of our Coffee Day shares. This was very unfair and has led to a serious liquidity crunch."

Summary of Corporate Governance

Risk management on its own cannot perform and be successful without solid corporate governance; risk management will just slip through the cracks of poor corporate governance. In any of the above examples of Yes Bank, Jet Airways, and Café Coffee Day, how and where would have fitted the risk management. For example, when are loans given across the table, and what risk assessment can be done? Similarly, when all the decisions are taken through a central place, what role risk manager will play?

A company can survive without risk management but cannot survive without proper corporate governance. Therefore, good corporate governance is a necessary condition for risk management to be successful.

NINE

Challenges are Thrown in Corporate Governance during COVID 19

This chapter is written with Dr. Purnima Rao, Associate Professor, *Fortune Institute of International Business, New Delhi, India*

Introduction

This chapter highlights the challenges thrown by COVID 19 during the last two years on corporate governance. Such challenges have highlighted the weakness in the working of Board, remuneration committee, the effectiveness of risk management and limitation of the risk management framework, corporate governance focusing only on shareholders and ignoring other stakeholders such as employees, taxpayers when Government bailout companies, liquidity challenges, etc.

Good corporate governance is a necessary condition for an organization's risk management to flourish. Corporate governance is a facilitator of the entire conduct of the organization. However, the successive crisis has exposed the weaknesses in corporate governance. In the current living creatures, COVID 19 has given maximum impact across the world forcing people to think beyond current practices and looking for changes for a higher level of sustainability. The chapter also looks at the changes that are required in corporate governance to handle a future similar situation better.

Challenges in Corporate governance

This section discusses the challenges in Board, remuneration committee, and risk management.

Board

The Board during the initial period at the start of the pandemic close to January 2020, could not foresee the coming risks and could not take mitigating action. Also, companies were perhaps not prepared for this kind of stressful situation. Some companies do perform stress testing; however, they are more for academic purposes and mitigating action plans are not prepared to deal with those risks. So as a result, Board could not steer the Company to safe harbors.

Grove, H; Clouse, M & Xu, T (2021)mentioned that the management and corporate governance system must accept their failure in handling the COVID crisis and there was a bias toward shareholders ignoring the workers. The focus of the Companies is to boost quarterly revenue and earnings to keep the stock price up. According to the Congressional Budget Office, the U.S. federal government has spent more than $4 trillion in 2020 to keep the U.S. economy afloat.

Similarly, during the 2008 economic crisis, corporate governance faced similar challenges in terms of the Board of Directors not being able to give sufficient time to full filling their duties. Many of the Board members were not coming from a technical background, and some of them had no banking experience.

According to Moody in 2005 stated that Lehman Brothers 4 out of 10 members were more than 75 years of age and only one had a financial background. The Board needs to have the right mix of experience and age. It was also reported after the investigation that the Risk committee did not meet regularly, Lehman Brothers met only twice each in 2006 and 2007. In some institutions, the risk committees were established shortly before they failed such as Bear Stearns. Board of Directors not performing serious performance appraisal. Some banks reported difficulties in recruiting non-executive directors with financial backgrounds.

Dick May & Chris Mackin (2020) has mentioned that large organization with large skilled leaders and workforce should be held accountable for the corporate failures during COVID 19. They identify the need to change the corporate governance due to the lack of ability of the Board, managers, and advisors to foresee or better react to the crisis. Gelter, M, and Puaschunder (2021) also highlighted the failure of the Board in dealing with the crisis

Remuneration Committee

It was noted during the peak of COVID that millions of workers lost their job and companies had challenges in paying their salaries. There was a lack of liquidity in the system and the remuneration committee was questioned on the role of handling the situation.

Grove, H; Clouse, M & Xu, T (2021)mentioned that many US business houses did not have enough liquidity to pay the salaries to the employees for one month after the COVID crisis. As a part of financial planning, families are encouraged to keep the cash reserve for six months to one year, but corporate did not have enough cash to pay the salaries of thousands of workers. The questions are raised on the role of the Remuneration Committee in this regard and pointed out that the US government is to bail out the companies just like the banks bailing out during the 2008 crisis. The remuneration committee did not play its role as cash was returned to shareholders in a form of a dividend and stock buyback option to keep the stock price high. He mentioned that the Board was self-serving.

Risk Management

During COVID 19, the risk management was also not able to perform up to the expectation as they could not highlight the expected risk. Risk function is the eyes and ears of the organization to anticipate and raise an alarm bell. They are like the captain of the ship looking for a possible iceberg and alerting the engine room. The risk professionals can smell the risk.

Kumar, S (2020) mentioned in the report of "Institute of Risk Management Covid–19 Global Risk

Management Response" that barring in the countries where Covid-19 reached in January and February, the world was waiting to spread the fire further and it did. Why don't our risk management frameworks have buttons which prompt taking immediate actions rather than leaving the actions to the decision-makers? It's like having an immediate sprinkler system as soon as a fire is visible or smoke is there. If we need to protect the world from the next disaster that may come anytime in the presence of global warming, we need to tighten up the risk management framework that everyone must agree on as a part of the national constitution. The losses to human life and economic cost are enormous, we have to have a sprinkler system and decision-making cannot be left to choose.

Bergener, J, and Filzen, JJ (2021) examined the risk literacy of business executives and found significant variations. They suggested that it would help the organization to identify its risk literacy that will help in developing the risk culture. They are of the view that risk literacy helps solve complex problems.

It is already identified during the 2008 economic crisis the importance of relevant experience and qualification.

In the Indian context, there is no mandated risk qualification for the appointment of risk professionals by any of the regulators. In recent times, the Indian Central Bank (Reserve Bank of India, RBI) has started mandating risk management qualifications for the appointment of CROs (RBI Circular dated 25th June 2021) in Urban Cooperative Banks.

Pagach, D and Wieczorek, M(2020) mentioned that pandemic risk was underestimated both in magnitude and frequency and suggested an improvement area under enterprise risk management. To facilitate good risk management, there is a greater role of CRO in communicating the risk information to the Board, management, and stakeholders. They further emphasized to increase the effectiveness of ERM, there is a need to improve the governance and risk culture.

The failure of risk management during COVID 19 at the global level stresses the need for risk management qualifications to help better understand risk management and apply it in the right context. There is also a need for standardizing the risk management qualification given different needs and too many providers.

There is also a need to increase the risk literacy of the Board members to guide the corporate ship better and it would be helpful to have at least one independent director with risk management experience and qualifications.

Suggestion for Improvement

Given the challenges in the emerging COVID environment, there is a greater need to improve corporate governance to handle the future situation better. Environment risk may pose an even more severe impact and the world should be ready and prepared to deal with it. Also, some of the techniques used in other fields such as aerospace or tracking of key risk indicators during the flight could be used in sailing corporate ships. Such fields have many more risk parameters and uncertainties.

Grove, H; Clouse, M & Xu, T (2021)mentioned that there is a need to rebalance the U.S. corporate governance to deliver economic security for all citizens and stakeholders, not just shareholders and the wealthy.

Dick May & Chris Mackin (2020) advocated that larger, publicly traded companies at risk of bankruptcy will only be improved if government relief is conditioned upon structural changes in equity ownership and governing control. They further say that the structural change should allow the creation of long-term profit-sharing with employees. Also, the choice of Board representative should take place in consultation with employees and independent Directors.

Gelter, M, and Puaschunder (2021) highlighted the need for nationalism and/or protectionism in corporate law. They mentioned that previously government ownership in the economy had a bad name because of its perceived inefficiencies, however, the same government is bailing out the companies. Now counties are not in favor of taking financial help from international investors with political motives, such as firms affiliated with the People's Republic of China. The EU and US governments are tightening the FDI rules. They have stressed the need to have government ownership for corporate nationalism.

There is a very strong voice coming about moving away from the shareholder focus approach to the stakeholder focus approach.

Conclusion

Corporate governance in its current form has holes that need to be plugged in to handle any future crisis. One key theme that is coming out is moving away from shareholder focus to stakeholder focus corporate governance. It also seems from nationalism that we are moving to square one.

References

1. Bergener, J and Filzen, JJ (2021), Is your C-suite risk literate?, Business Horizon

2. Pagach, D and Wieczorek, M(2020), The Challenges and Opportunities for ERM Post COVID 19: Agenda for future research, Journal of Risk and Financial Management
3. RBI/2021-2022/62 DOR.CRE(DIR).REC.26 /21.04.103/2021-22, dated 25th June 2021
4. Kumar, S (2020) "Institute of Risk Management Covid–19 Global Risk Management Response", PP 25
5. Grove, H; Clouse, M & Xu, T (2021), COVID reflection on corporate governance (special issue). Corporate Governance and Sustainability Review, 5(1), 94-106
6. Dick May & Chris Mackin (2020): Responding to the COVID-19 Crisis: Public Policy and Corporate Governance Considerations, Challenge
7. Gelter, M and Puaschunder (2021), COVID 19 & Comparative Corporate Governance, Fordham University, School of law

TEN

BASICS OF MODELS FOR RISK QUANTIFICATION

Introduction

The purpose of this chapter is to introduce how models are used for the purpose of risk quantification. The idea is to understand at the concept level and not to enter into the mathematics of the thing.

Why Models are Important

Risk is about the future; models help understand the risks of the future. One way is using the astrological technique that is based on the position of stars and natal charts to make predictions about the future. But this science is not developed to rely upon.

In the entire risk management process, it was discussed identifying risks and planning for mitigating action. One of the key steps in between the two is risk measurement of risk on the basis of which the company quantifies and assesses the impact. But without knowing about the future, the impact cannot be assessed.

Therefore mathematics and statistics provide tools to estimate the future (note the word estimate) and not predict. So whatever numbers mathematics or statistics provide are estimate about the future.

The estimate about the future comes from past experience (as the future is unknown) with the assumption that the future will behave in a similar way as the past. In some places, judgments are used to adjust past data for future use.

There are two ways to make estimates about the future, one is using the variable dependent models and the second is statistical models.

Variable dependent models

In variable-dependent models, there are two variables, one is the independent variable and the second is the dependent variable. The value of the independent variable does not depend on anything and the value of the dependent variable depends on the independent variable. For example, the weight of a person is dependent on the height of a person. So height is an independent variable and weight is a dependent variable.

There can be more than one independent variable for one dependent variable, for example, GDP is a dependent variable on the number of independent variables such as interest rate, inflation, production, exports and imports contribution from the service sector, etc. Such models are often referred as econometric models.

The simplest form of variable-dependent modes is a linear model such as $Y = M^*x + C$, where x is the independent variable and Y is the dependent variable. M and C are constants and their values are derived from the historic data.

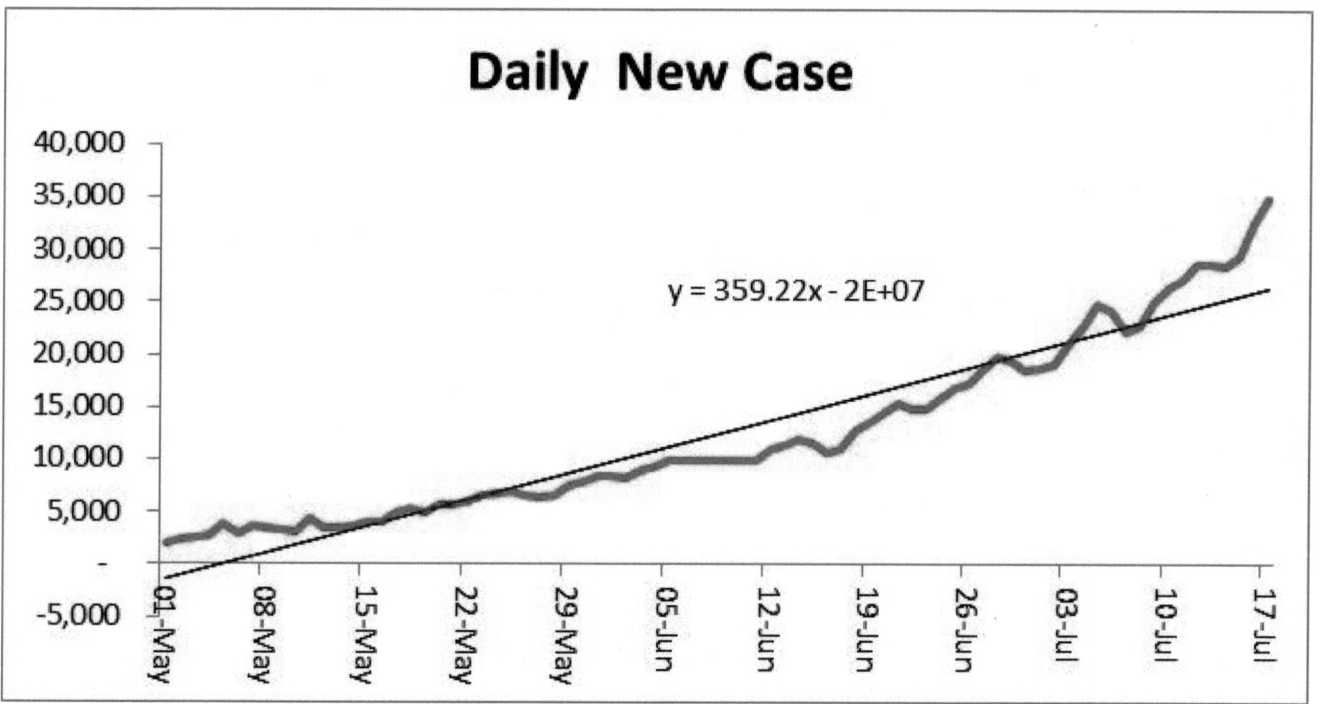

For example in the given graph, there is a development of daily new coronavirus cases between 1st May to 17th July 2020, in the given data shown as red line are actual data, a linear line which is a black is fitted represented by equation Y = 359.2x-2*10^7.

Forecast

Using the fitted line equation, if the dates are increased from 18th July onwards, it will start giving projections for new cases for the period up to 31st July as shown in the below graph.

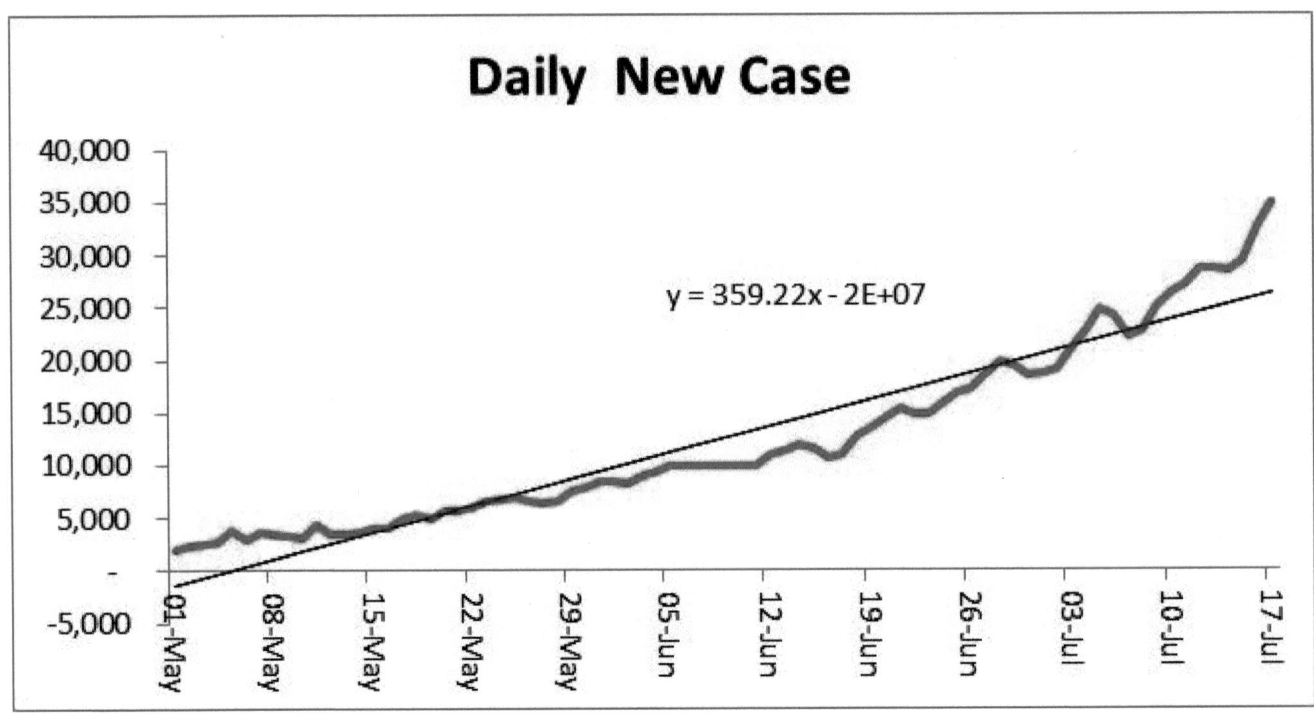

It can be noticed that the black line has increased up to 31st July and the dependent value which is a daily number of new cases can be read about the projected line 31st July. This indicates that the model Y = m*x + C gives us the projection for the future. The results that are coming out from the forecast should be read with care and should know the limitation of the model.

Limitation

There few points to consider when making forecasts using such models.

1. The projection assumes that the past trend will continue, so generally, such projections are good for a short-term period as in reality, the actual shape of data may change then the fitted equation will not give an accurate result.
2. Secondly, the slope of the curve can change which will change the equation and so the projection
3. Sometimes based on the shape of the data, different equations will fit.

Another Example

Let's consider another data set such as the ratio of daily increase to daily exit, it can be noticed that the data points are curvature in nature; here different equations will get fitted such as a quadratic equation. Based on the trend, one will expect that as the days increases, the ratio will fall further.

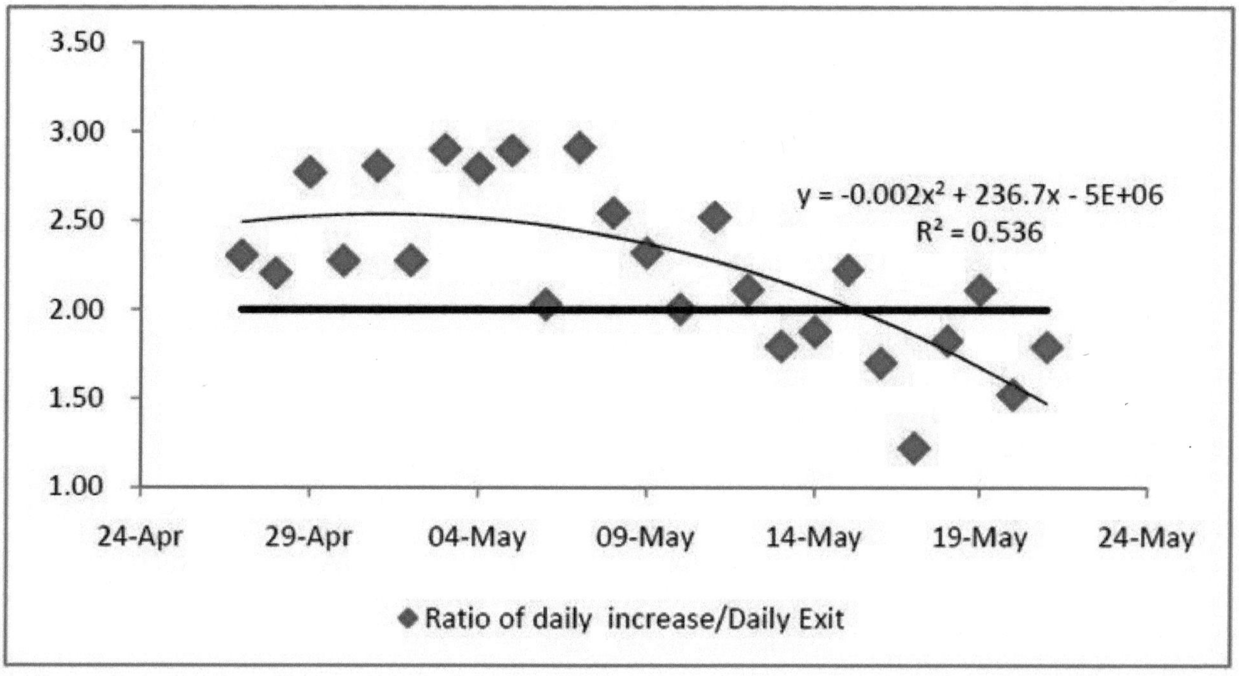

But that is not the case, see the change in the shape of the data as time progressed and the shape of the fitted curve has also changed. Therefore, one has to be very careful when using such techniques and which model to fit.

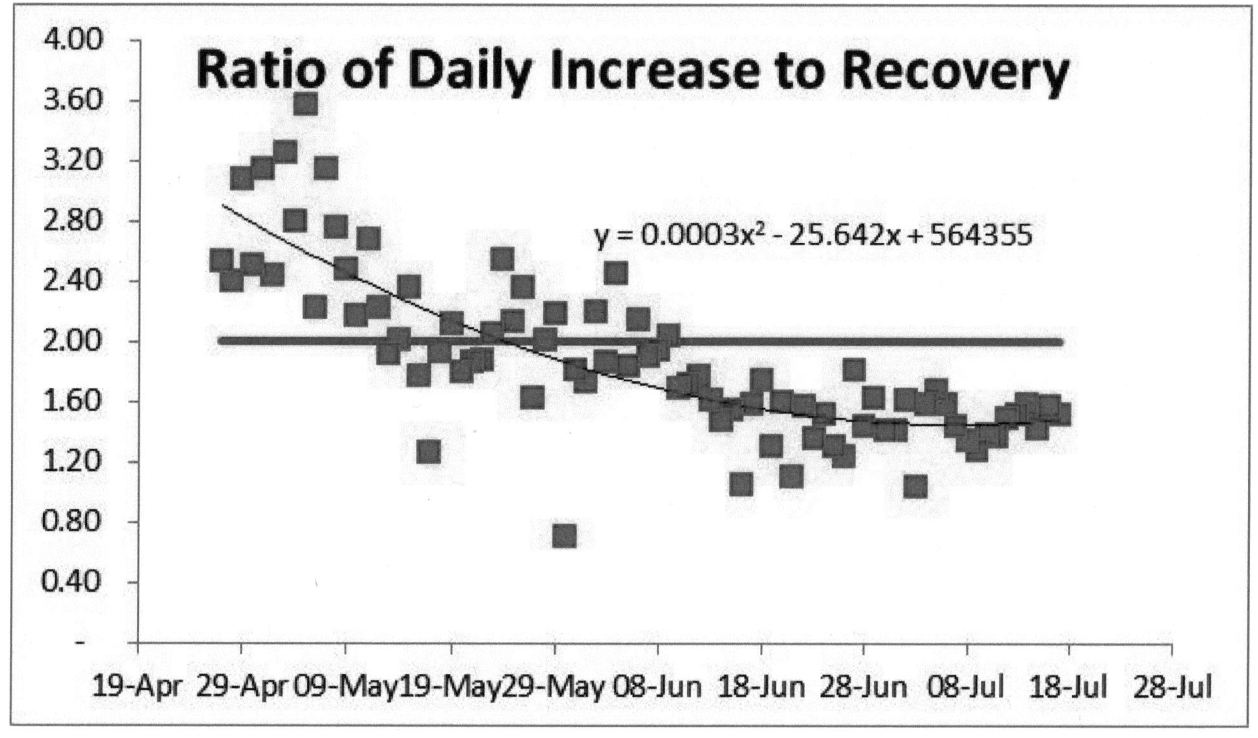

This demonstrates how such a model Works. There are several such models including econometric models.

Statistical Models

The statistical models are based on probability which is the likelihood, it says what are the chances of happening of an event. For example, if a coin is tossed, between the time, the coin is tossed and the time it lands, it is not known whether it will land on its head or tail, that's uncertainty. Instead of a coin, one considers any events that have only two possible outcomes, such as while going on the road, whether the accident will happen or will not happen. If one has to judge, what is the probability that an accident will take place, similar to what is the probability that the head will land?

The method is simple, one can start tossing the coin say 100 times and start noting how many times, the head comes and how many times the tail comes. one may find that 49 are head and 51 are tail, that is, 49% chance of head and 51% chance of tail but as a number of tosses increases one will find that there are equal chances of getting head or tail that is the probability is 50% for either head or tail.

Accident Example

In the accident example, one can exactly do the same thing and start noting say, how many accidents take place in a city out of a total number of vehicles on the road. This may come out to be daily 5000 accidents out of a total 10 lac vehicle (both are fictitious numbers), this comes out to be 5000/10 lac = 0. 5% chances of an accident on a daily basis and the probability of not happening the accident are 99.5%

In probabilistic language this example tells about the future, there are equal chances of falling head or tail in the future. The probability of an accident for tomorrow is 0.5% if all remain exactly like all previous days. So the historic estimate tells us the likelihood of the future with the inherent assumption that other things are constant.

In the above example, there were only two outcomes, head or tail, accident or no accident, however, in practical life, there are multiple events that may take place and we require the probability of each of the events.

Multiple Events

Let us understand one example of multiple events and how they can be used for practical purposes. Once, one example is understood, then the rest of the world will follow on similar lines.

Let's consider the example of return on the stock market and the following picture shows the actual annual return between 1991 to 2018. One can notice a wide range of annual returns on each of the years, it ranges from positive 2% to 82% and negative 5% to negative 52%. So, one can want to find the probability of different returns over the annual period.

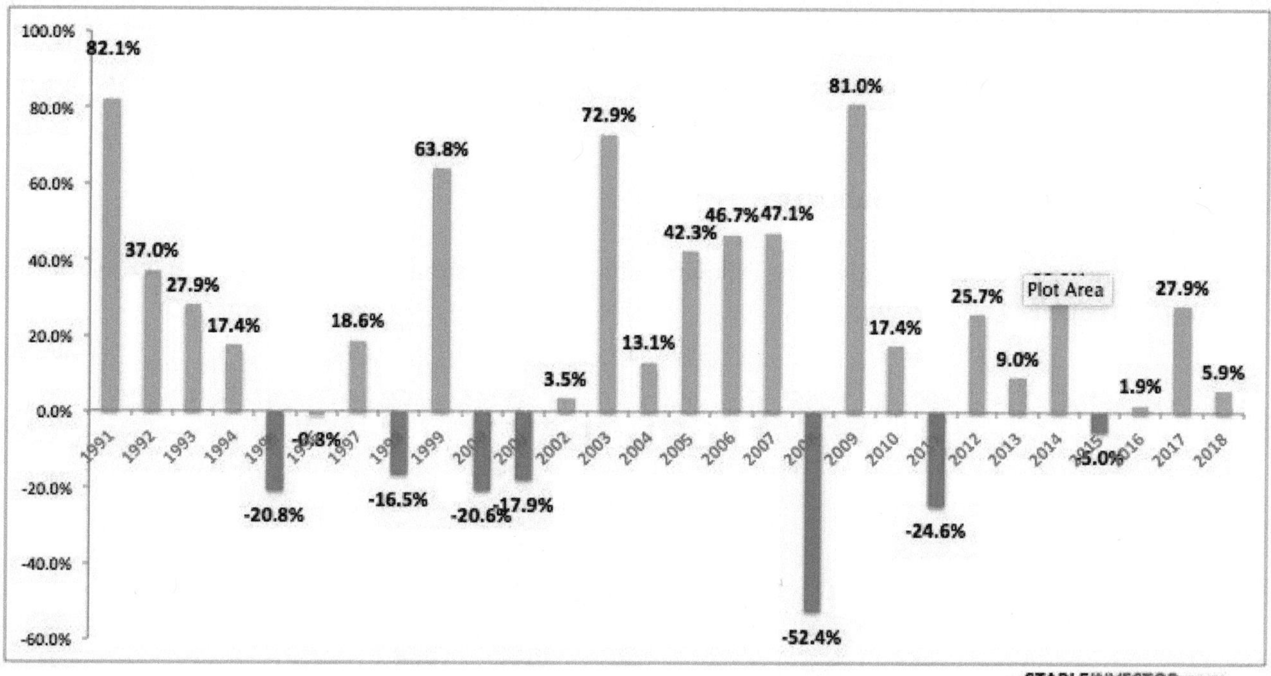

Class Interval

Recall the days, when statistics were first taught by making the class interval and doing the tally mark and if one does that we shall get something like this

Annual Return on Stock Market	Frequency	Probability
<-30%	1	4.0%
-20%--10%	2	8.0%
-10%-0%	3	12.0%
0%-10%	4	16.0%
10%-20%	5	20.0%
20%-30%	4	16.0%
30%-40%	3	12.0%
40%-50%	2	8.0%
>50%	1	4.0%
Total	**25**	**100.0%**

The frequency tells us that in one year, the annual returns were less than 30% and in one year, the annual returns were more than 50%. There were 5 years when the returns were between 10% to 20%. Note that the frequency is adjusted to give a particular shape to the distribution. The idea is to understand the concept rather than convert the raw data into distribution.

If the frequency is divided by a total number of years which is 25, then one gets the probability of getting a return in different brackets. For example, there is a 20% chance that my annual return will be between 10% to 20%, exactly the same as the probability of an accident example. Here one can see that there are multiple events of different returns.

The plot of Frequency and Probability

The plot of frequency and probability gives the following shape, which is the same in nature and it does not matter whether one plot frequency or probability

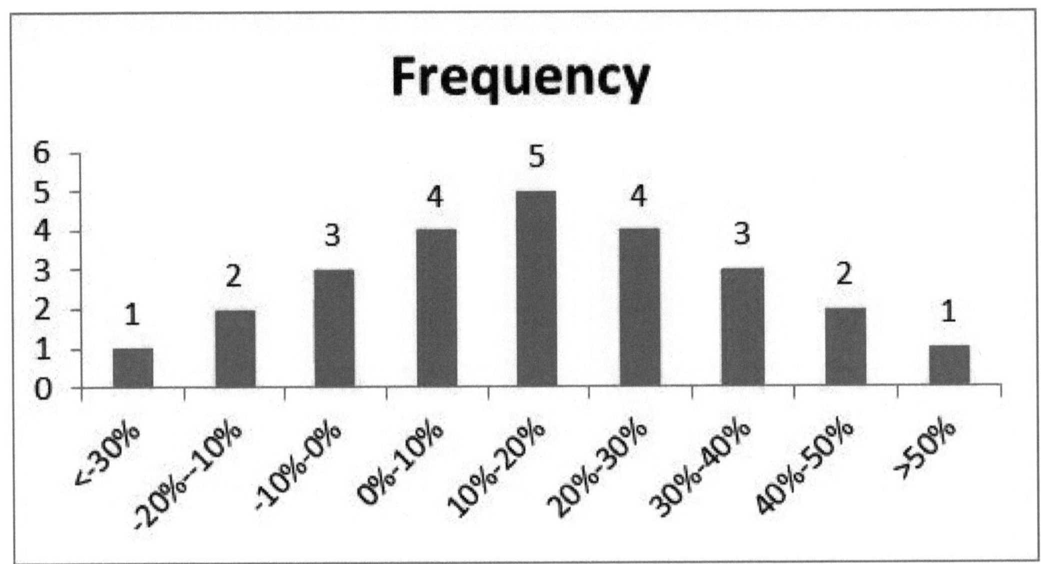

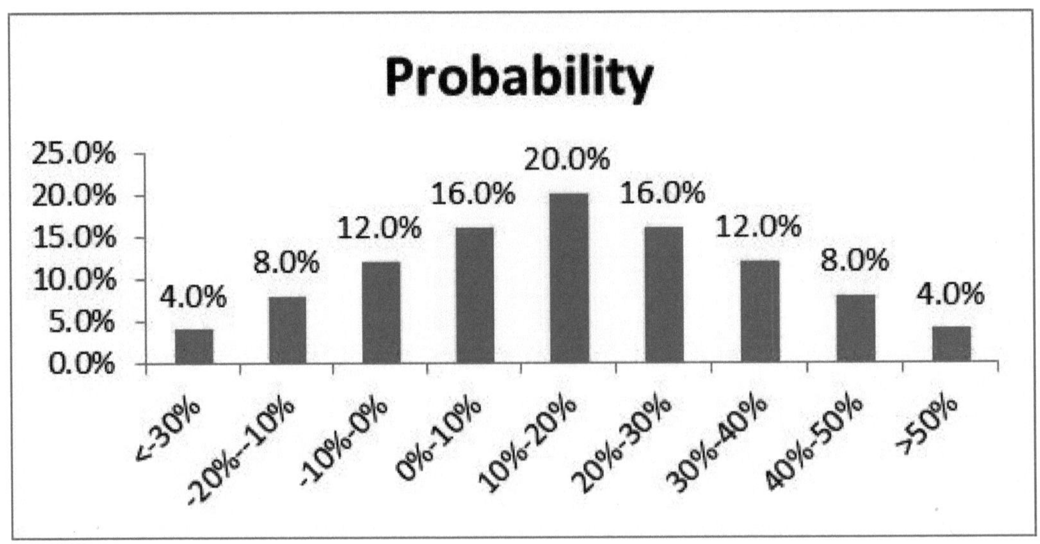

Such shape in the world of statistics is very commonly termed as **Normal Distribution** which is symmetrical on both sides. The average return would come out to be somewhere around 10%-20% which is the center and both sides are symmetrical.

Another point to note is that if one adds all the probabilities, one will get 100% or 1. So the sum of all probabilities for all possible outcomes within a set of events will always add to 1. Alternatively, one can understand this by looking at the frequency table and each frequency is divided by its total, so all the probability will add up to 1.

Discrete and Continuous distribution

In the above probability distribution, one can see the discrete annual return interval, that is, it is between say, 10% to 20%, 20% to 30%, etc. Such distributions are called **discrete distributions.** In the discrete distribution, one can define the probability at a point in time.

Continuous distribution takes the continuous value on the x-axis and the graph comes out to be smooth

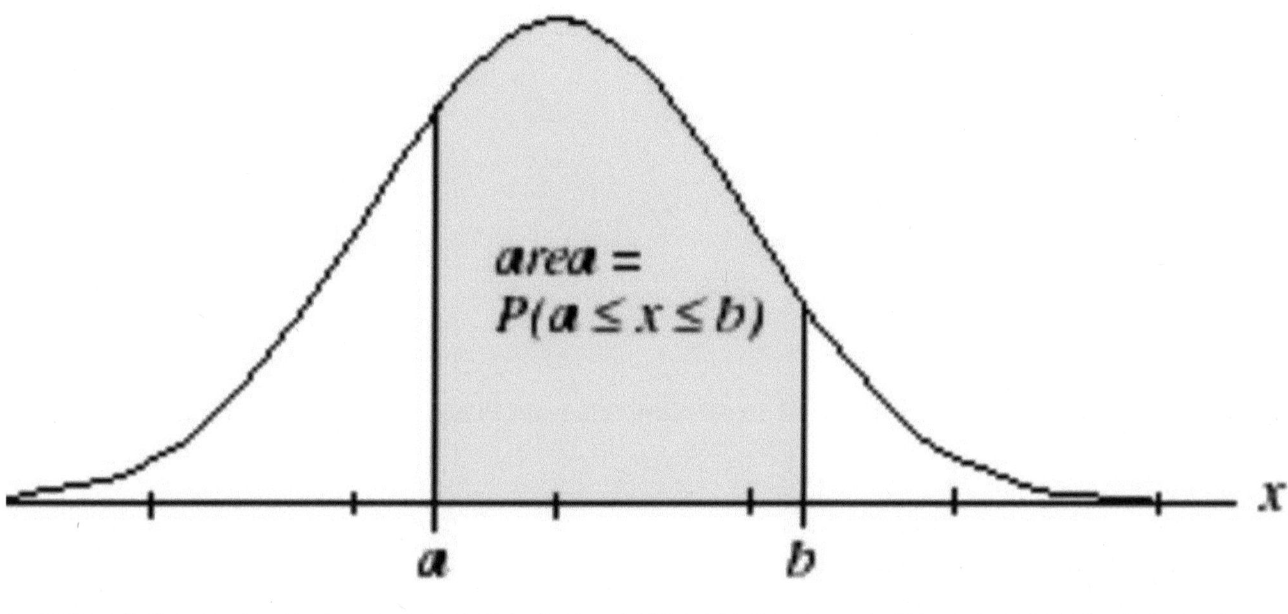

One can notice that on x-axis takes continuous values rather than discrete values and the shape of the curve is continuous in nature rather than bars. In this case, one cannot define the probability at any point in time, but one has to take the interval on the x-axis say between point “a” and point “b” and then the probability is defined as the area between the point “a” and point “b”

If one plots the above example on a continuous basis the figure will come as

Annual Return example on Continuous scale

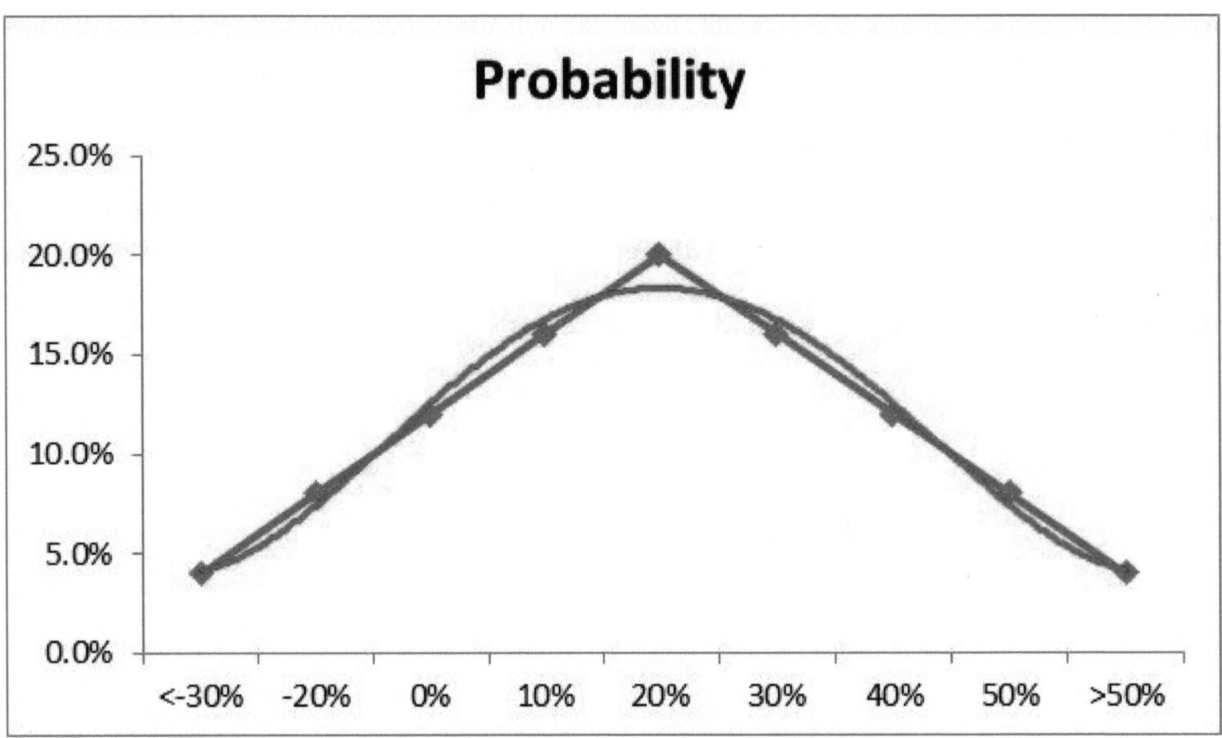

The same example of annual return is plotted on a continuous scale. Pl note the following points:

1. X-axis numbers are continuous
2. Blue lines are probability on a discrete scale
3. Redline is on a continuous scale fitted on the same data
4. On a discrete scale, one can define the probability of getting a 20% return as say 20% but on a continuous scale, one cannot calculate the probability of getting a 20% return. Instead, one can find the Probability of getting a return up to 20% or greater than 20% or between any intervals say between 0% to 5% as one can calculate the area between the two points.
5. On a continuous scale, at a point, we cannot find the area; therefore, the probability at any point is zero.
6. If we have to find the probability of getting the return up to -20%, then the probability will be the shaded area shown on the left of the vertical line on -20%.
7. If one has to find the probability of getting the return greater than 50%, then the probability is the shaded area on the right of the vertical line of 50%
8. If one has to find the probability of return between 30% to 35%, then the probability will be shaded area between the two vertical lines at 30% and at 35%.
9. The area is calculated using the integration technique used in mathematics
10. The red line that one sees is called the probability density function and using integration one can calculate the area between any two intervals.
11. It is important to note that the red line may have a different shape based on different events and hold the key in the calculation of probability

Application of distribution

Now the concept is ready to look into the application of probability distribution in different areas.

Please note that in the statistical function two things will change and the rest of the concepts will remain the same

1. One is, instead of annual stock return on the x-axis, there could be different events such as loss amount due to motor accident, loss amount due to hurricane, credit loss, or anything that can be thought of.
2. The second change is, based on the type of events, the shape of the curve will change, that is, the density function will change. The method of calculation of probability will remain the same.
3. So for any kind of application to be used, one must know the density function of the distribution and one can calculate the probability.
4. Recall from the example of the accident that the important point is to calculate the probability which represents the expected future event
5. The changes that may happen from the past to the future may be adjusted in the calculated value of probability that is coming. This will come from the judgment about the future. In Actuarial calculation, such adjustments are often used as actual experience changes compared to when the probability was calculated. This is the importance of monitoring experience which helps in updating the assumption for the future.
6. The Challenge that comes is for every event, probability distribution does not exist or data is not available and so how to arrive at probability. For example, there is no historic data to forecast the probability of Covid-19. There are very little data that how to ensure a Cricket Test Match?

Given this background, one can apply all statistical techniques at a concept level. To get the hands dirty, there are volumes of books written on different statistical distributions and the limitation and applicability of the distribution. However, from the understanding point of view, this basic concept suffices.

Let us look at some application of statistical distribution, their shape, and the logic behind each of those shapes.

Loss Distribution

There is a lot of application of loss distribution in the general insurance industry and also in the credit rating where the shape of the distribution could be one of the following. Notice the change in the shape of the curve compared to the one with an annual return.

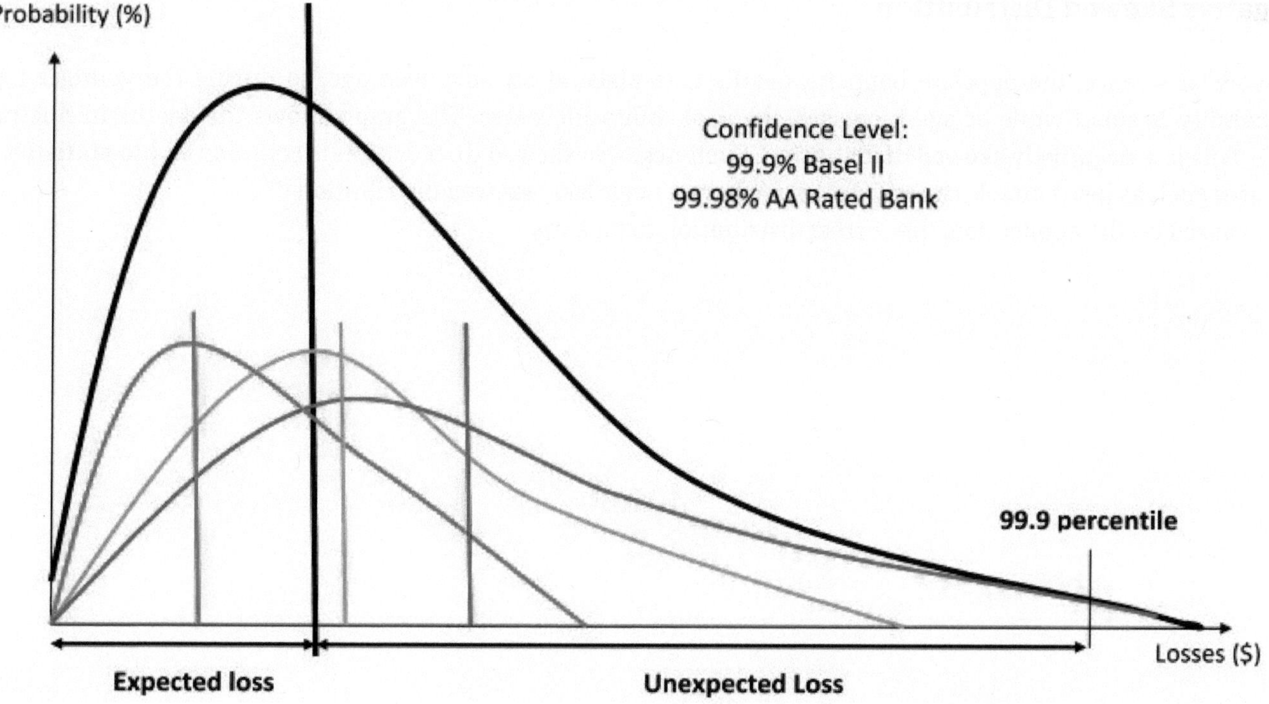

Based on the different types of events such as motor claims, liability claims, theft, accidents, etc may take different shapes within the shapes mentioned above. For example, one event may take the shape represented by a black line while another event may take a shape represented by a green line and some other by a red or orange line. Note for each of the distributions mentioned, at the same point on the x-axis, will give a different probability based on the types of the event.

Let's understand the shape of the curve. First note that on the x-axis, as a loss amount in dollar terms instead of annual return in our above example. The second one can see that shape of the curve has a hump in the beginning and then a tail on the right. This means that in reality, most of the claims are of small amount, the probability of such events is high and there will be very fewer claims will be of big amount on the right tail and so the probability of a very big amount is low. Such a shape of the distribution is called a **positively skewed distribution**.

For the practical purpose of calculation of probability, the method will remain the same, for example, if the company wants to calculate the probability of loss beyond "x" million dollars, then, one can calculate the probability as the area on the curve after the "x" million dollars on the x-axis.

Let's understand two concepts discussed earlier **Value at Risk (VaR)** and **Stress Testing**.

If the x-axis represents all the possible losses that the Company has suffered and wants to calculate VaR or Risk-Based Capital at say 99.9% confidence level. This means that from the beginning of the x-axis on the left to the vertical line on the right shown as 99.9 percentile represents that the area between these two points is 99.9%. So, if one picks up a dollar amount from the x-axis exactly at a point representing the 99.9 percentile will be the risk-based capital or value at risk. Let's say this amount on the x-axis is 1000 million dollars.

So, if the Company keeps 1000 million dollars, they have a chance of protection of 99.9% times.

And if it is written 99.9% Basel-II AA rated bank. This means that if the bank maintains the capital requirement at a 99.9% confidence level then such banks will have a rating of AA.

Let's look at the stress testing, stress testing is performed, how much capital is required, and if a situation comes when an event falls in the area on the right of the vertical line represented on 99.9%. Because VaR does not give us the capital requirement beyond the defined level of confidence level, stress testing is required. If a stressful situation may require a total of 1200 million dollars, that is additional 200 million dollars.

Negative Skewed Distribution

In medical science, the opposite happens, deaths take place at an advanced age, so during the younger age, the probability is small while as age increases, the probability increases. The graph shows the deaths in Australia in 2012. This is a **negatively skewed distribution**. Such negative skewed distribution is common in **bio-statistics**, most diseases such as heart attack, cancer, stroke, etc have a negatively skewed distribution

So based on the application, the correct distribution to pick up.

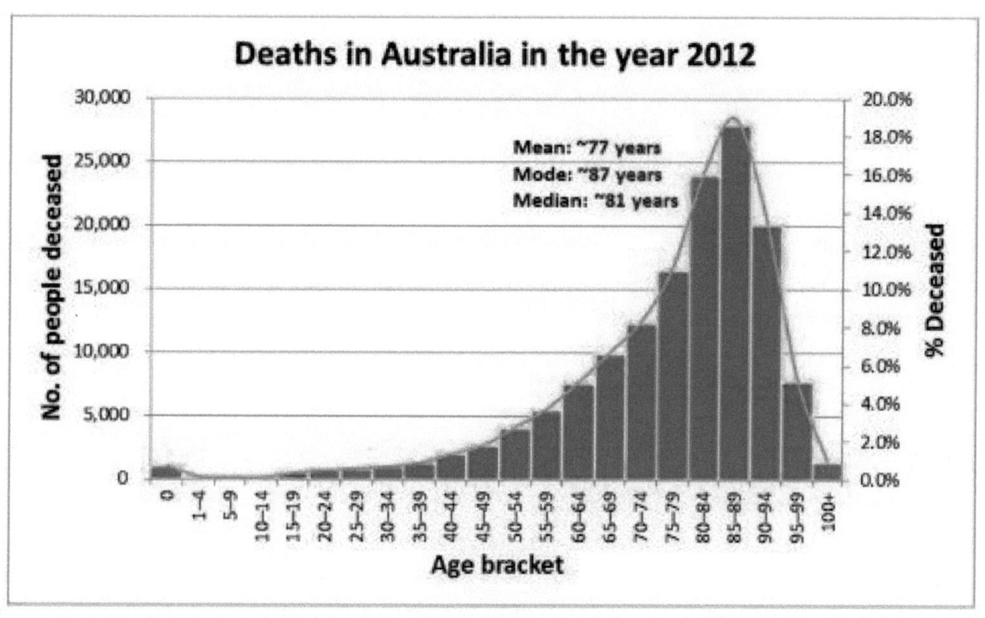

Credit Risk

In credit risk, the company calculates the probability of default that the one who has taken a loan may defaults and the company require the probability of the default. Such distribution looks like

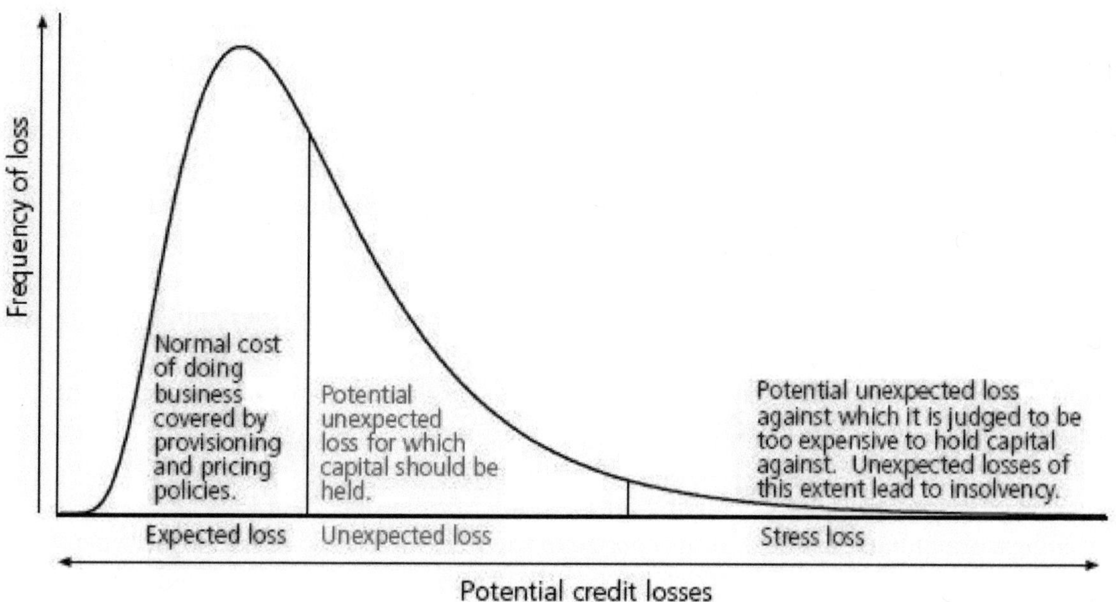

Enter Caption

One can see that on the x-axis are the credit losses and the shape of the curve is similar to loss distribution where the probability of a high amount of losses is small.

Credit risk or credit default risk associated with a financial transaction is defined as the expected loss of that transaction. It can be defined as follows:

Credit Risk = Default Probability * Exposure * Loss Rate

Where:

- **Default Probability** is the probability of a debtor defaulting on his debt payments. Such default probability is calculated from the distribution above
- **Exposure** is the total amount the lender is supposed to get paid. In most cases, it is simply the amount borrowed by the debtor plus interest payments. This amount is shown on the x-axis
- **Loss Rate = 1 – Recovery Rate**, where Recovery Rate is the proportion of the total amount that can be recovered if the debtor defaults.

Credit Risk, the Housing Bubble, and the Great Recession

Improper risk management by banks and other financial institutions was a key factor behind the **US housing bubble in the mid-2000s** that eventually led to the 2008 recession. **Commercial banks, investment banks, and other financial markets participants underestimated both the default probability and the loss rate** and consequently **underestimated the credit risk they were facing**.

In the lead-up to the recession, most lenders gave loans to individuals and businesses with questionable credit histories. The fact was most evident in the housing market, where easy credit led to house prices rising rapidly in the mid-2000s. Increased house prices meant borrowers could refinance their mortgages and borrow even more money, which fueled the bubble even further.

Interest rate Risk

For certain risks, other than statistical models are required to assess the risks. Interest rate risk and liquidity risks are two risks prevalent in the financial sector. Let's look at first interest rate risk.

Interest rate risk is the fluctuation in interest rate leading to a change in the value of assets and liabilities. It should be remembered that the value of assets or liability increases if the interest rate falls, while the value of assets or liability falls when the interest rate rises. Both the situations lead to a mismatch between assets and liability. Therefore assets and liability management is very common in the financial institution to manage the interest rate risk.

In the banking sector, assets (which are loans given) are of longer tenure compared to liability (which are deposits), so if the interest rate rises, the value of assets falls more than the value of liability leading to a mismatch between assets and liability.

In the insurance sector, liabilities (customer's policy term) are longer than assets (investments), so when the interest rate falls, the value of liability rises more than the value of assets leading to a mismatch between assets and liability, so fall in the interest rate is a risk in the insurance business.

The interest rate risk is measured by calculating the **duration** of assets and liabilities.

Duration is a measure of the sensitivity of the change in the value of assets and liabilities when the interest rate changes. For example, if the duration of the asset is 8 and the duration of liability is 9, then if interest rate changes, then assets value will change by 8 unit and liability will change by 9 units. So the gap between assets and liabilities will be 1 unit. Therefore, in the management of assets and liabilities, it is an endeavor to match the duration of assets and liabilities.

The other method of measuring the assets and liabilities gap is by matching the cash flows of assets and liabilities.

Liquidity Risk

Liquidity Risk is a risk of insufficient liquid assets to meet payouts forcing the sale of assets at lower prices, leading to losses. Liquidity risk may not threaten the solvency of the Company but may lead to default.

Liquidity risk may arise due to either an unexpected increase in liabilities or assets and stress and cannot be easily liquidated.

On the liability side, there are chances that the outflow from the financial system increases due to some untoward economic condition and there are more withdrawals from banks or insurance policyholders start surrendering the policy.

On the assets side, the liquidity risk may arise due to impairment in the capital market, increase in interest rate, lower than expected new business premium, lower than expected renewal premium, or default by the reinsurer. In capital market impairment, previous liquid asset classes become temporarily illiquid or materially less liquid for an extended period of time raising even a nominal amount of cash can prove to be difficult.

Another important source of liquidity risk is when assets are downgraded by rating agencies. The downgrading of the news spread very rapidly in the financial media and reaches the customers which may create panic among them leading to a higher level of withdrawal. This situation could be very dangerous unless management act quickly.

Liquidity risk is measured by either calculating the Liquidity Coverage ratio or testing the future cash inflow and outflow for say next 12 months' time and seeing whether the company has sufficient cash to payout. The companies also use stress testing.

The LCR is defined in the Basel committee recommendation as a ratio of

LCR= (Stocks in High-Quality Liquid Assets/Total Net cash outflow over next 30 Calendar days) >= 100%

For the institution to stay liquid, the LCR should be greater than 100% for the next 30 days. Based on the requirement, the institution may choose a time frame as one month, three months, 12 months, and 18 months. In insurance companies, this period is generally taken as 12 months, however, some also consider 18 months.

Other Risk

Here, quantification of key risks is covered such as credit risk, interest rate risk, and liquidity risk. Let's look at some other risks such as what tools are used for quantification. For operational risk, as it was mentioned earlier, qualitative risk assessment is used because so far no statistical models have been able to fit in the operational losses. However, some organizations and the consulting firms have tried to use loss distribution and scenario analysis to model operational losses. The results are mixed and no concrete evidences are available on its application. Intuitively, losses from operations can be modeled but yet lot of work to be done.

In insurance business, there are three risks; they are mortality, lapse and expenses. For mortality, there is a well established method of using the life table where out of cohort at age 0 is tracked until say 100 years and numbers of deaths are noted at each year and that become death rate at ach age. In every country, actuarial profession takes care of preparation of such mortality table after every 10 to 15 years time because mortality changes over time, so a new table is prepared. In between the time, the mortality rates are adjusted as per emerging experience.

For lapse and expense risk, the method is very simple, actual experience is measured against what was used in pricing and keep taking the corrective action so that actual experience become in line with pricing.

For equity risk, we have seen our first model on annual return on equity, the time period of calculation can change such as daily volatility or monthly volatility etc.

ELEVEN

Challenges in Embedding Enterprise Risk Management in The Indian Market

Introduction

Enterprise Risk Management (ERM) is about integrating the risk management process across the organization flowing right through the top of the hierarchy of the Board to the last employee in the ladder chain. For a successful organization, ERM should be well embedded within the daily working culture and decision-making process. To progress systematically, ownership of risks should be identified and allocated. ERM is like an entire body linked through the veins flowing blood, any broken links are recipe for disaster.

The key determinants of ERM are risk culture, three lines of defense, corporate governance, risk management framework, support of Board and Senior Management, etc. Well-developed determinants help in embedding risk management into the organization and also enable increasing the firm value. However, these determinants are often not so well embedded in many markets leading to challenges in the application of ERM. Therefore, many markets are not able to derive the full benefits of ERM despite regulatory push.

This chapter discusses some of the challenges present in embedding the determinants of ERM issues like corporate governance, independence of CRO, challenges in implementing three lines of defense model, lack of risk knowledge in the first line of defense, lack of risk qualification in the second line of defense, etc. The chapter also gives some suggestions based on the author's experience, evidence from literature and wider global activities to improve the embedding of ERM.

Corporate Governance

Good corporate governance is a necessary condition for an organization's risk management to flourish. Corporate governance is a facilitator of the entire conduct of the organization. There is a two-way connection between risk management and corporate governance, that is, good corporate governance helps in improving the implementation of risk management, and risk management also helps in improving some of the activities in corporate governance.

Deloitte conducted a global survey on risk management practices from March-September 2020 and published in 2021. The survey included 57 financial services industries (banking, investment banking, investment management, insurance, etc.) with participants from North America, Europe, Asia Pacific, and other countries. One of the results of the survey was that 89% of respondents said the risk committee of their boards has independent directors, with 32% saying the risk committee is composed entirely of independent directors and 37% saying that a majority of its members are independent directors. An independent director chairs the board risk committee at 86% of institutions.

This suggests the importance of independent director in different global financial firms A presence of independent directors provide more challenges during the Board meetings and it has been proven in the academic literature that the presence of independent directors help improves the Board's performance.

Failure of Corporate Governance and inability of risk management to apply

There are many examples of corporate failures in the Indian market resulting in millions of losses leading to termination of business, the intervention of central banks, loss of reputation, etc. The ICICI Bank-Videocon bribery case is an example of failure at the top in implementing ethics indicating that risk management is hard to work in such cases.

Another case of the PNB-Nirav Modi Scam happened in February 2018 resulting from collusion between the employees of banks and the external party. This is a clear failure of operational risk.

The Satyam won the Golden Peacock Global Award for good corporate governance at one point and colluded with auditors in the scandal in 2009. This was a failure at the top as well as of auditors; risk management was not perhaps present in 2009.

In another case of the Singh brothers, officials of Religare Enterprises Ltd took loans from banks and diverted the money to other companies.

In the case of YES Bank used to disburse loans to corporate borrowers who were rejected by other banks. The bank used to charge a huge upfront fee diverted to other companies set up by the owner. In such cases, most borrowers were defaulters at will.

Jet Airways was a promoter-led board due to banking a huge amount at the time of failure in 2018, the Company was India's second-largest airline with a 13.8% market share. In this case, the Board often serves at the wish and command of the promoter-chairman. Risk Management is challenging work when corporate governance is not working.

Actions for improvement

It has been observed in the Indian market that auditors are often blamed after every debacle. However, the role of the auditors starts after an adverse event happened when risk has crystalized, the only thing that can be done after is crisis management. To arrest the problem in advance, there is a need to act before the event and for this purpose, the role of the CRO becomes important. For this purpose, there is a need to strengthen the position of the CRO so that he can act independently.

Some of the suggestions below for improvement in ERM:

- CRO reporting to Audit Committee/Board
- Review of CRO to be done by Audit Committee/Board
- Possibly distancing of Risk Team from Business as an independent entity with access to all information
- Mandatory sign-off from CRO in all decision-making like pricing, business plan, merger acquisition, loan sanction, etc.
- Change in corporate governance on the distribution of powers to promoters driven CEO, for example, Jet Airways, YES Bank

Risk management embedding helps in improving the processes which can prevent an event like the PNB-Nirav Modi scam.

Other measures to improve corporate governance

- Proper minuting of all committee meetings preferably audio recorded better for evidencing in future
- Quality of challenge provided by the Board members evidenced through Board minutes

- Quality of challenge provided by CRO in the Committee Meetings- Evidence from RMC/ALCO minutes
- Mandatory inclusion of quarterly independent CRO risk report directly to Board,
- Quality of challenges raised by CRO in product pricing, business plan, key decision making, mergers, acquisition, etc.
- Inclusion of rewards based on risk performance to employees
- The CROs should be in conversation with Board members on the inclusion of risk-related remuneration components (Bonus and increment) in CEO and CXOs- 44% of Deloitte survey stated that Board reviews the incentive plan aligning with risk
- All the risks should be mapped to all CXOs based on their areas of expertise to have ownership and accountabilities
- Every CXO should sign off quarterly/Half-yearly/Annual compliance of risks that they own. Possibly an external party should independently review the embedding of risk management in the first and second line of defense and give the report directly to Board. Such report should form the basis of risk related bonus component for all CXOs and line below.
- Every function should have Risk Champions to enable improvement of risk management in the first line of defense and embedding of ERM.
- 70% of Deloitte respondents said that the Board help establish and embed the risk culture of the enterprise; promotes open discussions regarding risk

Evidence from Literature

A paper was published entitled "Risk management, corporate governance, and bank performance in the financial crisis" authored by Vincent Aebi, Gabriele Sabato, and Markus Schmid, published in the Journal of Banking & Finance, 2011. The authors raised questions about corporate governance during the 2007-08 financial crisis. The paper investigated the role of corporate governance in risk management whether the CRO in a bank's reports to the CEO or executive Board and whether this has improved the bank's performance during the financial crisis of 2007/2008.

The authors found in their investigation that where CRO directly reports to the Board of Directors rather than the CEO and exhibits significantly higher stock returns and ROE during the crisis.

A survey on LinkedIn was conducted in May/June 2021 with a question, "Do CRO Reporting to Board improve risk management". There were over 16,000 views, 155 votes, 122 votes stating that CRO reporting to Board improve the independence, while 23 stated that CRO is a part of business continue reporting CEO and 12 were not sure. The respondents were Risk Managers, CROs, Risk Advisors, Risk heads, etc. The responses were from India, Australia, the UK, Nigeria, Gulf, etc.

This clearly shows the inclination for CRO reporting to the Board from current sets of risk management professionals from different countries. Some of the risk professionals whose correspondence was made after the survey stated that such reporting would increase the independence of CRO. However, some views were divided where experts believe that CRO continues to report to the CEO.

A similar result is also visible from the Deloitte survey, which states that there are benefits of CRO reporting to Board as well as to CEO; indicating CRO reporting to CEO represents Seniority of his position while reporting to Board indicates his independence. The survey finds that in 70% of institutions, CRO reports to the CEO and 53% state that CRO reports to Board or Board level committee. The survey further finds that 63% said that conducting executive sessions with CRO is Board's responsibility. This indicates that some institutions may be considering strengthening the position of CRO by elevating its reporting relationship.

These results suggest a strong viewpoint of a global risk professional in elevating the CRO reporting relationship. However, some risk professionals believe CROs continue reporting to CEO as a part of the business. The debate continues.

Improving the effectiveness of the three lines of defense model

In the three lines of defense model, the responsibility of risk identification, quantification, and mitigation is the responsibility of the first line of defense, while the role of the second line of defense is to provide the risk management oversight, and the third line of defense, Audit, assure the Board. The first line is all functions, except, Risk, Compliance, and Audit, while the second line is Risk and Compliance and the third line is Audit.

However, this model is not working properly as one of the key reasons for not so effective ERM. The first line is the army responsible for risk management exercises is without arsenals in terms of risk qualification and risk training. They do not have a "What if" mindset, smell the risk when it is brewing, an idea about sources of ris**k** necessary for risk management. In this situation, the three lines of defense are ineffective. It is a new challenge for them to do their core job and ask the question, "what if" things go wrong, they have never done it, therefore, there is a greater need for investment in developing the risk management skills in the first line rather than in the second line. There is a need to have a clearly defined path of risk management development. If the first line does not work on the risk management, then the ERM model will collapse because it is based on enterprise-wide risk management, and three lines of defense will cease to exist.

Second Line alone cannot do risk management for the entire organization because of their small team size and lack of subject matter expertise. In the current setup, the second line can only provide oversight given their bandwidth. However, Risk Team must have some mandatory risk qualification on financial risk, enterprise risk, operational risk, IT risk, etc., such risk qualification helps in getting grips with the grammar of the subject. Such qualification can be linked to promotion criteria/appraisal cycle/career growth etc.

As per the Deloitte survey, 58% of respondents mentioned that they face significant challenges regarding the first line in getting buy-in from them and 53% said they face challenges in defining the roles and responsibilities between the first and second line. For the next two years, 49% of respondents mentioned that they have a high priority in transforming the risk management operating model of the first line of defense. As per the survey, the regulator expects, the first line to own the risk management but this is difficult to implement. The survey further explains that the first line may not have risk management expertise and also their incentives are linked to a business outcome rather than risk management. There is a greater need for tone from the top in accelerating the involvement of the first line in risk management.

So international scenario of embedding risk management in the first line of defense is going through a tough time in getting buy-in from the first line.

TWELVE

KEY RISK INDICATOR-A STRONG MANAGEMENT TOOL

Introduction

Key Risk Indicator (KRI) is a very strong tool for the Management and the Board to give an early warning signal to any emerging risks. It is therefore important to create the right risk indicators that can represent the emerging risks. KRIs are prepared for the most important risks to the Company that can have an adverse impact . Risks are futuristic so the KPI indicates where risk may crystalize.

The first step towards the development of KRI is the identification of risks.

Preparation of KRI

Any risk event does not occur on its own; there are always causes behind the risk events. So if we track the factors that influence the cause, we can come to know whether the risk will crystallize or not. For example, consider mortality risk- a risk defined as an actual number of deaths more than anticipated. Now to identify the KRI for mortality risk, we have to see what causes an increase in the number of deaths. Below are the factors that influence the increase in the number of deaths:

- The outbreak of a new disease or existing disease
- Changes in the weather condition lead to extreme heat or cold
- Change in lifestyle
- Pandemics
- Natural calamities
- Drugs/Alcohol

If we monitor these indicators, we can tell whether the number of deaths in the future will increase or not. If the factor gets influenced by the pandemic, this will result in "an event" of a higher number of deaths. The higher number of deaths will have an adverse impact on the Company's performance of say profit, impacting the performance indicator. They are referred to as Key Performance Indicators (KPI).

In the above diagram, cause leads to events and event leads to adverse impact on the Company. In the management of risk, "Cause" plays an important role both in the development of KRI as well as placing the controls. If the Controls are placed on the causes, the risk of event materialization can be addressed. However, the control factors may not be the same as KRI factors.

In the above example, except for the use of alcohol and drugs, none of the other factors can be controlled from outside and so cannot be used for the risk control (mitigation) purpose. Lifestyle change to a certain extent, control can be placed but may not be not fully addressed because individuals are not under anyone's control.

In the life insurance business, to address the mortality risk, underwriting is performed to assess the individual risks against the standard parameters. The lives are underwritten at normal rates only when lives are standard lives. The questionnaire is given in the proposal form and medical underwriting are linked to the health of the individual and family history (causes) that may lead to an adverse health condition.

Selection of KRI

The selection of KRI should be in such a way that can give an indication about the change in the likelihood or impact because the expected loss is defined as

Likelihood X Impact (Rupee terms)

In the example given above of mortality risk, we identified a couple of KRIs such as

1. The outbreak of a new disease will impact the likelihood
2. Changes in weather conditions may increase the number of deaths, impacting the likelihood
3. If an insurance company is writing too many protection businesses (Term Assurance), this may have an impact on the claim amount.

Casual Analysis

So cause wise analysis is very important in the management of risk. If suppose a Company is not performing well in meeting its revenue targets repeatedly, then the Company must perform a cause-wise analysis. This will help in identifying the KRI which can be tracked.

The reasons for poor sales could be one or more of the following reasons:

1. Inadequate size of the sales team
2. Incompetent sales team
3. Product not competitive in the market
4. The attrition rate of the sales teams is high
5. Customers lack trust in the Company/Brand issue

Based on the investigation, KRI can be picked. If attrition turns out to be the key reason of fall in sales, then attrition rate could be the KRI. Now Company can monitor the attrition rate as KRI and any increase in attrition rate could act as early warning signal for fall in the revenue.

Conclusion

KRI is a very strong tool in the risk management for early warning signal which can prepare the management and the Board to take early action. Care is needed to identify the key risks and indicator which are representative of the risks.

THIRTEEN

"INSURANCE RISK" IN LIFE INSURANCE

Introduction

This chapter discusses the insurance risks in the life insurance sector. The insurance risks in the life insurance sector are mortality risk, lapse risk, and expense risk. The purpose is to introduce these risks, their measures, and the mitigation process.

The chapter is structured by first defining each of the risks, then defining their measures, and then the risk mitigation process is explained.

Many of these risks are defined as a deviation in experience compared to assumptions made in the pricing. The pricing assumptions are specific to the insurance company which is not available in the public domain; therefore, it was difficult to give examples in this paper.

This chapter covers the following life insurance risks in the same order:

- Mortality for Life insurance business
- Longevity for Annuity business
- Lapses, where policyholders stop paying premiums and
- Expenses

The first mortality risk is covered.

Mortality Risk

The mortality risk is defined as actual claims higher than expected. The expected claims come from assumptions made at the time of pricing. When the product is priced, it is assumed how many lives may die based on the standard mortality table. The mortality tables are prepared by the Actuarial Profession. The mortality tables are based on the ages and how many lives will survive at each age out of the cohorts assumed at age 0. The cohort may be assumed as 100,000 or even more.

So, if say, for example, it was assumed at the time of pricing that 5 deaths will take place at age 40, while the experience suggests that the number of deaths in a year aged 40 is 7, then two excess deaths have taken place for which life company is to pay the claim for which they have not priced.

Similarly, if 4 deaths take place in actual, then there will be a profit of 1 claim because the insurance company is to pay only for 4 deaths while they have priced for 5 deaths.

As per the press release, the number of COVID-related death claims in India between 1st April 2021 to 9th June 2021were 190,601 compared to claims 162,892 for the period 1st April 2020 to 31st March 2021. These claims during the first quarter of FY 22 compared to the last full financial year were 17% greater. This is an indication of worsening of mortality experience due to coronavirus.

Early Claim Experience

When policyholders take insurance at the inception, they undergo the scrutiny of papers for both financial health and medical health as well. It is anticipated that the lives who have taken policies recently will exhibit lighter claim experience compared to those who have taken life insurance say seven years back. This is because over a period the selection effect of underwriting wears off over some time. The mortality studies suggest that the selection effect remains for at least two years in the UK, while in the US, the selection effect remains for a longer period say 10 years. After the selection period, the mortality rates are referred to as the Ultimate mortality rate. The claim experience during the select period is lighter than the ultimate rate due to the underwriting selection effect.

Early claims are referred to as when during the initial period of policy inception say in the first two to three years, the actual claim experience is worse than anticipated. This generally happens due to anti-selection. This means that policyholders select themselves against the Company. This generally happens when the policyholder does not disclose his own worse medical condition to the insurance company. As a result of poor health, an early claim arises which leads to loss to the insurance company. So anti-selection is adverse for the life Companies.

The measures of Mortality risk

A/E Ratio

There are a couple of measures of mortality risk, the first is the ratio of "Actual Claim" to "Expected Claim" often referred to as the A/E ratio. If the A/E ratio is greater than 1, this means that actual claims have been more than expected. And if this ratio is less than 1, then it reflects that the actual claims experience is better than anticipated.

As a general comment mortality experience moves more or less on predictable lines, where mortality experience improves over the period except during the period when stress events happen like a pandemic or natural catastrophe. So, for many Companies, A/E ratios are less than 1 both in the early years and later years. This comment is subject to no new diseases that have taken place or there has been a spurt of pandemics or any other claims in bulk.

For example, during the COVID 19 for most life insurance companies, the A/E ratio crossed the ratio 1. Because of this experience, the insurance companies increased their term insurance rates. Though this was mostly triggered by an increase in reinsurance rates which was also due to worse claim experience.

The A/E ratios in the insurance Companies are measured by policy year and also at an aggregate level combining all years. For a good claim experience, the A/E ratio should ideally be less than 1.

However, in practice, it is observed in some Companies that during the first two years, the A/E ratio is greater than 1, and in the later years less than one. This is an indication of high anti-selection.

High anti-selection is not good for the life Company indicating either poor underwriting or claim settlement or poor sales practices. All three need to be curbed for a good experience.

Reinsurance Premium Payment

The other measure of mortality experience within the Company is how much reinsurance premium is paid to the reinsurer and how much claims have been received from the reinsurer.

Life insurance Companies reinsure some of the high sum assured cases where a part of the sum assured is retained by the life insurance companies and the rest of the risk is passed over to the reinsurance Companies. So, when a claim arises, the sum assured retained by the Life Company is paid by them and the sum assured taken by the reinsurer is paid by the reinsurer. This way, life Companies may limit some of the high risks policies. For reinsuring risk, insurance Companies pay a premium to the reinsurance Companies and receive claims when such policies result in a claim.

So, during a financial year, if reinsurance claims received by the insurance companies are more than the premium paid, this indicates that the claims experience of reinsurance Companies is not good due to the poor portfolio of insurance companies. Such poor experience is a risk to the life insurance company in two respects, one is the future reinsurance premium rate, which may increase and there is a reputational risk to the insurance Company wherein an extreme case, the insurance company may not able to find any reinsurer to reinsure their policies.

This is exactly what happened in the Indian life insurance market when claims due to covid increased during 2020 and 2021 resulting in reinsurance companies increasing the reinsurance premium rates by 30% to 40%. This increase in reinsurance premium rates is ultimately passed to the customers in the form of increased premiums, particularly in the term insurance product.

This can be seen as an example from the experience of three top private life insurance companies in India, where due to COVID during FY 2020-21 and FY 2021-22 up to the quarter elapsed, the claims paid by reinsurer is greater than reinsurance premium received by them (**Figures in INR Cr, 1 Cr = 10^7**)

Table-1			
ICICI Prudential	Reinsurance Premium Paid by Insurance Company	Claims received by Insurance Company from Reinsurer	Net profit/Loss to a reinsurer
FY Q1 22	268	971	-703
FY 21	759	903	-144
FY 20	551	520	31
FY 19	351	328	23
FY 18	258	228	30

It can be noticed during FY 2018 to FY 2020, the reinsurance company made a profit while after the COVID, there is a loss. It can also be seen that the amount of loss during FY 22 is much greater than FY 21 even if only one-quarter of experience is available. This is due to the second wave of COVID in India during April 2021 to June 2021.

A similar experience can be seen in HDFC life. The data for FY 22 is for half a year.

Table-2		Figures in Cr	
HDFC Life	Reinsurance Premium Paid by Insurance Company	Claims received by Insurance Company from Reinsurer	Net profit/Loss to a reinsurer
FY H1 22	304	1173	-869
FY 21	461	640	-179
FY 20	483	346	137
FY 19	262	216	46
FY 18	193	174	19

These numbers are taken from L1 and L7 of public disclosure of each life insurance company from their website.

Table-3		Figures in Cr	
Max Life	Reinsurance Premium Paid by Insurance Company	Claims received by Insurance Company from Reinsurer	Net profit/Loss to a reinsurer
FY Q1 22	98	468	-370
FY 21	278	340	-62
FY 20	204	188	16
FY 19	156	123	33
FY 18	121	94	27

One noticeable point is quantum of loss in FY 22 is much greater than in FY 21 even though the time elapsed in FY 22 is either for one or two quarters. This could be due to the second wave of claims in India from April to June in FY 2021.

Mortality Risk Management

The mortality risk is managed by one or a combination of one or more following factors.

1. Underwriting
2. Claim Management
3. Reinsurance
4. Sales training

Underwriting

Every proposal that comes to the insurance company undergoes the scrutiny of papers for medical health conditions and the financial position of the customer. Financial position is assessed because insurance companies want to ensure that the customer can pay all the required premiums. The medical condition is assessed to ensure that the policyholder who takes the insurance policy conforms to the mortality assumption used in the pricing.

The risk to the insurance company comes from the fact that as age increases, the mortality rate increases, so at a higher age, the insurance company wants to ensure that the customer undergoes an adequate medical examination. So as age increases, the medical tests increase.

Another risk to the insurance company is with high sum assured cases, because, in the initial years, the premium is smaller compared to the benefits. So high or very high sum assured also warrants more medical examination.

For the customers, with high age and high sum assured, their medical examinations are more stringent.

Those customers who are in good health are accepted at standard premium rates, while the sub-standard lives are accepted either by applying health extra premium, or reducing the term of the product to limit the risk for a shorter period, or reducing the sum assured of the product, or proposals can be postponed. The amount of extra premium due to poor health conditions is applied based on the severity of the disease.

That is how insurance companies ensure that the mortality risks are managed through the underwriting

Claim Management

The underwriting is performed at the time of proposal; however, the claim management is performed at the time of death claim. Insurance Companies investigate claims, particularly the early claims for claim-related information such as to cause of death, history of disease if the deaths have occurred due to certain diseases, hospitalization papers if any, etc.

If the investigation at the time of claim reveals that some of the health-related information was concealed during the proposal time, the insurance company can repudiate the claim. The Indian regulator has made it mandatory that all the claims will be paid to the customers if the policy has run for three years. So, if claims occur after three years, the insurance company cannot repudiate the claim.

The regulator takes a strong view that there should be a very minimal decline of claims because insurance companies have all rights to check the health status of the customers whether they have suppressed any health-related information. Therefore, the three years condition is applied after that no claim repudiation will occur.

The claim management helps insurance companies in completing the loop of monitoring mortality experience. This helps them in understanding any gap in the underwriting process, improving the sales practices to prevent anti-selection, having a feedback loop to realign mortality assumptions in future product pricing, and in setting up assumptions for valuation purposes.

Reinsurance

Reinsurance is another tool to manage the mortality risk. Reinsurance is a process of taking insurance by the insurance companies from specialized reinsurance companies. Reinsurance helps insurance companies in accepting either a very large risk or insuring sub-standard lives.

For example, if there is a policy of Rs.100 Crore, the insurance company may not able to insure such a large sum assured on its own. This is because if such a large claim arises this may make small insurance companies insolvent. So, as an example in such cases insurance companies retain the risk of say 10 Cr and reinsure the rest 90 Cr. For Rs.90 Cr of insurance, the insurance company will pay a reinsurance premium to the reinsurance company. If a claim arises, then Rs.10 Cr will be paid by the insurance company and the rest Rs.90 Cr will be paid by the reinsurance company. This way an insurance company has limited its maximum exposure to Rs.10 Cr and is also able to write a large sum assured case.

Sales training

Sales training is one of the ways to manage the mortality risk by explaining to Sales Agents on importance of the selection of healthy lives. They are the first people who interact with the customers and can give very important information to the insurance company on their health and financial condition. They are the front-line underwriters.

Sometimes sales force sells the policies to sub-standard lives for meeting their sales target. There are incentives to the customer as insurance is available without disclosing poor health conditions at a cheaper price.

To manage such risk, adequate and relevant training is given to the sales force explaining how it adversely affects the company. At times agents are also debarred as a punishment for procuring new business.

Longevity Risk

Opposite to the mortality risk is the longevity risk, this risk is living longer than anticipated. In the annuity business, regular monthly payments are made to the customers till the time the customer is alive. If customers live longer than anticipated, the insurance companies are to pay the annuity for a longer period than assumed in the pricing assumption which is a loss to the insurance company.

To address the longevity risk, insurance companies assume an improvement in mortality assumption and build this margin in the premium at the time of pricing. However, the risk remains because if customers still live longer than the improvement assumed at the time of pricing.

While doing the risk-based capital, mortality and longevity risks have a negative correlation, therefore it is beneficial for insurance companies to keep both the term and annuity product in their portfolio. In the term product, the benefit is only paid when the customer dies.

Lapse Risk

A policy lapses when the policyholder stops paying their future premium. There could be many reasons for this, the policyholder does not want the insurance because he is getting cheaper insurance elsewhere, the policy has been mis-sold, the customer has financial problems, etc.

Lapse risk occurs when actual lapses are more than anticipated at the time of pricing. There is an adverse impact of high lapses on the insurance company's profitability.

The direct impact of high lapses is on the embedded value of the life insurance company as the profit loaded in every policy is lost due to non-payment of premium. A high lapse rate is an indication of either customers are not satisfied or mis-selling is happening or customers are facing financial hardships.

During the initial period of COVID 19 when people lost their jobs, the lapse rate increased in India. Also, during the 2008 economic crisis, a similar adverse impact was visible from to financial distress of customers.

The indirect impact of high lapses triggers the expense risk including high initial commission paid to agents because, after the lapse, a lower number of policies are in-force where fixed expenses are now spread over the lesser number of policies leading to an increase in per policy expense.

High lapses also worsen the mortality experience of the portfolio. This is because a policyholder lapses his policy when he believes that he is a healthy life and no longer requires insurance. So, on lapse, the insurance company loses healthy lives and the remaining insurance portfolio is of relatively poorer lives. So, if lapses increase, mortality risk also increases.

How to manage the lapse rate? One of the established methods of addressing the lapse rate is need-based selling. If the customer needs the insurance, they will not lapse his policy. So, the sales force should be trained for need-based selling and avoid mis-selling.

Another reason for high lapses in the Indian market is customers are not contactable once they change their living place and do not update their address with the insurance company. As a result, renewal premium notice does not reach the customers leading to discontinuing their policies. To address these issues, insurance companies recommend for direct debit option from the bank at the time of the first sale.

Financial health condition is checked at the time of proposal so that customer is in good financial health to pay all the future premium. This is referred to as financial underwriting.

Expense Risk

The expense risk also comes under the insurance risk and is defined as actual expenses more than expected. Other issues with the new companies are the expense overrun. This happens because during the initial years, actual expenses are very high and the same high level of expense cannot be charged from the customer because the premium will then be very high. So, a relatively lower expense is loaded in the premium to stay competitive. The difference between the actual expenses and loaded expense is the expense overrun.

The excess of initial expense is recovered in a later year referred to as the expense breakeven period. Such expense breakeven period could between 6 to 8 years for a life company. However, many insurance companies in Indian are still in the expense overrun phase after over 2 decades of operations.

Expense overrun is managed through control of operating expenses which is under the control of management.

Conclusion

Mortality risk gained prominence during the COVID pandemic where all the life insurance companies suffered mortality losses. Though the A/E ratio is not available due to company-specific information, worse mortality experience in the last two financial years can be assessed from insurance companies receiving more claims from reinsurers compared to the premium paid by them. The worsening of mortality experience in the Indian market has led to an increase in term insurance premium rates by 30% to 40%. This is one example of looping the mortality experience back to the assumption setting exercise.

The COVID also demonstrated the impact of worsening of the financial condition due to job losses into an increase in lapse experience.

Expense risk continues to be a challenge in the Indian life insurance market where many of the players are still in the expense overrun phase despite now close to two decades of operation.

References

https://timesofindia.indiatimes.com/business/india-business/life-cos-see-5-10x-surge-in-covid-claims-in-april/articleshow/83493244.cms

https://www.maxlifeinsurance.com/about-us/media-centre/public-disclosures

https://www.iciciprulife.com/about-us/investor-relations/yearly-public-disclosures.html

https://www.hdfclife.com/about-us/investor-relations

FOURTEEN

Risk Mitigation, Monitoring and Reporting in Life Insurance Business

Introduction

A business value is created by identifying the risks in the business and developing the risk mitigation plan. Only identification of risks is of little use unless an effective advance plan is developed and implemented to reduce either the likelihood or impact or both of the events. In this chapter, different methods of risk mitigation are discussed in the life insurance industry. The chapter also discusses the utility of monitoring of risks and reporting.

Risk Management Model

In the management of risks, it is important to understand the risk management model, so that it is clear how to approach to mitigate the risks.

Risk is an event in the future that disrupts the objective of the Company, the event does not occur on its own; it always has its cause and then the consequence. The event itself cannot be controlled, for example, accident is an event which cannot be controlled, What can be controlled are causes of accident such as high speed, quality of road, driving skills, condition of car etc which will reduce the likelihood of the accident. Wearing seatbelt cannot control the accident but it can reduce the impact post accident, but wearing seatbelt is an advance action and not post facto event.

So the fundamental of risk management lies in the controls applying to address either likelihood or impact or both. This is because severity of the risk is defined as

Severity = Likelihood * Impact

Based on the different controls applied, risks can be managed from high likelihood zone to low likelihood and similarly from high impact zone to low impact. When controls are applied on causes, it manages the likelihood while when consequence is addressed, it manages the impact and post event management helps in reducing the overall loss like rescue post accident.

Based on the different controls applied on causes and consequence, there are four ways through which risks are managed, they are

I. Accept the risk
II. Manage the risk
III. Transfer the risk

IV. Avoid the risk

The application of above four tools are used when

- Risks are accepted when the likelihood and impact is low
- Risks are managed when likelihood is high and impact is low
- Risks are transferred when likelihood is low and impact is high
- Risks are avoided when likelihood and impact both are high

Application of Risk Management Technique

In this section, following risks mitigation are discussed:

- Insurance risk
- Financial risk
- Operational risk
- Regulatory risk
- Reputational risk

Insurance Risk

First the discussion is on management of life insurance risks. The key life insurance risks are mortality, lapses and expense

Mortality Risk

The mortality risk is defined as actual claims higher than expected. The expected claims come from the mortality rate assumed in the pricing of the product. To manage the mortality risk, there is a need to identify and address the causes of higher actual claims, how the impact of higher claims can addressed.

The causes or sources of higher actual claims are

- Self selection or anti-selection
- Business sold to sub-standard lives
- Development of new disease
- Inadequate mortality assumption
- Catastrophic event
- Higher sum assured exposure
- Worsening of portfolio due to higher lapses of healthy lives

Self selection or anti-selection

Actual claims turns out to be higher than expected if the customers select himself by not disclosing his poor health condition, this generally happen to low sum assured cases where either there is a no underwriting or minimal underwriting. These cases generally have low likelihood and low impact, so insurance companies accept these lives. Such cases are managed through sample underwriting to identify the trend and behavior of the policyholder. If required, if the experiences of such cases are worse, then insurance companies may increase its vigilance on its source, location, pattern of life style etc. This helps in further reducing the likelihood of self selection. A sample claim investigation also helps in identify the trend and loop back to improve the point of sale underwriting. A point of sale underwriting is performed by the sales agent who sells the policies and gets first hand information from the customers. As a point of sale underwriters, agents may get health related information through his informal routes. Trainings may be given to agents for such underwriting.

Business Sold to Sub-Standard Lives

Businesses sold to sub-standard lives are deliberate attempt by the sales force to fetch the business either to benefit the customer or complete his sales quota. Such risks will have low likelihood and impact will depend upon the size of the sum assured. The likelihood is managed through the underwriting performed at a proposal stage. These underwriting will depend on the age and size of the sum assured. Lower age and smaller sum assured cases may pass through the underwriting net increasing the likelihood, but higher age and higher sum assured cases will get caught at the underwriting stage.

Lower age and smaller sum assured cases are analyzed either at claim stage or through the sample underwriting to complete feedback the loop to strengthen underwriting, mortality assumption and sales training. This helps in reducing the likelihood. If such cases are caught at the claim stage, then the claims to the nominee of policyholder may be repudiated.

Those sub-standard lives caught at the underwriting stage are rated up according to medical standards set by the Company in conjunction with reinsurance. This helps in charging the right price of the risks presented to insurance company in line with the pricing assumption.

Development of new disease

Such development will increase the likelihood of claim, so insurance companies manage such cases. The source of risk is not in the control of the insurance company but in the demography. The insurance companies manage this risk by:

- Apply exclusions for such cases
- Rate up the cases
- Perform analysis on the impact of the new disease on claims
- Take help of reinsurer to design underwriting and terms and conditions
- Not to accept the risk- decline (avoidance of risk)

Inadequate mortality assumptions

Inadequate mortality assumption is a more an operational risks because it may happen due to inadequate people and process. This may happen due to inadequate training or manpower skills resulting risks coming from "people" side. If the company has not set a proper process of review of assumption, then also there is a risk that the assumptions are inadequate. At times when the company is entering into a new market where they have no prior experience, there is a risk that the assumptions may be inadequate.

Inadequate mortality assumption is expected to increase likelihood; such risks are managed by the company through:

- Establishing proper assumption review mechanism
- Hiring skilled workforce

- Spending time and money on training
- Use of reinsurance experience when entering into new market
- Periodic review by internal audit and Risk
- External consultation
- Use of experience in other country's similar market

Catastrophic event

A catastrophic event such as earthquake, storm, flood, nuclear disaster etc increases both number of claims and cost of claim in a very short period of time. Such events are not in the control of the insurance companies. Some of the risks such as nuclear disaster and pandemic are excluded from the list of events resulting into claims. While many of the catastrophic events are not in the control of Insurance companies, but can limit the total damage. Such damage is controlled by taking catastrophic reinsurance, so such risks are transferred as these are high impact events.

In the catastrophe reinsurance arrangement, risks are insured at a Company level between certain limits, like loss between Rs.100 Cr and Rs.200 Cr will be covered under the defined catastrophe event. So in this case impact is managed by purchasing the catastrophic reinsurance by paying small premium.

High Sum Assured Exposure

Insurance companies write both small and large sum assured business; there is a risk to the insurance companies that if 10 large sums assured policies of Rs.1 Cr each result into a claim. This would mean total claim payment of Rs.10 Cr. The risk here is on impact. There is a possibility for insurance companies to write business up to the certain low sum assured only to limit the likelihood of large amount claims, but this will not be in line with good business decision.

So to address this risk, insurance companies purchase reinsurance with certain retention limits. The retention limit depends on the type of the product, but this may vary between Rs. 10 lacs to Rs.20 lacs in the Indian market. This means that for every policy with sum assured greater than Rs.20 lacs resulting into claim, first Rs.20 lacs will be paid by the insurance company and rest will be paid by the reinsurance Company. In above example of 10 claims of Rs.1 Cr each with retention limit of Rs.20 lacs, so in this case for each policies Rs.80 lacs will be paid by reinsurer and Rs. 20 lacs by insurance company. The total out go for the insurance company will be Rs.2 Cr and for the reinsurance company will be Rs. 8 Cr. This way insurance company has restricted its total claim payment.

Worsening of Portfolio due to higher lapses of health lives

If policyholder is healthy, either do not have a need for insurance or getting cheaper insurance elsewhere, they may lapse the policy. If many of the healthy policyholders are lapsing the policy, then the remaining portfolio will be with relatively sub-standard lives as policyholder with poorer health will not lapse the policy. Such activity results in increasing the likelihood of claims. To address this type of risk

- Insurance companies may at periodic interval re-price their product and offer enhancing the sum assured to its customer at no other extra cost. This will help in managing the increasing lapse due to cheaper product elsewhere.
- Such management actions may be taken for pure term products where premiums are relatively smaller

Lapse Risk

A policyholder lapses his policy because either he do not have a need for insurance that he holds or getting cheaper insurance elsewhere. Higher than planned number of lapses have adverse impact on recovery of fixed expenses loaded in the product. Also higher lapses erode the loaded profit resulting into lower overall profit.

The key causes or sources of higher lapses are

- Mis-selling
- Change in policyholder's need
- Liquidity drying up in market
- Equity market tanking impacting ULIP business
- Over insurance
- Poor fund performance
- Negative market news
- Contactibility issue

Mis-selling

Mis-selling is one of the key reasons of high number of lapses because policyholder when they realize that the product sold to them are either too expensive or not meeting their need or insurance have been sold in the name of other financial products such as fixed deposit. In such cases, the policyholder prefers to lapses the policy and often leads to complain resulting into the reputational risk.

Mis-selling increases the likelihood of lapses, so there is a need to place control mis-selling. Mis-selling can be addressed by

- Taking direct feedback from customers on the selling process and whether their needs were assessed before the sale
- Giving proper trainings to the sales force to understand the needs to customer and sell only relevant products
- Applying a mechanism to assess the needs of the customer as a part of selling process
- Regular reviews
- Action on erring agents to send the message of non-tolerance
- By giving reward if lapse rate is low or applying penalty if lapses are higher than required

Change in Policyholder's need

The policyholder may lapse his policy if his genuine needs have changed, this means his current need is not served by the policy he has taken. This may happen due to change in financial condition, increase in family size, and establishment of new liabilities or need of money. This activity is not in the direct control of the insurance company; however, they can take certain proactive measure by engaging with customer throughout the life of product. This helps in understanding the emerging personal and financial needs, so that they can pitch right product and retain the customer.

Though premium holiday is not an option under Indian life insurance industry, this can be used as a tool to address the distressed financial condition of the customers.

Liquidity drying up in the market

At times of distress economic condition, the market may become less liquid were there are restrictions on withdrawing beyond a certain limit of cash. Also in this situation, customers prefer to keep cash in hand than paying premium to the insurance companies. In this situation, the policyholder may lapse its policy.

The likelihood of such situation is low and insurance companies may accept the risk without taking any action.

The example of similar situation in India was late during 2016 at the time of demonetization.

Equity Market tanking

Insurance companies have investment guidelines from the regulator in which proportion investment is to be made. Equity investment is mostly made in the participating products and in unit linked business. The proportion of investment in equity under participating products is small, so the risk resulting from tanking equity market is very small and insurance companies may accept this risk. Also investing in blue chip stocks helps in reducing the market volatility.

Under the unit linked business, there is a risk of falling unit price when equity market is low; a sustained period of low equity market may force unit linked policyholders to lapse their policy in the view of getting whatever remain in the fund in the fear of losing the current fund value in coming days.

Such risk is not in the control of the insurance company; however, fund managers may continuously evaluate the emerging national and international parameters that can affect the unit price and advice the customers in advance to take proactive action. The likelihood of such event is low, but its impact can be high on unit linked policyholders. There is a no mechanism through which such risks can be transferred to the third party.

Over insurance

Over insurance is a situation when a policyholder has taken large number of insurance policies and paying high proportion of his income as a premium. This can lead to lapsing his policy in a slightest distress personal financial condition. This risk is addressed through the financial underwriting at a proposal stage. The financial condition of the customer is evaluated based on his income and other life insurance policies that he has taken. If the insurance company identify that the customer is adequately insured and he is paying relatively high proportion of his income as a premium, then his new proposal may be denied further insurance.

Poor fund performance

If the unit linked policyholders are not getting the value for money through the investment they have made due to poor fund performance, they would prefer to lapse the policy and move elsewhere. A sustained period of poor fund performance may result into mass lapses impacting the expense recovery and overall profitability.

Such risks are managed through internal review mechanism of fund managers and linking their incentives with the performance of the fund. The fund performances are also tracked with industry returns so that customers are aware about the fund performance. Such risks have low likelihood given the control mechanism.

Negative market news

Negative market news about the insurance company may compel policyholders to lapse the policy as a loss of trust. Such events have low likelihood but may have adverse impact if such event happens.

Proactive measures are required to manage the reputational risk so that negative news does not arise or manage such news if there is a need to address. A related such activity recently happened in the Indian banking market where one corporate bank was put under vigilance and restrictions were placed on the withdrawals. If such event happens with the insurance companies, there is a risk of mass lapse that can permanently damage the reputation and future new business. Such risks can only be managed.

Contactibility issue

Customers details are either not filled completely at the proposal stage or their details have changed over the period of time. This risk is prevalent in the Indian insurance market. The insurance companies have set up the retention team to address these risks. Sales agent training, use of digital mode of contact and regular touch base with the customers can help in reducing the likelihood of such event happening.

Retention activity

Insurance companies also undertake revival activities where the customers who have lapsed their policies are contacted to get revive their policy on favorable terms such as revival without underwriting or wavier of interest payment etc. Sometimes surendering policyholders are offered suitable terms such as paid up policies.

Expense Risk

Expense risk is defined as actual expenses are higher than expected. The expected expenses are loaded in the product at the time of pricing.

In the Indian market, most of the life insurance companies are running through the phase of acquisition expense overrun. This happens during the initial period of operations when the operating expenses are way higher than loaded in the premium. This is because actual high acquisition expenses cannot be loaded in the premium because the product will become too expensive for customers to purchase. So the higher acquisition expenses are recovered over the period of time. A typical time to eliminate expense overrun is around 5 to 8 years. However, many of the Indian life insurance companies are still in acquisition expense overrun phase. This is a typical challenge in front of Indian life insurance player. To address the issue of higher expenses, the Indian insurance regulator has brought expense of management regulation so that they can apply limits on the expenses that they incur.

The typical reasons of higher acquisition expenses are following

- Expansion during the initial period
- High cost of agency model development
- Increase in distribution cost
- Lower than planned volume

Other reasons of higher actual expanses

- Higher than planned lapses
- Change in product mix compared to business plan

Expansion during the initial period

During the initial period of life office development, there are many expansion cost such as rent, recruitment cost, system set up etc. These costs cannot be avoided and insurance companies accept the set up cost and try to recover slowly over the period of time.

High cost of agency model development

There are two types of insurance players in the Indian market, one with bank as one of the shareholders and second who set up the branches for the distribution of products. Those players with bank as distribution shareholder partners have relatively lower distribution cost compared to the one who open the branches on their own. The players with bank shareholders have a shorter expense overrun and many of such players in the Indian market have achieved expense breakeven period. While the other players who have set up their own branches are still running with expense overrun.

Such risks are accepted and apply the expense control to shorter then expense overrun period.

Increase in distribution cost

For the distribution of products, many life insurance companies collaborate with banking and non-banking financial institution, where they pay upfront development cost which increases the acquisition expense. As setting up of agency model is expensive, this method is typically used. To address the high upfront cost issue persistency clause are set up so that recovery of initial commissions can be made, if the distributor do not maintain a particular level of persistency.

Lower than planned volume

If the actual volume turns out to be lower than the plan, then the fixed expenses loaded in the premium takes longer to recover. Volume may get affected due to many reasons such as competition, frequent changes in product regulation, aggressive business plan, sales attrition etc.

Based on the sources of such events, the insurance players is to manage this risk by regular monitoring of sales volume, realistic business plan, competitive products, understanding the customers need and pitching the products accordingly etc.

Change in Product mix

The operating expense limits are set up during the business plan time with the assumption of different product mix. Different products have loading of expenses based on the assumptions made during the pricing. Such assumptions are made based on expected new business volume over the period of time. Longer actual deviation in the product mix sales will have adverse impact on recovery of expanses. So it is important to stay within the defined product mix decided during the business planning.

Financial Risks

The key financial risks in life insurance companies are the following

- Interest rate
- Equity
- Liquidity
- Credit
- Investment risk

Interest rate risk

Interest rate risk in life insurance companies are lower actual earning than expected. The expected earning rate comes from the interest rate assumed in the pricing. Different products have different severity towards the interest rate.

Under the unit linked products, the investment risk is passed to the policyholders, so this risk is minimal under the unit linked products.

Under the term products, interest rate risk is lower as there is a no maturity amount; however, some term products with longer tenure or with return of premium may have higher interest rate risk.

Under the participating products, annual bonuses are distributed, so if the actual earning rate is lower, then insurance companies can adjust the bonus rates to reflect the lower earning. So, participating products are preferred option in the management of interest rate risk. However, the policyholders expectations are created at the time of sale with loaded bonus, insurance companies is to manage such expectation and this can be done through distribution of regular and terminal bonuses.

Under the non-participating products, interest rate risk is maximum, because insurance companies contracted to pay the guaranteed maturity amount whatever may happen to interest rate from inception to maturity. The risk is if insurance company has priced such product with assumption 7% return over the 10 years period, and yield on the actual investment falls to 5% after three years, then accumulation of premium at 5% interest rate may fall short of maturity amount and insurance company is to pay the balance from their pocket.

Given the 90:10 profit route to the participating business and relatively smaller margins in the unit linked products, many players are selling high proportion of non-participating products in the Indian market.

Such interest rates are managed through

- Applying margin in the pricing rate of interest
- Applying derivative contract- Not too many players are using this due to the cost and other regulatory restrictions
- Withdrawal and re-pricing of products when interest rate falls beyond appetite
- Moving towards par and unit linked business
- Assets and liability management

Assets and Liability Management (ALM)

- Assets and liability management are performed often on quarterly basis to align with the Assets and Liability Committee meeting. Often the assets and purchased to match the duration of the liability so that when the interest rate changes, the change in the value of liability is of similar amount of as change in the value of assets. The other methods used in the management of ALM are cash flow matching and calculation of economic capital for interest rate risk.
- Interest rate movements are regularly monitored and triggered points are defined where insurance company may withdraw sale of new business, if the yield on the non-par fund fall below a particular level.

Equity Risk

Equity risk management is discussed under the lapse risk.

Liquidity Risk

Liquidity risk is defined as though the company is solvent have inadequate cash to payout the liabilities or liquidity is created by selling the assets at lower price resulting in losses.

Liquidity risk arises from both assets and liabilities sides. Assets side liquidity risk arises due to

- Investment in illiquid assets- such as property-

    - Limiting the investment in the illiquid assets through regular monitoring of liquidity position for next 12 months by projecting the emerging liabilities against the liquid assets. Such projection is also to be performed on stressed condition and make liquidity available. Stress testing is a prevalent tools used in other financial institutions such as in banks.

- Fire sale

    - Fire sale occurs when the company is to sell the assets when the yields are high at lower price to meet the emerged liabilities.
    - This can occur if the company has invested in long term bonds and not keeping enough liquidity to meet the emerging short term liabilities.

- Fall in the credit rating of third party from where money is due

    - When credit rating of the company is downgraded then that bond become illiquid as there are not too many purchasers available in the market. In this situation, if liquidity need arises, then cash crunch may occur.

- Bulk sales

    - To meet the liquidity, if the company is selling high proportion of stock, they may get the relatively lower price due to bulk sale in the market.

- Drying up line of credit

    - To manage the liquidity risk, insurance companies may tie up with banks to provide liquidity at a time of need. However, if there is a stressed economic situation, the bank may refuse the obligation.

- Concentration risk

    - Concentration risk in few stocks may result in liquidity crisis if there is a need to liquidate those stocks and market is in a distress situation

- Exchange rate risk

    - If the investment is in overseas assets, fall in exchange rate at the time of liquidity need may create liquidity issue. Overseas investment in Indian is not permissible.

Liability side liquidity risk arises due to

- Mass surrender

    - Mass surrender with guaranteed surrender value creates liquidity issue where the life company may need to sell assets at distressed price. To address such risk, regular stress testing is required to be done and keep the liquidity equivalent to the stress situation

- Large number of deaths/catastrophic event

- Insurance companies can make arrangement with the reinsurers to release the payment within a week of the claims arising if claim amount is greater that certain limit, say Rs. 1 Cr.

- When portfolio start maturing and ALM mismatch occur

    - When portfolio is maturing, the existing assets are matched with the emerging liabilities; so it is important to keep the liquidity available for any emerging stress liability payouts.

Credit Risk

Sources of credit risk

- Corporate bond issuers

    - The insurance companies invest in the corporate bonds to get higher return than the G-Sec, and so take credit risk. There is a risk that the bond issuers may default on interest payment or redemption payment or both.
    - In the recent times, there have been failures by the bond issuers resulting into credit risk materializing in the Indian market.
    - The risk mitigation of this risk is through investment in AAA rated bonds, regular monitoring of credit rating and keeping track of financials of the issuer of the bonds

- Banks

    - In a distress financial situation, like in recent times, one corporate bank in India have placed restrictions on withdrawals. So in the need to cash, the insurance company may not able to withdraw its assets from such banks, if invested.

- Reinsurers

    - Insurance companies reinsure its high sum assured business and there is a risk that Reinsurance Company may default, if they are not in good financial condition.
    - To address this risk, the reinsurance may be placed with AAA rated reinsurance companies and monitor the rating regularly.

Investment Risk

Investment risk is not able to meet the various limits sets in the investment regulation. The investment risks are managed through

- Audit of Investment Risk Management Systems & Process,
- Internal / Concurrent Audit

    - Audit of "Investment Risk Management Systems and Process
    - Internal / Concurrent Audit of Transactions
    - Appointment of Audit Firms for "Investment Risk Management Systems & Process"
    - Appointment of Audit Firm for Internal / Concurrent Audit of Transactions

  - Information of Audit Firm for Internal / Concurrent Audit to be filed with IRDAI

- Approval of investment policy by the Board
- Setting up of investment committee that meet quarterly and report to the Board
- Preparing Standard Operating Procedure
- Applying the regulatory investment limits in the investment system
- Review of limits by the Mid office

Operational Risk

Operational risk is the risk of loss resulting from inadequate or failed internal processes, people and systems, or from external events. This includes legal and compliance risk and excludes strategic and reputational risk. This widely accepted definition is from the Basel Committee on Banking Supervision, a group that promulgates international standards used by many banking regulators.

Risk Control and Self Assessment (RCSA)

Risk and control self assessment (RCSA) is a process through which operational risks and the effectiveness of controls are assessed and examined. This helps in risk identification and risk quantification. The primary purpose of RCSA is to have register of all the operational risks with the business, looking at the inherent risks, what controls are placed so that residual risks come down to within tolerance limit.

The impact of operational risk could be financial, customer or reputational. The inherent risks are assessed in terms of likelihood and impact which could be in any or on all three areas.

Based on the cause of the risks, appropriate controls are placed so that the residual risks are not outside the risk appetite defined by the Company.

In the management of operational risk, risk controls play a key role. It is therefore very important to map the various causes of risks correctly.

The residual risks are again assessed on likelihood and impact scale after the application of controls.

Regulatory Risk

Regulatory risk refers to the risks, costs and problems arising from new regulations/laws or modification to existing regulations/laws and is one of the greatest strategic challenges facing insurance industry today.

Insurance business is in India is tightly regulated with strict capital requirement for the insurance companies; the foreign direct investment is also capped at 49%, customer's protection is one of the key objectives of the regulator with defined illustration to be presented to customers at the point of sale. The investment norms are defined in detailed that all in the insurance companies are to adhere. The non-compliance with the regulation attracts warning and penalties.

Due to the young nature of the insurance industry, there are frequent changes in the regulation that may trigger areas of non-compliance resulting into regulatory risk. The change in the regulation may require system change, change in the investment norms, reinsurance arrangements, public disclosures etc. These changes in the past have resulted into compliance challenges with some players resulting into penalties and warnings.

The regulatory risks may be managed through:

- Adopt best practices before they are mandated
- Regular communication with the regulator on areas of challenges such as

  - Expense of management
  - Issues on falling business
  - Issues related solvency capital
  - Setting up new distribution partners etc

- Strict compliance with various regulation with zero tolerance with non-compliance
- Compliance with the product approved by the regulator in all respect
- Disclosure of noncompliance areas in the Risk Management Committee and to regulator; asking for the time in the areas where insurance companies are facing challenges

Reputational

Reputational risk management is concerned with protecting organisation's reputation, arguably the organisation's most valuable asset. Reputation risk arises when there is a situation, event or series of events that have the potential to negatively influence public opinion and the perceptions of other stakeholders.

Reputation risks arise when a company fails to meet stakeholders' expectations and they change their behaviour.

Reputation risks arise as a result of rumours about a potential hostile takeover or negative media reports about changes to the board of directors. „

Reputation risks also results as a possible consequence of other risks. This means that a corporate reputation can be damaged as a result of practically any type of risk, including poor corporate governance, unethical practices, cyber risks, compliance failures and dubious sales practices.

Reputation Risk Management

Building reputation revolves around conducting every business or transaction in the most ethical manner. For example, every time an insurance company sells a policy, processes a claim, enters into a contract, builds a new facility, or enters into litigation, it is making decisions that define its reputation. This reputation affects its ability to acquire new clients or even continue servicing existing relationships. Thus, it is essential that it conducts its every transaction in a very professional and efficient way, in compliance with its core values & business ethics and ensuring enough focus on customer centricity i.e. delivering value to the customer. Also, apart from the business, every enterprise has some social responsibilities which it must discharge.

- Curbing any mis-selling practices carried out by its agents/ advisors and insisting on informed sales.
- Delivering all promised services to the policyholders.
- Maintaining timely and efficient communications among policyholders, regulator and other stakeholders.
- Establishing strong enterprise risk management policies and procedures throughout the organization.
- Instilling ethics throughout the organization by enforcing a code of conduct for the board, management, and staff.
- Complying with current laws and regulations and enforcing existing policies and procedures.
- Responding promptly and accurately to queries by policyholders and the regulator.
- Establishing a crisis management team to carry out tasks (as mentioned below) in the event there is a significant action that may trigger a negative impact on the organization

Risk Monitoring

Risk monitoring is the process of tracking and evaluating the levels of risk in an organisation. This discipline helps in tracking and evaluating the effectiveness of risk management strategies. The findings by risk monitoring processes can be used to help creating new strategies and update older strategies which may have proved to be ineffective.

The purpose of risk monitoring is to keep track of the risks that occur and the effectiveness of the responses which are implemented by an organisation. Monitoring also help to ascertain whether proper policies were followed, whether new risks can now be identified or whether previous assumptions are still valid. Monitoring is vital because risks are not static.

The key risk monitoring processes in life insurance are

- ***Actual Versus Expected***- Actual experience of mortality, expense and lapses are observed against the expected experience and ratio is calculated as Actual/Expected. If the ratio is greater than 1, it means that the actual experience is worse than expected. The emerging experiences are used in updating the pricing assumption to reflect company's own experience.
    - The experience is used as a lead indicator of insurance risks
- **Liquidity**- Liquidity experience is monitored over the next 12 months period by projecting the expected liability against the emerging liquid assets. Any shortfall in the assets needs to be bumped up.
    - Stress testing is also performed to assess the stressed liquidity position.
- **New business monitoring**- Monitoring of new business helps in ascertaining how the company is ding against the business plan. The monitoring helps in evaluating whether any new strategies are required to meet the new business target. This is generally tracked in the different risk updates to the Company
- **Assets and liability** positions are tracked in the ALM meeting on quarterly basis to asses thee mis-match between the duration of assets and liability. This helps in deciding how the assets to be purchased in coming months to match the liabilities
- **Breaches**-Regulatory and internal limits are set and monitored to stay compliant with the regulation and stay within the risk appetite of the Company. Any breaches are highlighted in the risk management committee and remedial actions are framed.

Risk Reporting

Risk reporting is a communication of the risk management process of risk identification, quantification, management and monitoring to different stakeholders such as senior management, Risk Management Committee, Audit Committee and Board. This help in taking the informed business decision and drawing up mitigating action to achieve the business objective. The risk reporting in life insurance industry in India may take following routes:

- **Risk register**- A Risk Register is a tool for documenting risks, and actions to manage each risk. The Risk Register is essential to the successful management of risk. As risks are identified they are logged on the register and actions are taken to respond to the risk.
- **Review and Challenge Process**- Review and challenge is a process through which the risk function evaluates the risk analysis performed by the first line of defense and provide the feedback on the same. Through this process, risk communication takes place when second line of defense provides the feedback.
- **RCSA**- RCSA is a Risk Control and Self Assessment process performed by the first line of defense for operational risk in conjunction with second line of defense. During this process which sometimes takes in a workshop like manner, the feedback is given during the workshop itself.
- **Audit Committee/ Risk Management Committee/ALCO**- These are quarterly committee meetings occur in the Indian life insurance industry where all operational, insurance, financial, reputational and regulatory risks are

presented to the respective committee. This includes the identified risks, mitigating actions, breaches etc so that Board can take a final call on the risks of the Company.

FIFTEEN

Overlap between Second and Third Line of Defense for Risk Management

Introduction

The purpose of the chapter is to assess the level of any overlap between the second and third lines of defense in the global market. The level of overlap influences the independence of the two lines and the maturity of risk management and audit function. The data is obtained by conducting a poll.

Three lines of defense model are popular across the world in addressing the risks and giving assurances to the Board about the controls in place to manage risks in the organization.

Luburic, Perovic, and Sekulovic (2015) mentioned in their paper that out of the three lines of defense, the first line of defense is business line management who manages risks in the organization. This includes the mid and front-line managers who are the risk owners responsible for implementing and maintaining the effectiveness of internal control. They further state that the second of defense are risk management professionals responsible for developing risk management policies, helping the first line of defense in risk identification, quantifying risks, managing, monitoring, and reporting of risks. The third line of defense is internal auditors providing reliable assurance of risk management system and internal controls to the Board.

For three lines to function effectively, there is a need to separate each line to create distinction in performing their roles. The role of risk management in the second line of defense is to give an independent opinion about the risks identified. Independence is very important because the opinion is without the influence of either the first line or the third line.

However, it has been seen in many markets that there is an overlap between the second and third lines of defense by combining the two functions. The integration of second and third line invalidate the purpose of three lines of defense model because both second and third line cannot function independently. In this situation, if the combined function is headed by the same person, it could be a challenge to give assurance to Board without some bias.

A similar study was conducted in Maltese credit institutions by Borg, Baldacchino, et al (2020) to explore whether integrated assurance function on three lines of defense is workable or not? They found through the study that banks were in favor of separate three lines of defense model but some non-credit institutions were in favor of integrating the internal control system. Their argument in favor of integration was reducing the duplication of work and enhancing the collective work by "cross-sharing information".

To understand the level of overlap between the second and third lines of defense, a survey was conducted to assess the position in different countries.

Survey Poll

The survey poll was conducted in August 2021 to assess whether companies have combined risk and audit functions or not. The purpose was to assess the acceptance of a separate three lines of defense model or integrated assurance function. Such integration of assurance function is also a reflection of lack of risk maturity model in an organization. A simple question was asked whether their organization has a separate risk and audit function or a combined risk and audit function.

205 votes were polled with 175 giving vote that their company has a separate risk and audit function (85%) while 30 votes were polled that their Company has a combined risk and audit function (15%).

The votes were polled by senior professionals such as Head of Internal Audit, Chief Risk Officers, Compliance officers, Head of information security, Director, Chief Actuary, etc. The responses are from almost all the major countries such as India, UAE, UK, US, Canada, Namibia, Greece, South Africa, etc.

Discussion

The survey indicates that in most of the organizations and most of the countries, there is a separate second and third line of defense, with 85% in favor and 15% against. However, in some companies, still, the two lines are combined.

A high percentage of responses about a separate line of defense is an indication of independence and level of maturity towards enterprise risk management. Mushsyaf, Saipul et al (2021) established that the three lines of the defense model play an essential role in realizing the effectiveness of risk management in the company. They further identified that the effectiveness of risk management is dependent on the effectiveness of three lines of defense.

Some of the comments given by participants are captured below.

"If Risk is not independent and the CRO does not report directly to the Board, the organization is not serious about the effective management of risk."

Another respondent wrote that *"The fact that the question is being asked indicates that organizations still have blurred lines of segregation between risk and audit. I've seen this change but, in some organizations, this is truer for operational risk where the roles and understanding blur with the audit. But it is changing."*

Mabwe, Kumbirai; Ring, Patrick; Webb, Robert (2017) undertook the study of looking at the three lines of defense model in the operational risk in UK financial services. They found many interviewees stating about the blurring of the first and second lines of defense. They also found that the second line of defense whose role of providing the oversight is doing the role of risk management for the first line. This results in second-line losing the independence and creating gaps between theory and practice.

Kumar, S (2021) also identified similar blurredness between the first and second line of defense in his paper. Further, the same situation is observed in the Indian financial market where the second line of defense is doing most of the risk management work of the first line. One of the reasons observed is due to a lack of risk management expertise with the first line of defense.

The third response was, *"If both Risk and Audit are combined and I've seen organizations where they have a Risk & Audit Director, then you have a situation where they're marking their homework. Furthermore, it becomes a very mechanical process of checklists and box-ticking."*

The respondent indicates the challenges when the two lines are combined and exercise becomes more compliance-oriented. However, the poll result suggests that the combined assurance activity has been reduced.

The fourth response, *"It cannot be a combined one. Every risk is a separate risk about its threats and vulnerabilities."*

The fifth response, *"We see the big gap in this lack of separation during project initiation and execution. ACRO assists the business to avoid audit findings before the fact and this has a positive effect on cost-saving and benefits realization"*

The sixth response, *"While it is true Risk is level 2 and Audit is level 3 control, however, to build the culture across enterprise and industry, initial combined effort makes more sense. In a matured industry like Banking and Insurance, segregation is worthwhile, however, at large synergy will be more meaningful. I will also like to add Internal Audit is also changing dynamically from its traditional role and is moving into a business enabler role where they help management in ease of doing business ensuring compliance, predictive analysis for achieving business objectives etc. with this risk profile can get merge and will in turn help organization implement the concept without increasing the cost significantly and also get IA more acceptable in the organization. It will be a win-win for all."*

The above comment has some reflection of study made in the Maltese credit institution where both the voices were observed from banking and non-credit institutions of keeping separate and combining the two lines respectively.

Conclusion

There is clear evidence from the people who participated in the poll that their companies have a separate second and third line of defense in many countries and many companies. However, there are still a minority of companies in some countries running with combined risk and audit functions. The implication of combined function is about the quality of assurance given to the Board which can be tested empirically.

References

1. Borg, Glen, Peter J. Baldacchino, Sandra Buttigieg, Engin Boztepe, and Simon Grima. "Challenging the adequacy of the Conventional 'Three lines of Defence'model: A case Study on Maltese Credit Institutions." In *Contemporary Issues in Audit Management and Forensic Accounting*. Emerald Publishing Limited, 20202.
2. Luburic, Radoica, Milan Perovic, and Rajko Sekulovic. "Quality Management in Terms of Strengthening the „Three Lines of Defence" in Risk Management-Process Approach." *International Journal for Quality Research* 9, no. 2 (2015): 243-250.
3. Muhsyaf, Saipul A., Susi R. Cahyaningtyas, and Elin E. Sasanti. "Three Line of Defense: An Effective Risk Management." In *18th International Symposium on Management (INSYMA 2021)*, pp. 85-91. Atlantis Press, 2021.
4. Mabwe, Kumbirai; Ring, Patrick; Webb, Robert (2017) in their paper "Operational risk and the three lines of defense in UK financial institutions: is three really the magic number?" published in the journal "Journal of Operational Risk"

5. Kumar, S. (2021). Risk Culture Is a Necessary Condition for Enterprise Risk Management to Succeed. *Academia Letters*, Article 2464. https://doi.org/10.20935/AL2464.

SIXTEEN

Risk Culture is a Necessary Condition for Enterprise Risk Management to Succeed

Introduction

Risk culture is essential for the success of enterprise risk management (ERM). Enterprise risk management is different from silo risk management where risks were mainly managed by one department. Enterprise risk management means that the risk management is integrated from Board to the last employee of the organization. This is much easier said than done. This means that every employee of the organization has a role to perform as a risk manager; this is essentially the essence of the three lines of defense model. It is not just important for a business to achieve the sales objective and other key performance parameters, but the real question is long-term sustainability which comes from managing the risks.

This chapter touches upon the different aspects of risk culture which is a building block of the success of ERM currently prevailing essential for developing a good risk management practice.

Current Position of Risk Culture

In many financial organizations across the world where Chief Risk Officer (CRO) position is mandated by the respective regulators. This means that the Company has a dedicated risk management function headed by CRO. In all such organizations, Board is the owner of the risk management where the baton is passed to the CRO to lead the race of development of risk management.

In all such organizations, enterprise risk management is practiced. This means that various components of ERM such as risk management processes, policies, integration of risk management across the Company, setting risk appetite, three lines of defense model, strategic risk management, etc. are practiced in the Company. However, there are different levels of embedding of risk management across different organizations which differentiate them among themselves in risk management terms. One of the key components of ERM is the risk culture, that is, how every employee uses risk management in practice. Under the three lines of defense model, the first line of defense is all employees except in risk, compliance, and audit function and they are the primary risk managers. The audit is the third line of defense and Risk and Compliance are the second line of defense.

It is widely believed in organizations that the job of risk management is of Risk function which is not fully true. The job of risk management in an organization is the first line of defense as they are the owners of the business objective and they have to identify the risks that can impede the achievement of their objectives. Further, the first line of defense is the subject matter experts, therefore, they are better placed to identify and manage the risks.

The role of the second line is to provide the risk oversight and not to do the job of risk managers. They can help the first line in understanding the risks and challenges upon what risks have been identified along with comments on mitigation action.

This is an ideal scenario; however, realities are far from ideal. In many organizations, risk management is performed by the risk function with very little idea of the first line that they are the risk managers. In some organizations, risk management is somewhat embedded but risk function is still playing a key role in the risk management exercise.

The best litmus test can be performed by asking the employees working in the branch office about risk management. They would mostly refer to the risk management performed by someone sitting in Head Office.

In such a situation, the three lines of defense model are not working well or working with a minimal efficiency and this is where the fundamentals of ERM start crumbling because risk management is not fully integrated across the organization.

Under this situation, the full benefits of risk management will not come. Therefore, there is a great need to develop a risk culture.

Further, underdeveloped risk culture is a breeding ground for operational risk. Operational risk results from the failure of people, process, and systems resulting in losses. Therefore, underdeveloped risk culture will impact all three drivers of operational risk. Under a risk-based capital regime, there is a regulatory requirement of keeping additional capital for operational risk. Therefore, it can be seen that risk culture has a direct impact on capital requirements.

Development of Risk Culture

The most important requirement of ERM to succeed is for the first line to think like a risk manager. There is a difference between doing a regular job and thinking like a risk manager. So, it is like double hatting for employees. Doing the regular work is perhaps easy because that is where their education, training and experience have been so far and make them experts in their areas. So, when thinking like a risk manager, one has to question, their own work from a "What if" point of view. This is not easy. It is like doing the job and thinking about what can go wrong and finding a solution. That is where a change is required for ERM to embed.

There is a need to develop a mechanism for how to approach the problem at hand with a "what if" mindset, and this is where entire risk management training is required to educate the entire workforce.

This is the reason why despite many CROs believing that ERM is well embedded in their organization, the branch guy will still not able to tell who is a risk manager.

There are many components of the development of risk culture within an organization. Though there is a requirement for proper training in the first line about risk management, the biggest human attraction towards learning is incentives and remunerations. It has been found is many developed markets that the inclusion of incentive in the pay structure help improve the risk management practices.

Though at first hand, it may look like a cost center, but in a long term, it is an investment on risk management as better ERM help improve the shareholder's value. This has been proven in many academic literatures and implemented in many developed markets.

Conclusion

Risk culture is essential for fully embedding ERM within an organization; the exercise should continue till employees at branch office able to identify the risk in their own work. It is just like the last screw of the engine is tight.

SEVENTEEN

HOW DIGITALIZATION CAN HELP MANAGE RISKS IN INSURANCE SECTOR

Introduction

Digitalization such as big data, artificial intelligence, the internet of things, cloud computing, and Blockchain is an enabler in the insurance sector. The key areas from where some of the risks in the insurance sector arise are customers, claims, cross-selling, churning, mis-selling, fraud, etc. Such areas often lead to the cropping up of operational risks. Digitalization helps in managing such risks.

Key Digital Areas

The key digital areas that are impacting the insurance industries are

- big data,
- artificial intelligence,
- the internet of things,
- cloud computing and
- Blockchain.

Big Data

There is no standard definition of big data; however, it is a collection of data that is huge in volume, yet growing exponentially with time. It is data that is so large and complex that none of the traditional data management tools can store it or processes it efficiently. Big data is commonly mentioned as '3V", where first V is referred to as "Volume" is assigned to the size of data, second V is referred to as "Velocity" indicates the pace of data being generated and processed and third V is "Variety" focuses on the diversity of data, which can be structured, semi-structured or unstructured. In recent years, now 3V has turned into '5V". The fourth V is "Veracity" referred to as inconsistencies and uncertainties in data concerning quality and accuracy. The fifth V is "Value" which is the utilization of data into meaningful use.

To perform the big data analysis, the insurance company is to install data lakes. Data lakes collect data in their original format from different sources whereas data warehouses are a repository of structured, filtered datathat has already been processed for a specific purpose.

Data lakes are therefore able to store unstructured data, which is not possible with data warehouses. Hence, data lakes are useful in increasing the number of efficient possibilities to find patterns and correlations in data.

Artificial Intelligence (AI)

Artificial intelligence (AI) is referred to the simulation of human intelligence in machines that are programmed to think like humans and mimic their actions. In AI the machine exhibits act like the human mind such as learning and problem-solving. Machine learning and deep learning are a part of AI. Machine learning is the study of a computer program that improves automatically through experience. Deep learning is an AI function that mimics the workings of the human brain in processing data for use in detecting objects, recognizing speech, translating languages, and making decisions. Deep learning AI can learn without human supervision, drawing from data that is both unstructured and unlabeled.

Internet of Things (IoT)

The Internet of Things (IoT) is a system of interrelated devices, internet-connected objects, mechanical and digital machines, objects such as smartphones, wearables, etc that can collect and transfer data over a wireless network without human-to-human or human-to-computer interaction. The IoT has a unique identifier for each participant to transfer the data over the network

The "Internet of Thing" is a combination of "internet" through which the data is transferred over the network, whereas "thing" is an object such as a device, connected appliances, Smart home security or wearable health monitors, etc.

An IoT is web-enabled smart devices that have processors, sensors, and communication devices to collect and send data. The devices mostly work without human intervention. An IoT can use AI and machine learning to act on the collected data to make use of it, either through supervised or unsupervised learning. When data is collected, big data tools can be used.

An IoT helps to automate the processes, reduce the labor cost, reduce waste and improve service delivery thereby reducing the cost of the product.

The application of IoT in the insurance industry requires the integration of the existing system with web-enabled devices along with increasing data storage capacity. The collected raw customer data from IoT requires sufficient capacity and knowledge to translate the results into insurance products, by employing a data analytics tool.

Cloud Computing

The Cloud computing service providers offer external computing and storage capacities that enable flexible access to pooled computing resources such as networks, servers, storage capacities, or applications. Cloud computing is the delivery of different services through the Internet. These resources include tools and applications like data storage, servers, databases, networking, and software. The front end enables a user to access data stored in the cloud using an internet browser.

The benefits of cloud computing are the reduced IT costs by eliminating the capital expenditure of buying hardware, software and setting up and running on-site datacenters. It also helps in reducing the cost through the round-the-clock electricity for power and cooling, the IT experts for managing the infrastructure, etc.

From an insurance company's point of view, it is necessary to integrate cloud computing into existing IT infrastructures. In this regard, a lack of compatibility of legacy systems with cloud computing is often challenging. In an ideal situation, insurance companies should aim to replace legacy systems, which present a major challenge. The resulting IT landscape is furthermore required to overcome data privacy and data security concerns in the context of cloud computing.

Blockchain

Blockchain technology is a protocol for the secure transfer of money, property, contracts, and identity credentials through the internet without requiring a third-party intermediary such as a bank or government.

Blockchain technology makes it difficult to change or hack information. This is a digital ledger of transaction which is distributed across the computer system.

The application of Blockchain in the insurance sector is many folds through which claims can be settled without any intervention of a third party which will improve transparency, follow regulation, and also reduces cost.

Key Sources of Risks in the Insurance Sector

Products

Like in any other business, insurance businesses thrive on selling their products which helps in managing the risks of the customers. Such risks could be life, health, property, vehicle, fire, etc. Therefore products are a very key component of the insurance business; however, most important is that the products should meet the needs of the customers. Some insurance is mandatory such as a vehicle, however, others are not and dependent on the needs of the customers. Unlike the banking business, where the customer himself walks to the bank branch, the same does not happen in the insurance business. Therefore, the products should be manufactured in such a way that meets the needs against the price the customers pay.

Underwriting

Underwriting is a process of selection of risks by the insurance company based on whether the risks presented by the customer conform to the risks taken in pricing. Such selections are made based on the customer's health condition, medical reports, and financial capacity to pay the insurance premium. Underwriting is a first stage of applying the filter which risks that insurance Company considers that they do not accept.

Claims

The claim made by the customer is the real benefit of the product that a customer purchases. Therefore, the claims payment should be hassle-free and the Company should honor the claim. During the claim process, it is ensured that the details are given by the customers at the time of proposal matches when the claim is made. This is done to avoid any possible fraud.

Mis-selling

For customers trouble may arise when he makes a claim realizes that the product he was sold was not what he intended to purchase. This is mis-selling quite rampant in the insurance industry as agents are to meet their business targets and sell the wrong product. Sometimes in the insurance sector, some insurance products are sold as other products such as mutual funds or fixed deposits.

Customer Complaints

When the customer's needs are not met or the wrong product is sold or claims are not paid, then customers make a complaint. The customer's complaint should be resolved amicably and quickly. However, many times customers are not satisfied which results in dissatisfaction and impact the future sale of new business of the insurance company.

Churning of business

Churning of business happens in the life insurance business when the renewal premium of the customers is used as selling a new policy to the same customer. This results in lapsing the customer's first policy without his knowledge and this is done by agents to meet their selling new business quota. In this situation, both the customer and insurance company loses money.

Cross-Selling

Cross-selling is an opportunity when a new product is sold to the same customer based on his needs. This generally happens when the first policy sold is of low premium and the existing customer's database is used to sell another product.

Policy lapsing

When a customer does not pay a renewal premium, the policy is lapsed or surrendered for cash value. When a policy lapses before the end of its original term, the insurance company loses the money.

Fraud

The legal definition of fraud defines it as means misappropriating assets or by deliberately misrepresenting or concealing material facts relevant to some financial decisions or by abusing responsibility, a position of trust (Section 17 of Indian Contract Act, 1872)

Insurance fraud is committed by either policyholder, intermediary or internal employees. These are performed by suppressing information and making inappropriate claims. In insurance, fraud is generally related to either information or financial transaction made either by customers or agents, or internal employees.

Insurance fraud occurs when any act is committed with the intent to fraudulently obtain some benefit or advantage to which they are not otherwise entitled or someone knowingly denies some benefit that is due and to which someone is entitled.

Mitigation of Risks due to Digitalization

A better understanding of customers due to the large volume of information:

A better understanding of customers due to large volume help understand the customers across demography, customer segment, their behavior, lifestyle, occupation, education, etc. This information is useful in understanding the likely impact on mortality of the customers because as seen from the above risk section that these factors impact the mortality rate. So an analysis of data using big data technology will be useful in better understanding the mortality risk

Customer behavior on the cause of lapse of the policy

Understanding customer behavior is useful in knowing what our customers need so that the right product can be pitched, this will help in reducing the lapse risk. Also, it has been seen policyholder's behavior has a direct relationship with lapse rate. Customers also lapse the policy due to changes in their economic condition, so analysis of the emerging economic position concerning customer behavior would be useful in predicting the lapse rate.

More knowledge about customers helps in greater interaction

More knowledge about the customers can help in establishing the interaction between the information presented by the customers at the time of proposal (underwriting) and when claims results. This will help in managing the mortality risk. This will help in reducing frauds.

Analytics convert the information into understandable results such as knowing buying decision-Up-selling/ Cross-selling;

Big data can help to buy behavior of the customers which can help in position the right products to the customers and also in cross-selling. So such analysis provides an opportunity to the insurance companies in increasing their business volume which in turn helps in managing the expense risk.

Big data helps in establishing **a correlation between large numbers of variables** helps in understanding customers better compared **to the traditional method of analysis.** This can help in establishing a correlation between different risk factors such as lapse and mortality, volume and expense, customer behavior, and lapse.

Improvement in insurance product Customer satisfaction and reputation risk

Such big data analysis helps in customer satisfaction which helps in improving the reputation risk. As seen from the risk section that reputation risk is a consequence of other risks. So when other risks are managed, helps in reducing the reputation risk.

Rate making and underwriting

As mentioned in the above section, underwriting is a process of selection of risk, so big data helps in analyzing the risk better thereby

- Tailor-made products- Customer satisfaction and improvement in reputational risk, the financial impact
- Cross-selling and up-selling-Impact on financials
- Better investment decision-Financial risk
- Operational excellence-Operational risk

Conclusion

There is sufficient evidence that digitalization has helped the insurance sector in managing the risks. However, one important point to keep in mind that the risks that arise due to the adoption of digitalization should also be managed simultaneously.

EIGHTEEN

RISK MANAGEMENT AND DIGITIZATION

Introduction

Risk is inherent in every business because future uncertainty may not help meet objectives. A slight deviation from meeting business objectives may be acceptable within risk appetite, but a significant departure could be catastrophic to the business. Thus, it is essential to assess the expected deviation level and plan for mitigating action, which is central to risk management. Therefore, risk management practices reduce earnings volatility, surprises, capital enhancement, add shareholder value, help in better decision-making, etc.

This chapter is about the role of digitization in risk management. So first, let's look at some of the challenges in risk management addressed through digitalization.

Challenges in Risk Management

For most business failures across the world, the key reasons are failure of risk identification when risk is approaching the business. The classic example was COVID 19, where many organizations did not react when COVID struck in early December 2019 and in January 2020. Also, during the 2008 economic crisis, businesses ignored initial signals of risks. However, no risk appears suddenly, and its information is primarily present. Therefore, to succeed in risk management, one must spot the risks and identify their correlation. For example, liquidity risk may arise in a bank due to an increase in credit risk. Similarly, under the term insurance products, the portfolio's mortality experience may worsen in the insurance sector due to the rise in lapse rate where all healthy lives have stopped paying a premium. Similarly, it is essential to keep an eye on the emerging risk, as the signals of such risks are very feeble, and the velocity of the risk may catch the institution on the wrong foot.

In the organization, risk identification is often a manual process. The manual method requires a systematic thinking process to approach risk identification. Otherwise, risks may be missed out. The challenge in the manual process, the data is often analyzed late, resulting in risks crystallizing.

In the organizations where risk culture is not well developed, employees are often in the denial mode when risks are highlighted to them; the most often response is "it won't affect us," and many of the live risks are left unattended. Such organizations also lack a "what if mindset."

Organizations also face challenges when data is scattered, lacking a unified view to assessing risk correctly. For example, during COVID 19, insurance companies depended on the exclusion clause in the policy bond that the pandemic was not covered. Different governments and regulators ordered to pay such claims leading to many court cases. Such claims are paid, which were not priced is a straight loss.

The correlation of risks is another area that requires CRO's attention. A big shock in a system sends ripples in different economic areas that directly impact the financial institution.

CRO needs to re-assess the Company's risk profile due to such events and raise the risks to the management and the Board for corrective action. Such re-assessment of risks is possible when CRO has an automated system that can re-calculate the risks in the wake of such events. Therefore, the availability of an integrated risk information system in one place is critical for CROs to assess the risks, draw correlations and make real-time risk-based decisions.

How digitalization can help in averting some of the above challenges

Digitalization is a way forward in managing some of the key challenges that an organization faces in the management of risk. Organizations require integrating a risk information system that can provide all risk information at the CRO's fingertips. This will help him slice and dice the risks, understand the materiality of risk, and correlate between them. This also helps identify critical sources of risks which is a breeding ground for various threats. For example, adverse economic activity is a source of interest rate risk; a sound information system monitors economic activity that helps in advance spotting the interest rate risk. A new trend is observed where organizations have started integrating publicly available data from their websites to their own database helping in competitive pricing of products, early determination of risk, analyzing market trends, taking competitive advantage, and making an informed decision. The availability of the digital tool help in automating scrapping the data from public websites to taking the information into their data system. In this way, risk can be identified in an automatic way. Because of the automation of risk identification, some of the personal human biases also get reduced.

Organizations are integrating Data Science, Data Analytics, Predictive modeling, Big Data, Artificial intelligence, the Internet of things, and Cloud Computing in making risk-based decisions. Such analysis helps in getting more knowledge about customers' demands of products, pricing, analyzing competitive trends, predicting risk, etc. For example, big data is a collection of structured or unstructured data that is huge in volume. None of the traditional data management tools can store or process it efficiently. This helps in understanding the customer behaviors, more significant customer insights, identification of trends, quantification of risk, and help understanding correlation between risks.

Machine learning (ML) is the study of a computer program that improves automatically through experience and prediction based on an algorithm. Artificial intelligence (AI) refers to the simulation of human intelligence in machines programmed to think like humans and mimic their actions. Application is on increasing trend- help in prediction, fore-warning, emerging risks. For example, in the aviation sector, ML/AI is also used to predict the possibility of accidents.

The Internet of things is a system of interrelated devices, internet-connected objects, mechanical and digital machines, smartphones, wearables, etc., that can collect and transfer data over a wireless network without human-to-human or human-to-computer interaction. As a result, it automates processes, reduces labor cost, reduces waste, and improves service delivery, thereby reducing the cost of the product. The application of IoT in the insurance industry is immense like data transfer for health insurance, motor insurance, and life insurance.

Cloud computing is external computing and storage capacities that enable flexible access to pooled computing resources such as networks, servers, storage capacities, or applications. Applications like data storage, servers, databases, networking, and software. Benefits reduced IT costs by eliminating the capital expenditure of buying hardware and software and setting up and running on-site datacenters, cost of electricity and cooling, the IT experts for managing the infrastructure, etc.

Conclusion

Many of the challenges raised above, such as risk identification which is the first step of risk management, is addressed through digitization, where inferences can be drawn from the data analysis. For example, falling economic activities could indicate an increase in the inflation rate or a change in the interest rate that may impact the financial institutions. So, emerging risks can be addressed through data analytics. ML and AI are used in many areas for predictive purposes. The challenges of correlation of risks can also be addressed through digital devices as the calculation of correlation would be easy with available data that can be plugged into the predictive model for better results. Human biases or human opinion can also be reduced by using digital technology, as data will give better evidence about the emergence of risk. However, it is essential to use human judgment to conclude the results because a blind trust in the model could be dangerous, as seen during the 2008 economic crisis.

Such data integration will also address the scattered data that the organization may have.

Overall, the adoption of digital technology will help organizations in the management of risk, save costs and increase the value of the firm.

NINETEEN

PANDEMIC RISK AND INSURANCE SECTOR

Problem Statement

The pandemic event has re-surfaced some of the challenges that otherwise remain in the backdrop such as the exclusion of uninsurable risks, the expectation of the government and regulator from the insurance industry in paying claims. Pandemic risk event leads to a complex web of correlation of risks. How these risks are to be priced keeping in line with the expectation of customers, regulators, and all other stakeholders. Insurance is a long-term contract and makes all these calculations much more complicated than linear equations.

Fine prints

Insurance is an understandably easy avenue where financial dependencies are passed from customers to insurance companies, but many may not be knowing that all risks under the sun are not covered, because some risks are not priced or difficult to price.

At the onset of the pandemic during 2020, many insurance companies around the world were facing dual challenges of searching the fine prints in the policy bond about coverage of pandemic, and on the other hand, there was an increasing expectation from the government on honoring the claims. The reputation of the entire insurance industry was at risk.

By June 2020, more than 450 lawsuits were there in the US, when insurance companies denied the claims covering small businesses interruption due to COVID. This was painful when business houses paid the premium for many years thinking all business interruption risks are covered.

Many regulators directed the insures to pay the claims irrespective of risk covered or not. Insurers argued that the reason pandemic claims business interruption losses, were not covered by their policies because the losses associated with pandemics are uninsurable correlated risks.

Correlated risks are losses caused by perils that result in numerous losses occurring in the same geographic area at approximately the same time

Insurers argued that to cover all COVID-19 business interruption losses would bankrupt the insurance industry.

Challenges

The challenges of the insurance industry do not end here. In the insurance business, no one pays claims out of their pocket, the claims are paid out of the premium collected. If the insurance company has either not priced the risk due to whatever reason, then from which kitty, they will pay the claims to the customers. This is because those risks that have been priced and customers have paid the premium, also come to lodge the claim.

Here the question boils down to how does the insurance company deals with the exclusions? During the normal day of working an exclusion seems like a distant event, it will never come but when it comes, it haunts.

Should the exclusion be written in a bold letter with a font of 14 to be visible to all customers, should this not be advertised in bold that pandemic risks are not covered so that the customers are aware of which risks they are paying the premium?

Here there seems to be a hidden assumption that the insurance company believes that the customers have read the policy condition and the customer believes that risks are covered and he has paid the premium. Does two wrong make one, right?

Both the things are not correct, if risks are not priced and the insurance company is paying the claims, it means that shareholders are paying out of their profit or from the cost of capital. Now, when risks were not priced, then why it was not told to customers in the clear term?

Now perhaps it is a time to think about exclusions like marketing material and written on the front page in bold, what risks are not covered, this will create both clear expectations for regulators and government but also for customers for which risks they are paying the premium. Exclusions perhaps are no longer to be kept in the smaller font.

There may be a need to make customers understand why some of the risks cannot be priced.

Correlation of Risks

The emergence of risks posts the onset of pandemic not necessarily follow any order whether first, it is demographic or economic. Within a month, all the risks will start triggering. If the sequence of events in India is to be followed, by the mid of March 2020, the equity market was bleeding red, its impact on the insurance Company's solvency was visible, many players had 20 to 30 bps solvency lower corresponding to the previous reporting period.

The 10-Year G-Sec bond yield in India was 6.5% as of 1st January 2020, by July 2020 the yield fell to 5.8%, and by mid of May 2021, the yield is still at 6%. Such a fall in the 10-year G-Sec yield has an impact on non-participating traditional products which have a customer's guarantee on maturity.

The rise in death claim led to reinsurance Companies increasing the reinsurance term insurance rates by 30% to 40% which were later passed to customers. All the summary of risks were visible in GDP with a contraction of 7.7% during FY 2020-21 over the previous year.

All the three risks equity, interest rate, and mortality have occurred together. There are two more equally important risks for the insurance industry is the persistency risk and expense risks have both internal and external factors.

How does the correlation of risks are taken into the pricing of risks? The traditional model of pricing of risks does not allow all the correlations of risks in premium. Some correlations of risks are allowed between mortality and persistency. There are other tools like stress and scenario testing (SST) but that remains mostly linear with no cross-over of risks. Further, there is no way to load the cost of correlation of risks into premium using SST under the traditional method of pricing. Think about fall in interest rate risk due to rise in mortality due to some or other catastrophic risk?

When SST results are interpreted, from practical point of view, they are left with some management action while when all stressed risks are taken together, they are mostly assumed will not occur and no actions are taken. And that is where the tail risk is? It occurred in 2020.

Conclusion

The question is we have experienced the pandemic risks and its impact, such experience should not go waste. There could be many areas to reinvent ourselves in managing the risks of this order. It is projected by Swiss Re that in 30 years' time, the global GDP may be adversely impacted by 18% due to climate change if no actions are taken. This warning is another imminent catastrophic event with global impact. Assuming, the event will occur, how the risk will be priced in the premium of long-term products? Even in the banking sector, there are long term fixed term loan, how this risk will be incorporated? Plus, there will be many correlated risks?

TWENTY

APPLICATION OF SOCIAL MEDIA TO MANAGE RISK

Introduction

This chapter discusses the application of social media which was learned during the 2011 Thailand flood originally written by three authors Laddawan Kaewkitipong, Charlie Chen, and Peter Ractham (2012). This study captures how people used social media for their slef-use when other modes of information sharing were down during seven months flood from July 2011 to January 2012. The motivation of highlighting this story because such methods can be used elsewhere because environment is taking a hit at a global level and disaster due to the environment is a plausible scenario in any part of the world. If it is not a flood, then there can be some other natural event that can take place and when it is known how social media is used in the past in some other countries, a similar application can be used anywhere.

The missing link here is no framework is developed as to how social media will be used in such a situation. This where policymakers come into the picture and extend the work.

The Event

Rainfall in March 2011 over the area of northern Thailand received over 300% above average level of rain. Bhumibol Dam in particular received 242.8 mm of rain, well above the normal 25.2 mm. Since January the dam had accumulated 186% above normal water. During May of 2011, a substantial amount of rain started and due to the tropical storm later on the situation worsened leading to flooding in many areas. Heavy rain continued during July and August due to the El Nino effect. By September 2011, most of the areas were under the effect of floods. By the beginning of October, most dams were already near or over capacity and were being forced to increase their rate of discharge, potentially worsening downstream flooding.

According to Sousounis, Peter (2012) in his blog wrote that from July 2011 to mid of January 2012, flooding continued in many parts of Thailand until mid-January 2012. The flood was so heavy that out of 77 providences of Thailand 65 were declared under flood impacting 13.6 million people in total. Reports suggest that up to 3.3 million structures were affected nationwide, including at least 750,000 residential properties. According to the World Bank, the flood caused an estimated USD 45.7 billion in economic damage, making it the world's fourth costliest disaster in terms of economic losses.

The Thai government considered this 7-month long flooding the worst in terms of the amount of water and people affected. However, the disaster's impact could have been minimized if warnings had been issued by the government earlier and correct measures taken before its occurrence. The insufficient response to the flooding zone further aggravated the crisis. After the crisis, the slow path to recovery was also heavily criticized, the public began the self-rescue process by turning to social media.

This is a huge impact on any country due to the natural event; it is difficult to imagine raining in some of the key cities in India like Mumbai, Delhi, or Chennai, etc for such a long where the cities are not equipped to deal with. It has been witnessed heavy rains in some parts of Indian cities in the last few years for few days leading to a grim situation. The key question of interest what if a similar situation arises in some of the Indian cities due to some or other natural events. How to deal with it?

During these situations, some of the key concerns are the dissemination of information, whereabouts of the people, the ground-level situation in different areas, how to get food items, etc. Generally in such a situation, the traditional model of information system fails due to network issues and damage of infrastructure. Also, the level of preparedness by the government authorities matters a lot.

Use of Social Media

July is a rainy season in Thailand, as a preparation for the rainy season, the Thai government monitored abnormal changes in the weather condition together with precipitation levels in the atmosphere. Such preparation was like any other year. They also set up a website to improve communication with people before the rainy season.

During the crisis, the government primarily focused on TV as the main source of information to keep local agencies aware of the ongoing flooding development. Government agencies also used Social media as a secondary channel to disseminate flooding information.

The national government agency also collaborated with online social communities to establish the Thailand information center to disseminate information.

Many online social groups in Thailand were formed when they got little help from the government in dealing with persistent flooding. More than 50 Facebook groups were formed during the crisis and most of them were established in Bangkok because it was the least affected city. These social sites did a great job in updating information and news about water levels in different affected areas, and the whereabouts of missing loved ones. Live pictures and videos sent by people from the affected areas were quickly updated on these social sites and shared among community members. This useful information enabled government agencies to prioritize the allocation of their limited resources.

Social media such as Facebook, Twitter, YouTube helped in bridging the gap in response time between on-site and online crisis response activities because of their instant connectivity on the open platform.

Social media was used in various situations during a crisis because of its information-sharing capability. People could share information, coordinate various disaster relief events, and collaborate to execute those events.

The Thai flood disaster was similar to the Haiti earthquake in terms of how people accessed and disseminated useful information through social media sites by using their mobile phones. In both situations, the traditional means of landline communication were either damaged or destroyed. The landline network and other electronic devices were unusable regularly. Also, people were always on alert and had to be on the move, thus the traditional networks such as television or newspaper were not very useful. Hence, access to social media through mobile networks was critical to information dissemination for most users during a natural disaster. Messages posted on social media became an alternative solution to improving the desperate and helpless situations faced by the public.

After the flood, people started recovery activities on Facebook and Twitter. They used these two media to send out moral support to each other and the victims. YouTube was used to share funny and homemade video clips with victims to help reduce their stress levels during the recovery process.

Conclusion

This is a great application of social media proven in one part of the world and can be very handy in other parts of the world as well. It has been now been 10 years since this disaster and now social media has increased its base in terms of more apps and more users so its reach can be wider and deeper.

There is a difference between random use of social media and systematic use of social media and that is where a framework is required on its use during the crisis. During a crisis, a quick response is required and every passing minute can be crucial, therefore a crisis management framework is required to use social media where the policymakers may have to chip in and create some framework.

References

Sousounis, Peter (2012) https://www.air-worldwide.com/publications/air-currents/2012/The-2011-Thai-Floods--Changing-the-Perception-of-Risk-in-Thailand/

Laddawan Kaewkitipong, Charlie Chen and Peter Ractham (2012), Lessons Learned from the Use of Social Media in Combating A Crisis: A Case Study of 2011 Thailand Flood Disaster, *Thirty Third International Conference on Information Systems, Orlando 2012*

TWENTY-ONE

THE 'INTERNET OF THINGS' AND THE INSURANCE SECTOR

This article discusses how IoT can help insurance companies better assess risk to help enhance the customer experience.

Risk assessment 'information' is the key that quantifies both likelihood and severity. Insurance works on the concept of pooling of risks where all information is required about the risks itself so that the pool is as homogenous as possible. Heterogeneity in the pooled risk are sources of variation resulting into large volatility in the claim experience resulting into fluctuating profits.

Underwriting is a process where insurance company gather all possible information to charge right premium to the customers based on risk presented and create homogenous pool of risks.

The challenge with the insurance companies is that information submitted at the time of application may or may not be correct either knowingly or unknowingly. This brings unassessed risks into the insurance company bucket that may result into adverse claim experience leading to losses. At times, the cost of collection of risk about the customers may be proportionately higher that may not allow insurance companies collect all risk related information and rely on the customer's declaration which is done on good faith.

Some of these challenges can be addressed through digitalisation such as Big Data, Internet of Things (IoT), cloud computing, machine learning and artificial intelligence (AI). These technologies can help in continuous gathering information about the proposal and insured that can help better assess the risks and price accordingly.

This article discusses how IoT can help insurance companies better assess the risk and give customer greater experience. Insurance proposal ask for customer's data at the start of a policy, but IoT devices help to regularly gather data about the insured through the life of a policy. They do this they collect, transmit and share information related to the risk presented. This helps in informed underwriting decision making, automated claims processing, reduced administrative cost, greater customer satisfaction etc. The IoT device also help in forewarning about the risks that may crystalise at customer's end leading to better customer experience and reduced insurance cost. It is estimated that the administration cost is reduced by 30% where some benefits are passed to customers reducing premium by 25% [1].

Insurance challenges

The Customer's insurance process starts with proposal is submitted to the insurance company that have details about the risk factors about the risk that customer is presenting. Insurance company perform underwriting process that assess the risks presented conforming pricing assumption and charge premium accordingly. The insurance company perform the underwriting based on the evidences produced by the customer such as age proof, income statement, health condition, medical reports etc in life insurance. At times, this information submitted by the customers are not always correct; however, due high administrative cost of verifying given details particularly in lower premium policies, insurance company do not verify all such information and underwrite. Such cases in the insurance terms are referred as anti-selection or self-selection.

As insurance is a contract written on utmost good faith, when claim arises and insurance company identifies that the information given at the time of proposal was not correct, they have a right to repudiate the claim because the premium charged at the time of underwriting was lower due to higher risk actually presented.

The decline in claim leads to customer's dissatisfaction, increased customers complaints, and regulator do not like it. All this leads to adverse press publicity, court cases and loss of reputation, which have adverse impact on future new business of the insurance company. Further, all these anti-selection resulting into unanticipated claims leading into higher losses, increased administration cost and greater cost of capital.

How IoT help in addressing these risks

IoT is a system of interrelated computer devices that transfer data over a network without requiring human-to-human or human-to-computer interaction. This device is placed to the object exposed to risk help insurance company to collect, transmit critical data on real-time basis. Such object can help the insurance company at the time of underwriting decision making by directly receiving the information from the source and removing the chances of human intervention in submitting the required documents. Also, the IoT helps in automated claims processing because the claimant can share the claim related information directly to the insurance company from the site of an accident or from the hospital where death has taken. This helps in reduced administrative cost and greater customer satisfaction leading to more future new business for insurance company.

These connected devices help the insurance company in gathering accurate information about the risk which subsequently helps in charging appropriate premium through initial or renewal underwriting process. Such better gathering of information helps in classifying risk in a more homogenous group. The direct submission of documents required for the underwriting helps in reducing the chances of anti-selection and thereby creating a more homogenous pool of risk, which will have lower claim volatility. Such reduced anti-selection increases the claim settlement rate and reduced administration cost which otherwise often spent on claim investigation and longer time spent. A better claim experience results into insurance companies allow discounts and vouchers to customers particularly in health insurance.

In motor insurance, the connected devices help the insurance company as well as customers who are alerted when a risk cross a particular limit and inform the customer about the likely impact on his renewal premium if he takes a particular route to reach his destination. For example, based on camera, GPS, and accelerometer the driver is alerted about the likely accident if he takes a particular route based on the traffic density, speed of vehicle and driving behavior of that day

For a home insurance, the insured are alerted for possible theft, taking mitigation action on the possibility of flood, thunderstorm or likely change in the temperature. IoT is very useful in health insurance where there is a continuous flow of information between insurance companies and insured through the connected devices giving real-time feedback about the health to customers, when to go for medical examination and necessary special medical tests. This can save the life of customers as well as cost to the insurance company.

IoT helps insurance companies in automating initial and renewal underwriting process, instant approval of claim, more accurate assessment of risk that reduces the claim management cost and optimize the additional margins that an insurance companies otherwise to keep for claim fluctuation. This further enhances the customer experience and increases the satisfaction and hence higher reputation

Conclusion

In summary, IoT bridges the information gap between the insured and insurance company which traditional method of collection of data do not work. Traditional method works on utmost good faith basis, but human behavioral issues create information gap. The application of IoT is still in a developing phase and many other areas in insurance yet to be tapped such as in life insurance. The overall impact on the insurance company is reduction in fraud and anti-selection, optimisation of capital due to lower volatility and higher profitability. Customers on the hand is also benefited by getting alerts when risks are about to crystalise. However, the digitalisation brings newer risk of cyber-attack and collapse of system. Many global insurance players have recognised IT and digitalization as one of the key emerging risks.

TWENTY-TWO

HOW AUTONOMOUS VEHICLES WILL SHIFT INSURANCE DYNAMICS

There's no doubt that the widespread introduction of autonomous vehicles will create an unprecedented shift in modern society. Among the largest adjustment will be felt in the insurance space.

Self-driving cars will change the dynamics of motor insurance over the next two decades [1] and beyond. This is because the risk factors associated with autonomous vehicles will change along with emerging experience of accident rates that informs the motor insurance technical premium costs, related to collision. Other perils like theft, damage etc may not change but due to the technological development, theft cases may decrease.

One of the fundamental changes with autonomous car insurance will be a shift of focus from driver to technology, influencing resulting accident rates. It is expected that the accident frequency will likely to reduce by 80% by 2040[1], which will be a substantial reduction. Today, accidents that are caused by human factors contribute 90%-94% of total accidents [1], [4]. The accident frequency is expected to reduce, but the forecast severity is less certain. There may be additional repair cost of for hardware, software, battery, sensors, cameras and more, but the average speed of collisions may also be lower.

The insurance will shift from personal car insurance to product liability because if a vehicle is driven by a driver, personal auto coverage applies. However, for autonomous vehicles, the liability will transfer to the manufacturer supplying the technology. According to the Accenture and Stevens Institute of Technology [2] report, by 2040, personal line insurance will fall by 40%, and product liability insurance will increase by 14%.

The change in the motor insurance scenario will develop over time depending on the level of automation. It is estimated that by 2035 US roads will likely have 23 million fully autonomous vehicles[1]. However, full automation development will be gradual. There are six levels of automation, starting from the manual version to fully autonomous vehicles. In the fully automated version, the car adjusts to different situations using sensors on its own. There will be no driver's seats in the highest level of automated cars but only the passenger's seats. The passengers are to mention only a drop location, and the vehicle will drive to the destination. Even the driver's licence will not be required in such a case, but the software may require approval from the traffic authorities.

What will change?

In Australia, the current risk factors for motor insurance include the driver's driving history, make of a car, cost of the car, age and gender of the driver, type of insurance policy, geographical location and more. The premium in the insurance sector is determined by the cost of pure risk and the loading for administrative expenses, commissions, cost of solvency, taxes and profit margins. The cost of the pure risk is determined by the risk factors mentioned above. With the driverless car, the risk factors will change, and most of the other elements of premiums will stay. The changes in the risk factors that are likely to come from collision and non-collision reasons are

Collision:

1. Change in accident rates (frequency)
2. the cost of repair of technology (sum insured)
3. Increase in risk of technical malfunction

Non-Collision

1. Increase in cyber security

    a. Ransomware to hold the vehicle under control till payment is made to unlock software
    b. Criminal or terrorist hijacking through remote control
    c. Misuse of personal information/data privacy

2. Change from personal liability to product liability

    a. Coverage of internet connection by the insurer
    b. Software bug
    c. Algorithm defect
    d. Hardware failure
    e. Sensor failure
    f. Camara failure

3. Infrastructure

    a. Cloud server system
    b. External sensor, signals, communication

These risk factors changes will change how motor insurance is looked at now. New and unknown risks will emerge, and older risks will become history. The shape of the car mechanics will change who will also be equipped with knowledge of software engineers. Car insurance will become technology insurance with more focus on hardware and software. The repair cost may increase as hardware and software repair expenses could be greater than the current engine and other repair costs, but it may reduce if average collision speeds reduce. The focus will change from the quality of the present-day engine to the quality of the software and other accessories like sensors, cameras and a third-party provider of cloud. This change will generate massive data, which will be one of the critical drivers of the future of car driving and insurance.

Internet service will at the heart of the entire traffic movement system. The cyber threat will be one of the key risks as any interruption in the internet service will disrupt the entire traffic system on the road resulting in a massive traffic jam. Traffic jams will be a new risk factor that insurance companies have to deal with by considering the pricing. Risk managers will need to learn to address newer risks for their management and upgrade themselves with other emerging changes.

Other types of new risks include when an accident occurs due to mishandling by the owner, resulting in the software misbehaving, leading to an accident. Policy terms and conditions will be essential for such risks and could be subject to dispute. In traditional insurance, few policyholders read the policy bonds and file claims leading to litigation as claim conditions are not insured. With so much technical jargon in autonomous car insurance, the car owners' may not fully understand the policy conditions. As a result, litigation can increase, leading to more law firms acting on behalf of customers.

Some other challenges are expected to emerge where an autonomous vehicle could be hacked. For example, ransomware could hold the vehicle hostage under control until payment is made to unlock the software. Other challenges could be criminal or terrorist hijacking through remote control or misusing personal information/data privacy. This will bring a paradigm shift in motor insurance, and it is difficult to say whether the reduction in accident rates is likely to offset these newer risks or newer risks will pose other challenges for pricing and risk management.

Actuaries must prepare themselves for the entirely new world of risks and modeling statistical distribution and their correlation. The introduction of digitalisation in motor insurance will shift the traditional actuarial books towards a combination of understanding the data architecture, data modeling, data analytics, artificial intelligence along with core actuarial principles.

Ethics is another issue that needs to be addressed with autonomous cars. Such cars are likely to reduce the accidents. However, the accidents will not be eliminated. When an accident occurs with the driver in the driving seat, the driver is responsible for their life and death. However, with autonomous cars, the decision to react in the accident situation will be made by the computer program codes written by programmers[3]. Who will be saved in such cases of accidents? Who will decide? How can the programmers decide on the lives of the individuals sitting in the car? The codes written in different manufactured cars will be from other companies, and how the overall decision at the time of the accident will be made on the lives of the passengers who do not have any control. Should the life of humans rest in the hands of machines based on the interaction of data, so-called intelligent software? Another ethical issue will be the massive radiation that the entire human race will be exposed to? Has there been any study that proves that such radiations are safer?

Summary

There will be a paradigm shift in the future of motor insurance with the introduction of autonomous cars. Car insurance will become technology insurance with more focus on hardware and software. This will change the risk factors determining motor insurance premiums.

There will be a shift from personal car insurance to product liability insurance. The focus will move from current garage-based mechanics to hardware and software centers. Internet and data will be the new life bloodstreams of car movements and insurance. Internet services and cyber security will be new drivers. Traffic jams could be a new phenomenon due to internet congestion.

Actuaries need to add digital knowledge along with modeling techniques of new risks that will be more correlated. Risk managers are to learn on how to mitigate new emerging risks, which will be different. Ethical issues will emerge.

References

1. https://home.kpmg/cn/en/home/insights/2015/06/automobile-insurance-in-the-era-of-autonomous-vehicles-o-201506.html
2. https://www.accenture.com/_acnmedia/pdf-60/accenture-insurance-autonomous-vehicles-pov.pdf
3. https://vce.usc.edu/volume-4-issue-2/the-ethics-of-self-driving-cars/
4. https://www.bcmlawyers.com/what-percentage-of-car-accidents-are-caused-by-human-error/

TWENTY-THREE

Analysis of Impact on The Indian Reinsurance Market Due to COVID-19

Introduction

This chapter is about the reinsurance claim experience in the Indian life insurance market resulting from the death claims before and during COVID-19. The chapter highlights the losses in the reinsurance industry suffered due to the impact of COVID-19. For this analysis, the top five reinsurance companies are considered. Based on the 2019-20 IRDA annual report, these five reinsurance companies accepted 78% of premiums among the branches of foreign reinsurers from the Indian market.

The chapter also analyses the claim experience of each of the life insurance players which contributed to the losses to the reinsurers. This includes the top 16 players ranked on new business premium income for the FY ended March 2020-21 contributed 98% of the business.

The chapter highlights the importance of right pricing and reserving the long-tail risk, adopting the prudent risk management approach, and lessons learned for other risks.

All the data on the life insurance industry is taken from public disclosure on Company's website from forms L-1 and L-7 (IRDA Public Disclosure). The reinsurance data is also taken from the public disclosure on the reinsurance Company's website (Given in references) from forms NL-1, NL-2, and NL-5.

Reinsurance Profit/Loss from Life Business in India

Insurance companies use the reinsurance tool to transfer the mortality risk to reinsurers since its inception, however, reinsurance companies in India opened their Indian branch office around the year 2016-17. So, the reinsurance profit/loss data from the reinsurance companies' websites is available since FY 2017-18. The chart below shows the operating profit/loss of the reinsurance business from life insurance for the three years FY 2017-18, 2018-19, and 2019-20. All the figures in INR are in the unit of Crore. 1 Crore = 10^7.

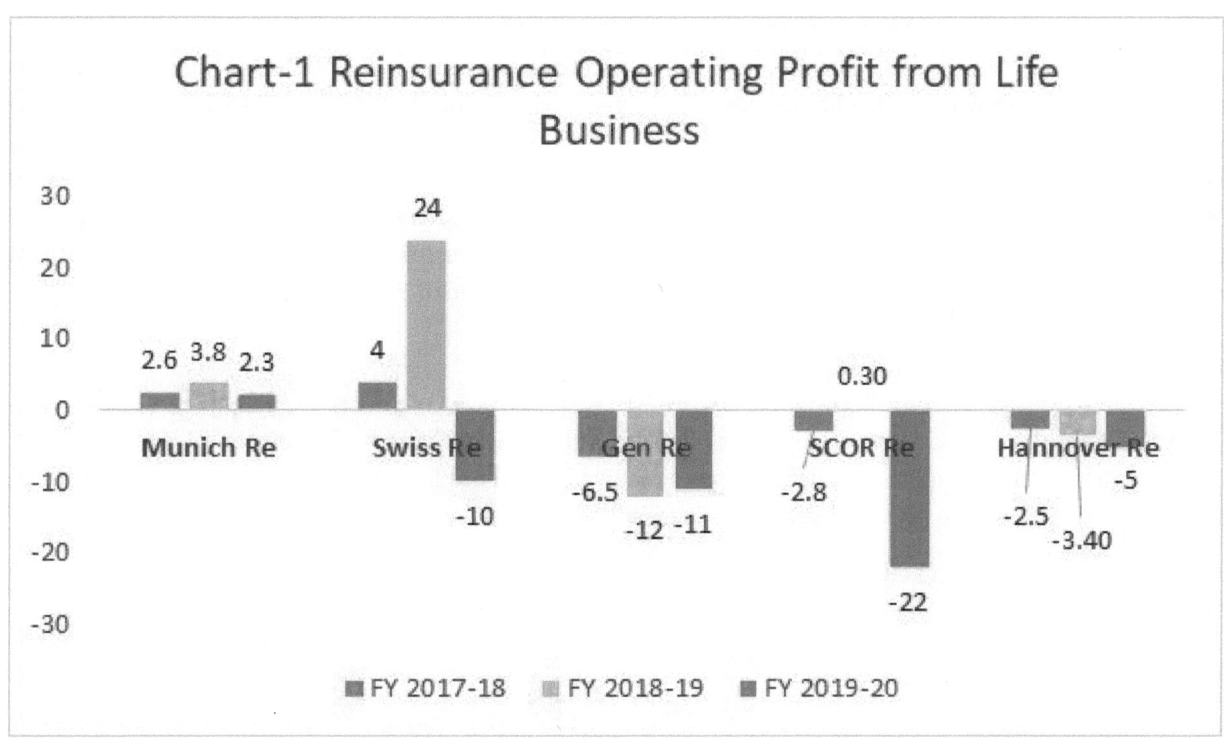

The above operating profit/loss position from their life business is before the inception of COVID-19 in the Indian geography. Munich Re made small profits in all three years while Swiss Re made profits in 2017-18 and 2018-19 and loss in 2019-20. The other three reinsurers made losses in all three years except SCOR Re making a very small profit of Rs.0.3 Cr in 2018-19.

After the strike of COVID-19 in the Calendar year 2020 in India, the losses from the Indian life insurance business started coming to think and fast. The chart below shows the losses from the reinsurer in the FY 2020-21

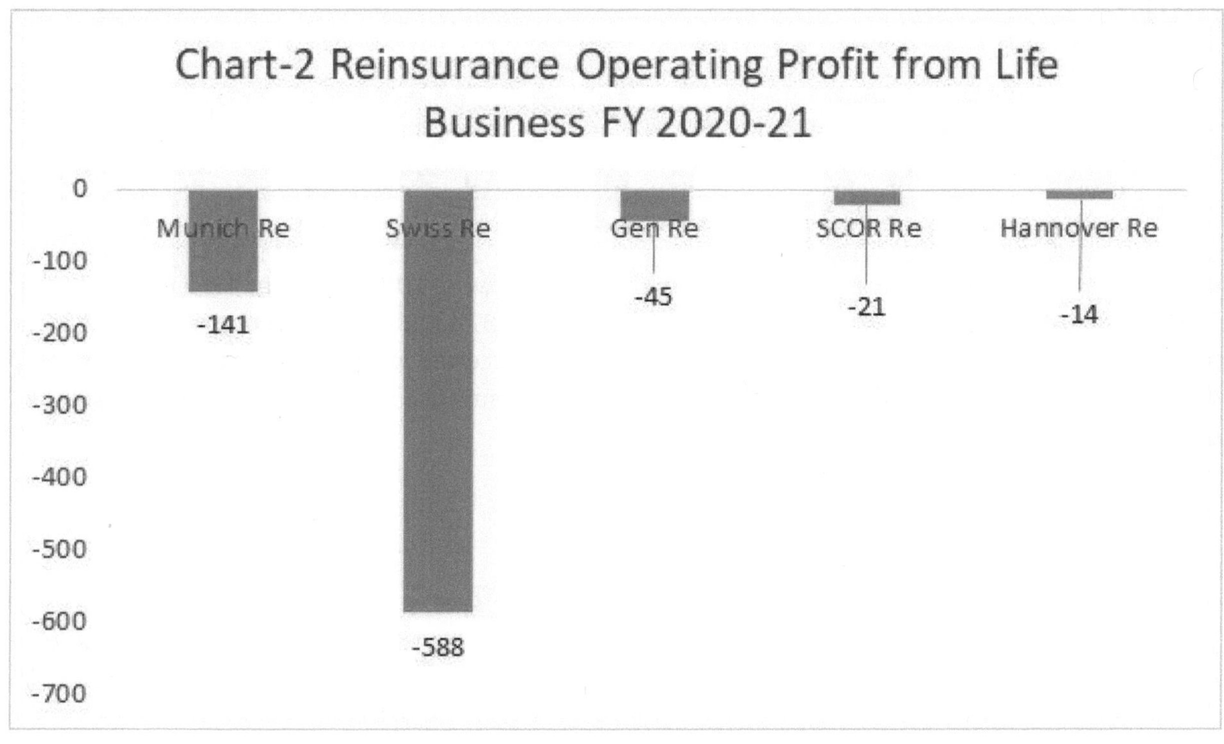

For all the reinsurers, the quantum of loss due to death claims triggered by COVID-19 is proportionally very high compared to the profits they made in the previous three years. Given that before FY 2017-18 profit/loss figures were not available, there could be a possibility that COVID-19-related death claims might have wiped out the entire profits made from the Indian reinsurance operations. Given the extent of loss triggered by the bigger reinsurance players, it may take a couple of years in the future to recover the losses from the death claims from COVID.

Post the impact of COVID, the reinsurance companies in India are taking the corrective action of tightening underwriting norms and increasing the term insurance rates to the tune of 30% to 40%.

Comparative Industry Death Claims

Graph-1 below shows the comparative death claims in INR in the unit of Crore for the period of H1 FY 2020-21 and H1 FY 2021-22. It can be seen that all the industry players received a higher claim amount in H1 2021-22 compared to the corresponding same period the previous year. This is largely due to the second wave of COVID-19.

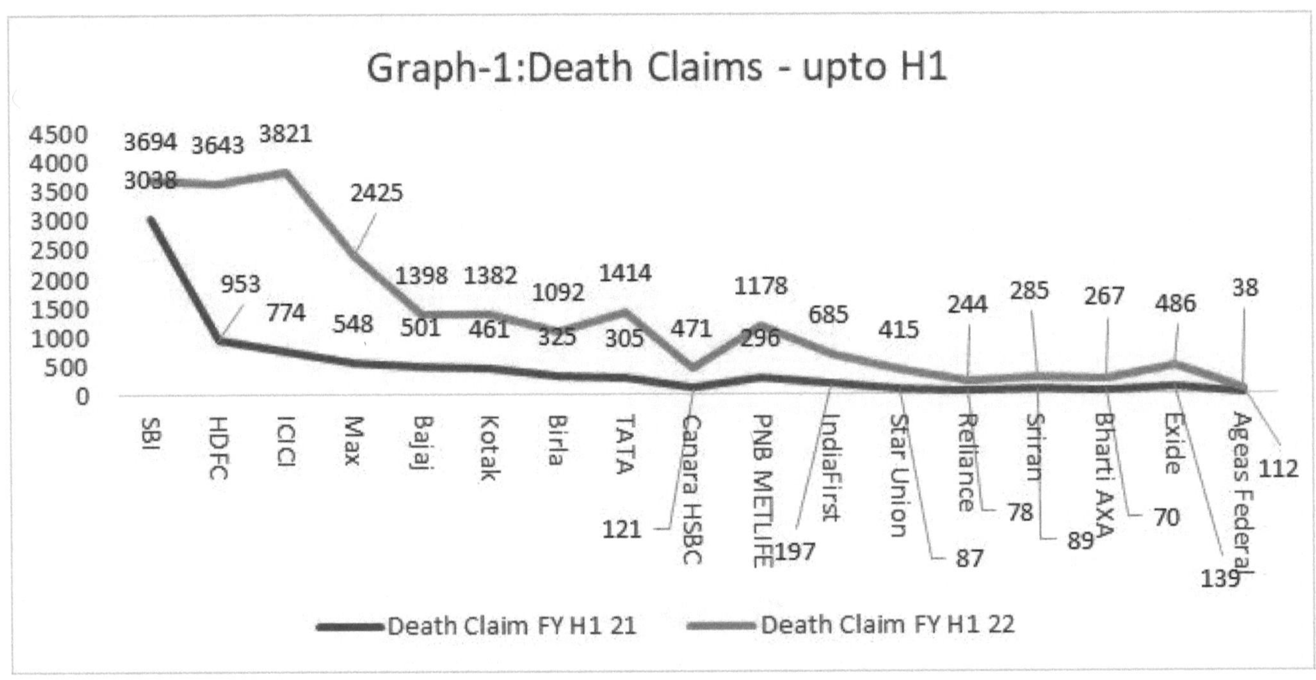

Graph-2 below shows the percentage increase in death claims between H1 FY 2021 and H1 FY 2022. It can be seen that on average the Indian life insurance industry received around 187% higher claims compared to the same period of the previous year. Except for one player, all the industry players received around 3 times more claims compared to the previous year. In Rupee terms, the claims received by the life insurance industry were around Rs.8000 Cr in H1 2021 which increased to Rs.23000 Cr in H1 2022.

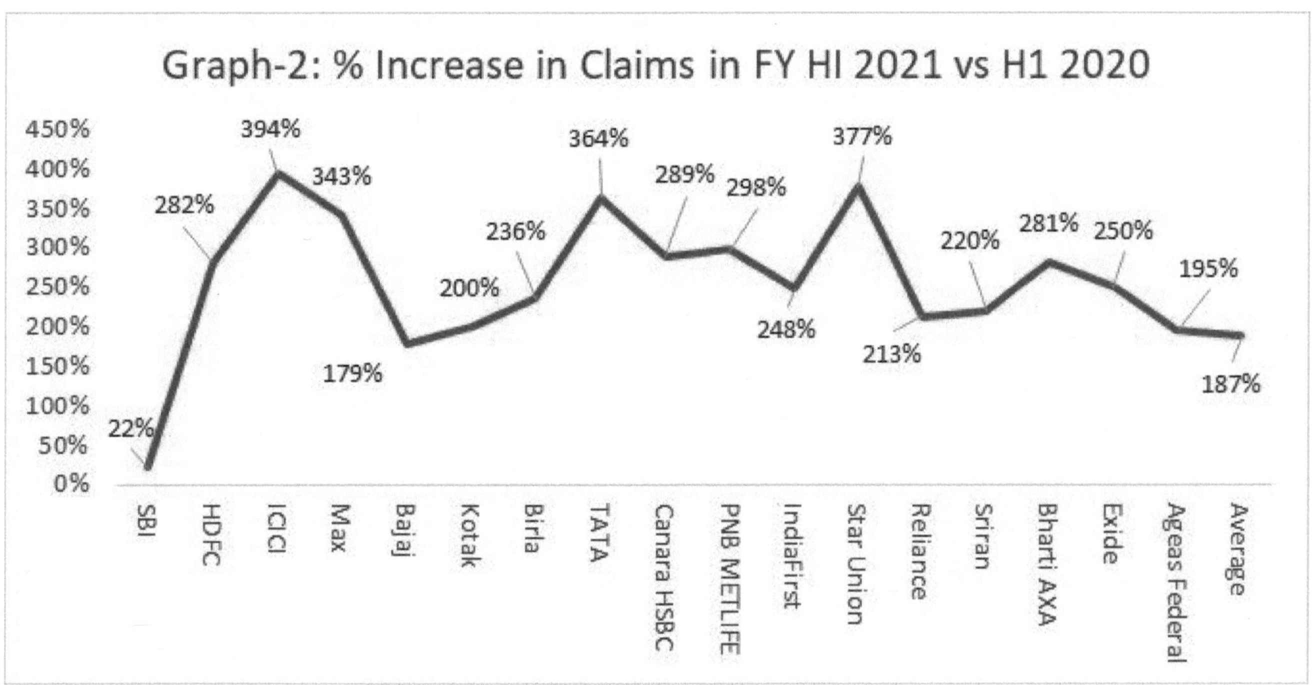

Reinsurance Experience

The reinsurance claim experience from the industry is captured by the reinsurance premium ceded by the insurer and claims received by them from the reinsurer. The reinsurance premium ceded is captured from form L-1 and reinsurance claims received by them are from form L-7.

For the clarity of understanding in the paper, if the premium ceded to the reinsurer is greater than claims received from them then it will be termed as "profit" to the reinsurer. And if the premium ceded reinsurer is less than claims received from them then it will be termed as "loss" to the reinsurer

Chart-3 below shows the difference between premium ceded to reinsurer and claims received from them (in INR unit of Crore) for the three financial years 2017-18, 2018-19, 2019-20 and cumulative position of three years.

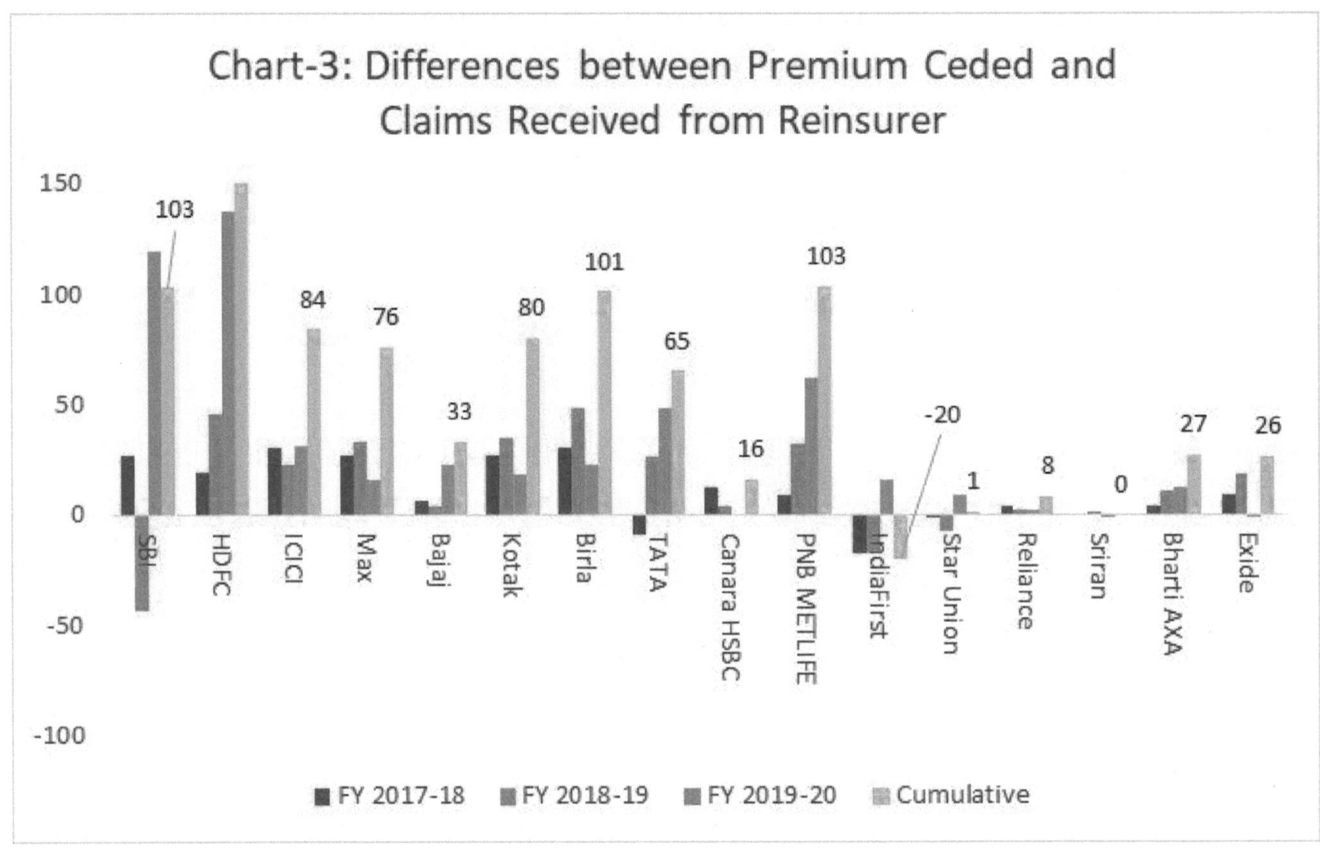

It can be seen that for most of the players, the reinsurer earned a profit, that is, the mortality claims experience for reinsurance companies was favorable. There are few stray years when some of the players gave losses to reinsurer while at a cumulative three years level, except in one case, there is a profit for reinsurance. It can be concluded that the reinsurance companies had favorable mortality experiences from the Indian life insurance market for the above three years period. This can be confirmed from the experience of Swiss Re and Munich Re shown in Chart-1 above.

Graph-4 below shows the difference between premium ceded to reinsurer and claims received from them (in INR unit of Crore) for financial years 2020-21 and the H1 period of FY 2021-22 after the strike of COVID-19.

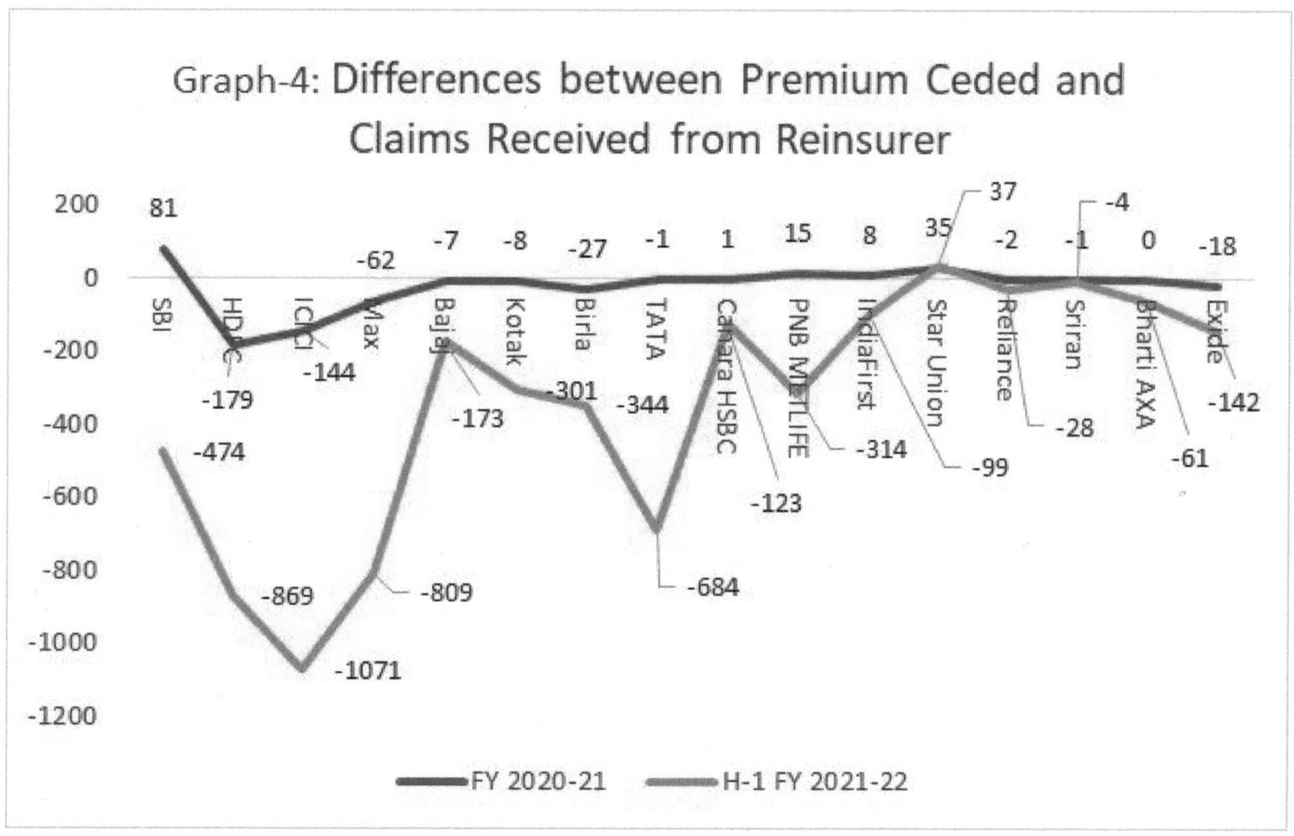

It can be seen that after the strike of COVID-19 first wave in 2020, most life insurance players suffered adverse death claim experiences in the FY 2020-21 which is evident from the reinsurer losses. However, the quantum losses for the reinsurer in the first six months of FY 2021-22 are way above the entire full year of reinsurance experience for FY 2020-21. This was due to the second wave of COVID-19 in India during 2021 and also could have some spillover death claims from the previous financial years 2020-21. It seems that once the entire financial year 2021-22 gets over, the death claim experience will further worsen especially when Omicron's third wave is just around the corner in India in December 2021 (at the time of writing).

Graph-5 below shows the cumulative profit or loss position for the reinsurer position for the last four and a half years from FY 2017-18 to H1 2021-22.

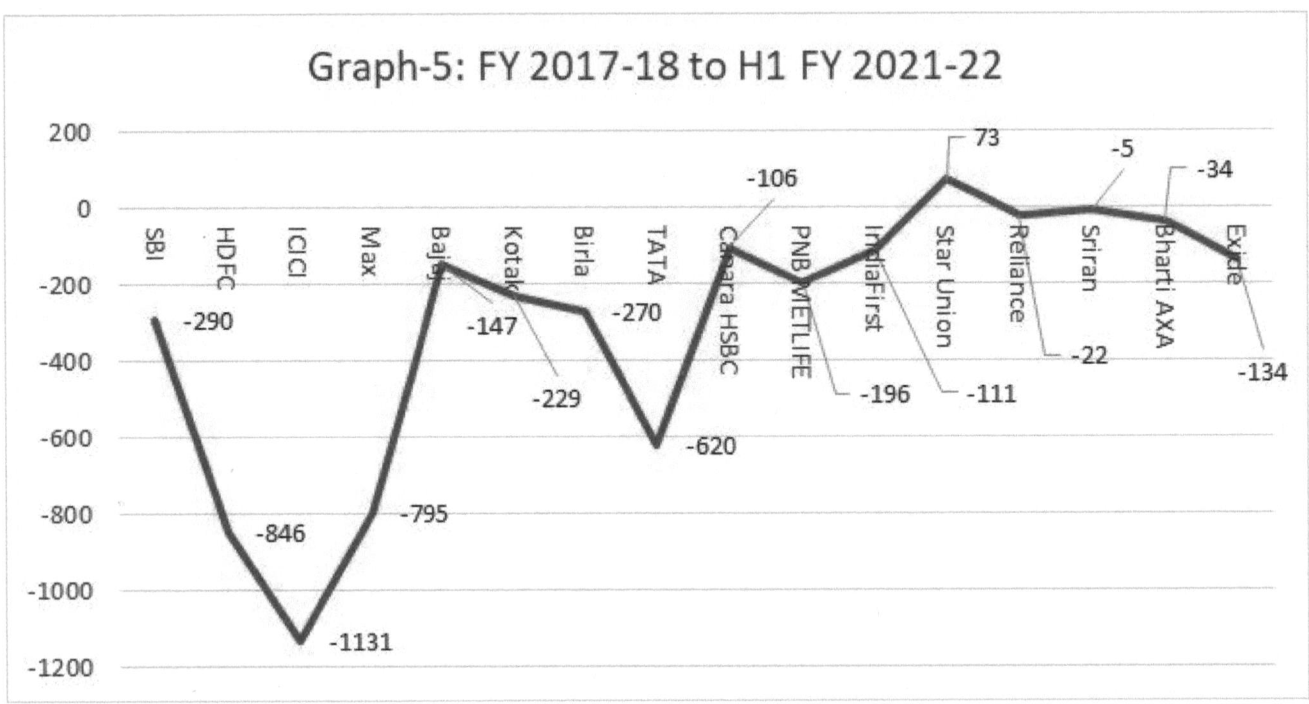

It can be seen that except for one player, all the life insurance companies have given cumulative losses to the reinsurers.

Such losses to the reinsurers in India have led to an increase in reinsurance premium rates by 30% to 40%. Many reinsurers have stopped writing group term business which has higher mortality concentration risk.

Discussion

The above experience throws light on the following aspects.

1. Benefits of risk transfer
2. Importance of right pricing and reserving
3. Lessons to be learned.

Benefits of risk transfer

Customers pass their risk of early demise to the insurance companies. Insurance companies in turn pool the risk and price according to the risks presented. Some of the risks accepted by insurance companies are high-value risks or small values of risk that become aggregately high or sub-standard lives. In the process of risk management, when the likelihood of occurring of risk event is small but the severity is high, the risk management tool used is the transfer of risks to the third party (Hopkin,2018). Such high-value risks or aggregated risks are transferred to the third party as reinsurance companies. Reinsurance companies specialize in the management of mortality risk with the help of their global experience in medical research and on the causes of human mortality (Mourik, 2018). Reinsurance companies pool the risks from different insurance companies and price accordingly. They charge premiums from insurance companies to insure their risks. When a death claim arises from a customer's reinsurance company pays their part of the risk covered to the insurance company which in turn settles the claims with the customer. This way high-value risks or sub-standard risks are shared between insurance and reinsurance companies.

Under normal circumstances when there are no stress events on mortality, the actual mortality experience is favorable compared to the expected claims experience. This is evident from Graph-3 where the reinsurance companies were in a profitable position among almost all the players.

However, after the strike of COVID-19 in 2020, the mortality stress event materialized with a high number of deaths among the customers. The benefit of risk transfer of managing the high-value claims was realized by the life insurance players in India evident from losses to reinsurers shown in Graph-4. The advent of COVID-19 increased the claims 3 times the normal situation shown in Graph-2 and Graph-7.

There are clear benefits of risk transfer to the third party, this works well at the micro-level; however, at the macro level, the risks are just transferred from one party to another party. Therefore, there is of the great importance of right pricing the risk and charge from the customers.

Importance of right pricing and reserving

The losses given by the pandemic COVID-19 start the debate whether the reinsurers loaded the pandemic risk-related premium into their reinsurance rates or not? And whether long-term reserving was taking place for such events or not? This is also true for life insurers whether, in their pricing, catastrophe risk premium was charged from customers or not and in particular pandemic risk?

Term insurance product has led to most of the losses to the reinsurers because this is the cheapest product in the market that cover the pure risk of death for the long term. Term insurance is a very price-sensitive product and ever since the opening of the Indian life insurance market in the year 2000, the term insurance premium rates have fallen continuously. There are a couple of reasons for that, the mortality experience generally improves (Burger et al 2012) over time (at a rate of 0.5% to 1% per annum) (Purushotham,2011) which is reflected in the benefits passed to customers through a reduction in premium rates in new products, the new reinsurers that entered in the Indian market had competitive pricing for term rates to capture the business and third is the advent of online insurance business further brought the term premium rates down on the premise that more sophisticated customers operating internet will exhibit better mortality experience.

The question is, given the long-term nature of the term insurance business, were the benefits of aggregate improvement in mortality passed too early to customers? In hindsight, it is easy to say but long-tail risks are always present in such products and insurance companies manage these risks by separately purchasing the catastrophic risk cover. The challenge with such cover is that the risks are covered for events like earthquakes, Tsunami, Flood, Storms, etc which give rise to claims over the next couple of days (for example 3 to 5 days), and not for risk events that extend over months or years like pandemic-COVID. When events like pandemic strikes have an impact over a longer period, the catastrophic risk cover does not trigger and insurance companies do not get the benefits of such cover. Further, the catastrophic risk cover has the limitation that it has upper boundaries of the claim amount and any claim beyond the upper cap is to be paid by the insurance company.

Fortunately for the insurance companies, their term insurance business was mostly reinsured with low retention cover and so their burden of the mortality risk was taken by reinsurance companies.

It is therefore important to price the long-tail risk with low in likelihood and high in severity into the premium charged from customers and reserve separately for such events. At the global level, different discussions are on to address the pandemic risk, however, there could be some other risks that can turn out to be catastrophic in the future. Are insurance companies loading premiums for climate risk that may occur 15 to 20 years later and reserving for that is the next question to debate?

Lessons to be learned

Risk management has a simple principle in mitigating risks, that is, plan for managing risks when it is brewing because, after the event strike, the organization or a country can only do crisis management. If risks are left with no action, risks are slowly brewing, for example, in hindsight when the benefits of mortality improvement were passed to the customers, risks were slowly building up. Another classic example in the Indian life insurance market is the interest rate risk where the high maturity guarantees are given to the customers on long-term saving products. Many life insurance players are trying to manage this risk with derivative contracts, but under the macro risk events, the entire economy gets impacted and there is a circular impact on the market. A sustained low economic environment in the future may trigger interest rate risk impacting both insurance and the banking system. The question is not about not writing such a product but about creating a balance between competition and risk management.

Conclusion

The paper concludes that COVID-19 has made a substantial impact on the Indian life insurance market with claims increasing around three times of normal claims pattern. However, due to low retention limits by the life insurance companies, reinsurance companies have taken the hit and suffered the losses that have wiped out the profits of the last many years and it may take a couple of more years in the future to recover the losses. As a result of these stressful events, the reinsurance companies in India have increased the term insurance rates in the range of 30% to 40% and tightened the underwriting norms.

The paper also highlights the importance of prudent risk management, and the importance of right pricing and reserving and take the action on the risk when it is brewing.

References

Hopkin, P. (2018). *Fundamentals of risk management: understanding, evaluating, and implementing effective risk management*. Kogan Page Publishers.

Mourik, T. (2018). Mortality risks, reinsurance, and risk-based supervision. *South African Actuarial Journal, 18*(1), 1-15.

Burger, O., Baudisch, A., & Vaupel, J. W. (2012). Human mortality improvement in evolutionary context. *Proceedings of the National Academy of Sciences, 109*(44), 18210-18214.

Purushotham, Marianne, With Improved Mortality Confirmed, The Question Becomes, "What Adjustments Do Actuaries Need to Make?" The Actuary Magazine, August/September 2011, Volume-8, Issue-4, Society of Actuaries, USA

Wendy Kriz (2021) https://www.barnett-waddingham.co.uk/comment-insight/blog/covid-19-impact-on-the-reinsurance-market/

IRDA Public Disclosure https://www.irdai.gov.in/ADMINCMS/cms/NormalData_Layout.aspx?page=PageNo764&mid=31.1

Reinsurance public disclosure

https://www.munichre.com/en/company/about-munich-re/munich-re-worldwide/india/financial-reports.html

https://www.swissre.com/investors/indian-public-disclosures.html

https://www.scor.com/en/scor-se-india-branch

https://www.genre.com/contactus/gen-re-india-public-disclosure-en.html

https://www.hannover-re.com/1198312/india_publications

TWENTY-FOUR

LEARNING FROM HISTORY-A RISK MANAGEMENT PERSPECTIVE

Introduction

Though risk management and its application in the corporate world are new, its essence is very old. One must remember that risk is always about the future and the future is always unknown. There is no idea what will unfold in the future, however, some ideas about the future can be assessed based on past data, present information, and judicious judgment about the future. The life insurance business which is about long-term assessment of risk is based on similar methodologies. The life insurance businesses have been successful throughout the world based on actuarial principles.

To address any risk, it is very important to first identify the risk, assess its likely impact, and plan for preventative action now, to minimize the impact of the risk, should risk materialize. Risk assessment requires a mindset with a vision to anticipate the future based on certain key risk indicators of the present which always emanate important information about the expected future.

In the very recent past we witnessed economic slowdown resulting from reduced economic activities, the key question that is addressed in this article is, could this have been anticipated to address the economic risks to take mitigating actions earlier than later.

Glimpse to Recent Past

The Gross Domestic Product fell to 5% in the Q1 FY 2019-20 corresponding to the same period of the previous year; obviously, its parameters such as private consumption, investment, government expenditure, and net exports performed adversely. The consequence of the slowdown was seen by job losses in different sectors of the economy, reduced earnings impacting business adversely, etc

The key question is, does this happen all of the sudden or certain trends were available which was overlooked? Let's see some trends in the key economic indicators in the next section.

Historic Data Indicators

Let's look first at a high level, how does the GDP was performing over the the period in the below graph

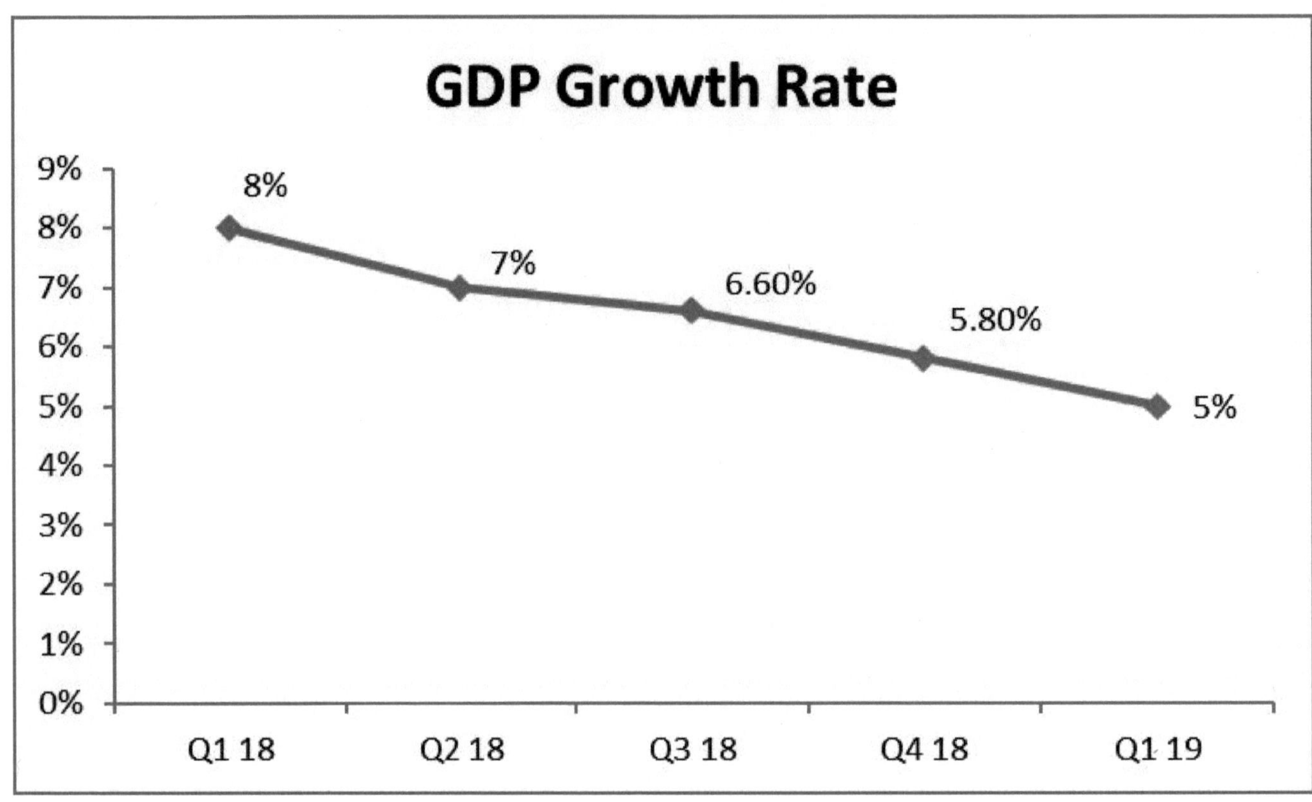

It is evident that the GDP declined over the last four quarters and the performance in Q1 FY 2019-20 is not all of sudden, some initial indications were available in the second quarter of FY 2018-19.

Let's now analyze some components of GDP over the last couple of years to look at the underlying factors. Under the **consumer economy**, look at the year-on-year growth in sales of a **passenger vehicles** from January 2014 to August 2019:

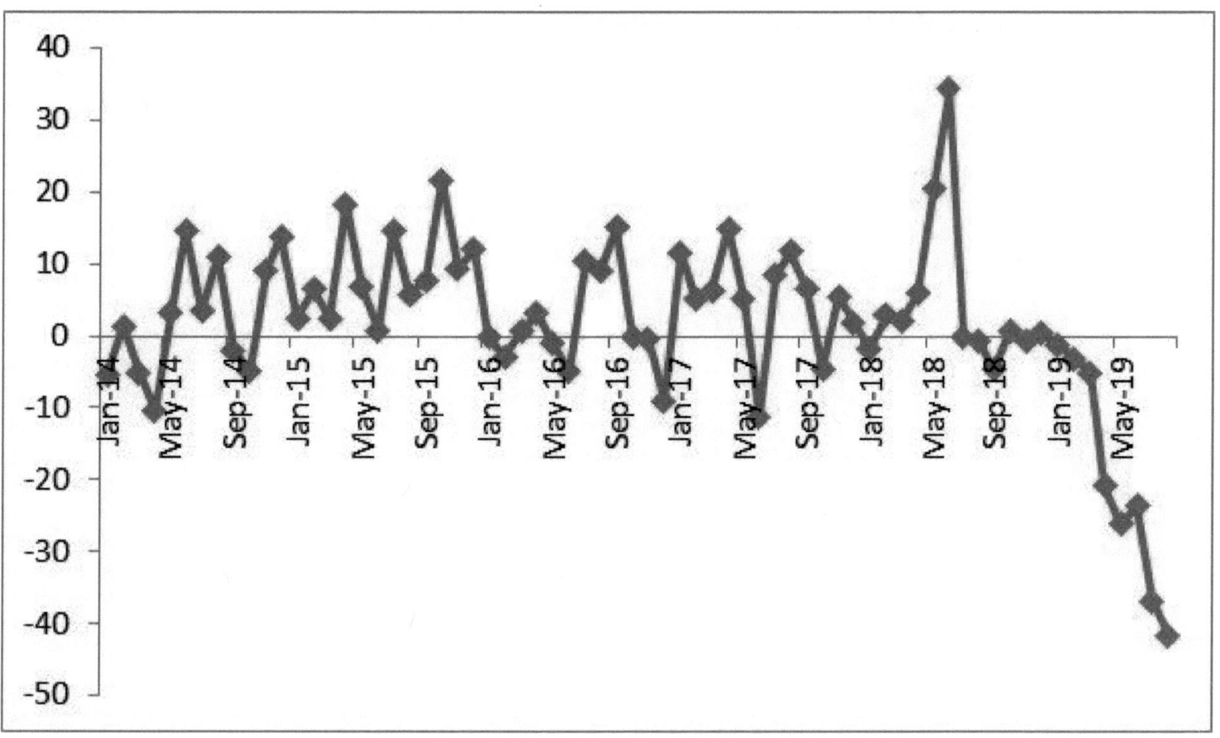

The early sign of volatile sales was visible way back in mid of 2017 ending with sustained negative growth from July 2018.

In the same category of the consumer economy, the year-on-year growth in **tractor sales** is shown in the graph below:

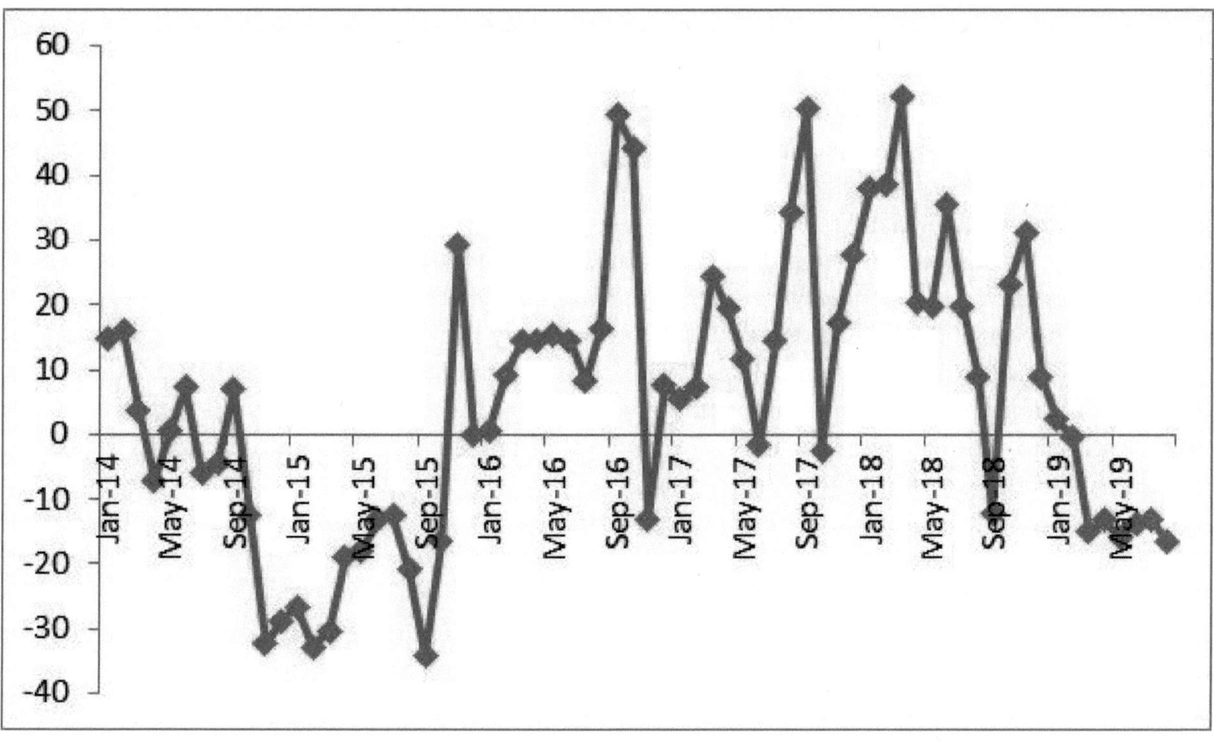

In this category as well, early signs of volatility were recognized in 2017 followed by sustained negative growth from January 2019.

Under the **industrial sector**, let us look at the **core infrastructure sector** comprising electricity, steel, refinery products, steel, crude oil, coal, cement, natural gas, and fertilizers. The graph below shows the year-on-year growth in the index of these eight core sectors

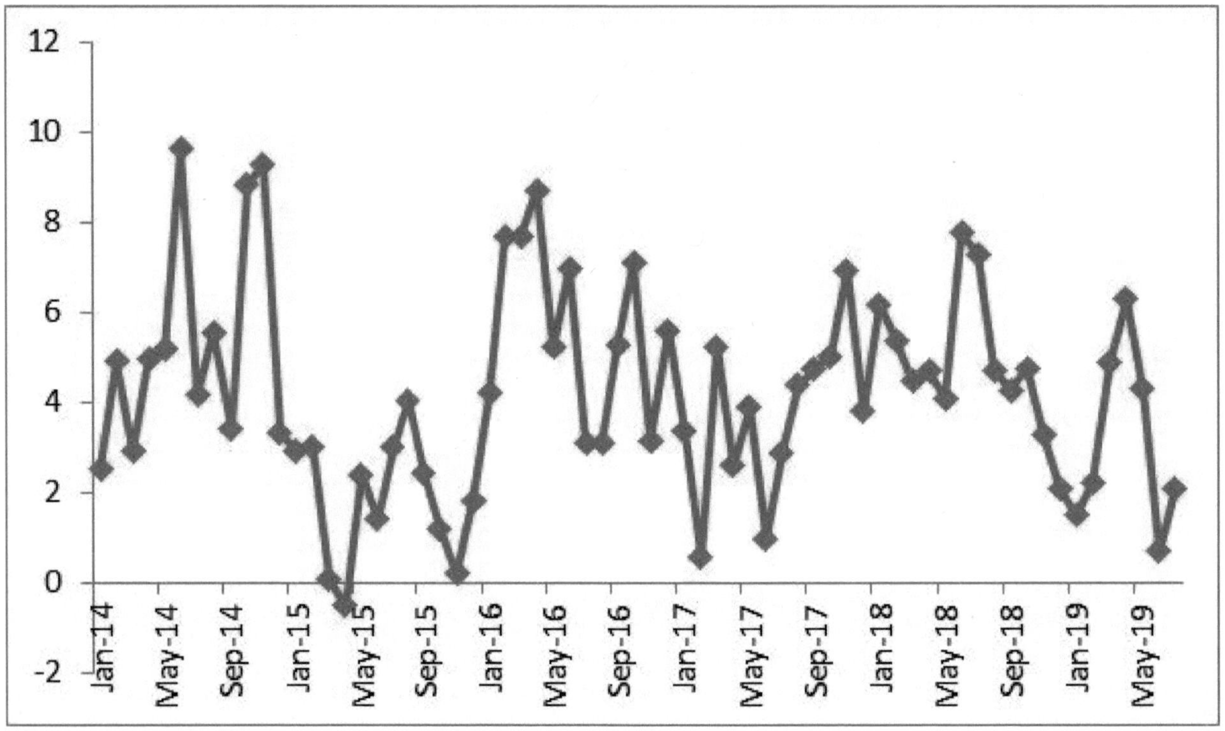

There are two downward sloping trends here, one is from May'16 to March'17, and the second is from May'18 to September'18 till August'19

The above indicators indicate that some early symptoms of the economic downturn were visible in the economy much before Q1 FY'20. Any such sustained downturn is a risk to economic growth. Early signs of adverse symptoms are like an indication of early poor health requiring immediate action; the delay in taking remedial action is like allowing the disease to settle down in the body.

If we use the concepts of risk management, then keeping an eye on the future is very important. As an example, in many of the core economic sectors, there were early signs of volatility were present way back in 2017. Now assuming we are in 2017 and there are volatile monthly annual growths in key sectors, then the risk mitigation plan should be prepared in 2017 and use the time between 2017 to 2019 in the implementation of those prepared action plans.

The observations of key economic indicators are very important for the corporate as they are the key sources of risks that adversely harm the business output. It is just not enough to monitor the internal Company-specific risks as economic risks can give bigger and longer shocks.

Apart from the economic indicators, the new emerging risk is a change in the climate showing its impact through excessive rain in different parts of the country. It may be noted that the excessive rain trend started a few years back and its frequency and spread in a different part of the Country is increasing ever since. This is not a good sign for both country and business together as we may get caught in deep trouble in the next couple of years when the impact of climate change is more severe.

Recently, we saw a spike in crude oil following a drone attack on Saudi Arabia's oil well shooting the oil prices in India; it was a good indicator of the likely rise in inflation and subsequent ability of the Central Bank to further reduce the policy rate further. Any sustained oil crisis could have an adverse impact on the economy and business model. The good sign is the oil crisis is over; however, this parameter may be tracked for future reference.

Recently International Monetary Fund has warned about the global economic slowdown, this parameter should be tracked as our economy is no more insulated from the external world. Any international slowdown will impact the export, flow of foreign funds to India for investment, fall in the stock market, etc. This may in turn further slow down Indian business-impacting both the top and bottom lines. The time is now ripe to monitor this global indicator to take remedial action on business now. This remedial action could be changed in the product design, change in the target market, cost rationalization, and change in the business model to cater to the emerging need if the global slowdown impacts the Indian market.

Tracking the Indicators

Continue tracking of risk indicators be it economic or Company specific is very important for the success of the Company. This helps in nipping the risk at its bud; there is no point in waiting for the indicators to get red. There is also a need to add more indicators such as risks emanating from demographic factors, environmental factors, and factors that have never been tracked but may cause entire disruption of the business such as failure of the internet. If the internet fails, many businesses depending on online will collapse.

Environmental risk is the most dangerous risk that may wipe out entire economic progress if remedial actions are not taken now. The time has come to track the environmental risk in businesses. Excessive rain during 2019 in different parts of the country breaking records of 100s of years is a warning signal. This warning signal is akin to or more severe than economic indicators that were missed in the distant past.

It is important to identify the right indicators representing the risks, sometimes some decisions lead to impacts that come out in a form of indicators much later on the time scale. For example, no one anticipated the impact on the economy of the demonetization decision taken way back in 2016. It took around three and a half years to begin its impact visible. This is where a judicious judgment is important using information available at present" along with the historic data. If there were the proper mechanisms of risk management in business houses were there along with tracking of economic indicators, these three and a half years would have used in taking mitigating action.

There are economic generator models are available that can be used for the purpose of anticipating the future along with the judgment. Along with the economic generator models, predictive models can also be used for projecting the future. The need is to develop futuristic thinking and a "what if" mindset. The developed economy has instituted corporate governance guidelines based on their adverse experiences in the past. The key question is can we avoid something like the 2008 crisis in India?

Someone may argue that it is easy to comment in the hindsight on the risks that materialized. That is the message to learn from history and prepare for the future and start taking mitigating action now from emerging risk indicators. No event in the world happens all of sudden and some information is always available giving hints about the future. If we wish to minimize the adverse impact of the risks, the time is now.

Quantification of Risks

It is very important to quantify the risk on the scale of likelihood and impact as this helps in identifying the top risk requiring more urgent attention. If sales of passenger cars are showing more negative growth compared to two-wheeler sales, then immediate action is required to boost passenger vehicles.

There are at times some risks that are low in likelihood and very high in impact; for example, the failure of the internet has a low likelihood but its impact could be devastating. The treatment of this risk will be different compared to the risk of falling sales in a passenger vehicle.

Conclusion

Risks does not occur in isolation and suddenly, it always give early warning signals; it could be a different matter that we have not developed and implemented robust risk management framework for its mitigation. The key to future risk mitigation is to keep all eyes and ears open and act early, time may be short in future to address risks.

TWENTY-FIVE
FLOW CHARTS

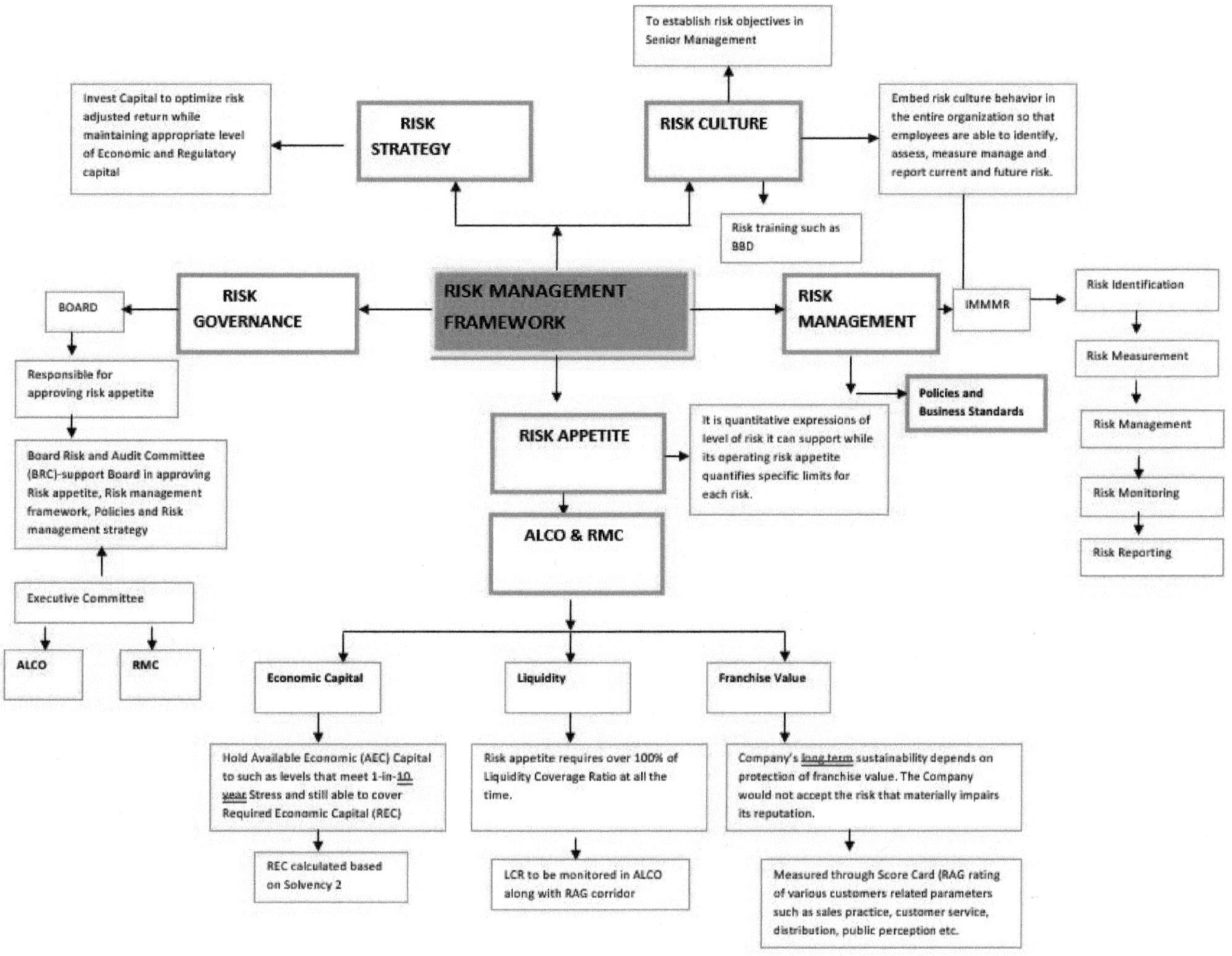

To establish risk objectives in Senior Management

Invest Capital to optimize risk adjusted return while maintaining appropriate level of Economic and Regulatory capital

RISK STRATEGY

RISK CULTURE

Embed risk culture behavior in the entire organization so that employees are able to identify, assess, measure manage and report current and future risk.

Risk training such as BBD

BOARD

RISK GOVERNANCE

RISK MANAGEMENT FRAMEWORK

RISK MANAGEMENT

IMMMR

Risk Identification

Risk Measurement

Risk Management

Risk Monitoring

Risk Reporting

Responsible for approving risk appetite

Policies and Business Standards

RISK APPETITE

It is quantitative expressions of level of risk it can support while its operating risk appetite quantifies specific limits for each risk.

Board Risk and Audit Committee (BRC)-support Board in approving Risk appetite, Risk management framework, Policies and Risk management strategy

ALCO & RMC

Executive Committee

ALCO

RMC

Economic Capital

Liquidity

Franchise Value

Hold Available Economic (AEC) Capital to such as levels that meet 1-in-10 year Stress and still able to cover Required Economic Capital (REC)

Risk appetite requires over 100% of Liquidity Coverage Ratio at all the time.

Company's long term sustainability depends on protection of franchise value. The Company would not accept the risk that materially impairs its reputation.

REC calculated based on Solvency 2

LCR to be monitored in ALCO along with RAG corridor

Measured through Score Card (RAG rating of various customers related parameters such as sales practice, customer service, distribution, public perception etc.

Risk Management Framework

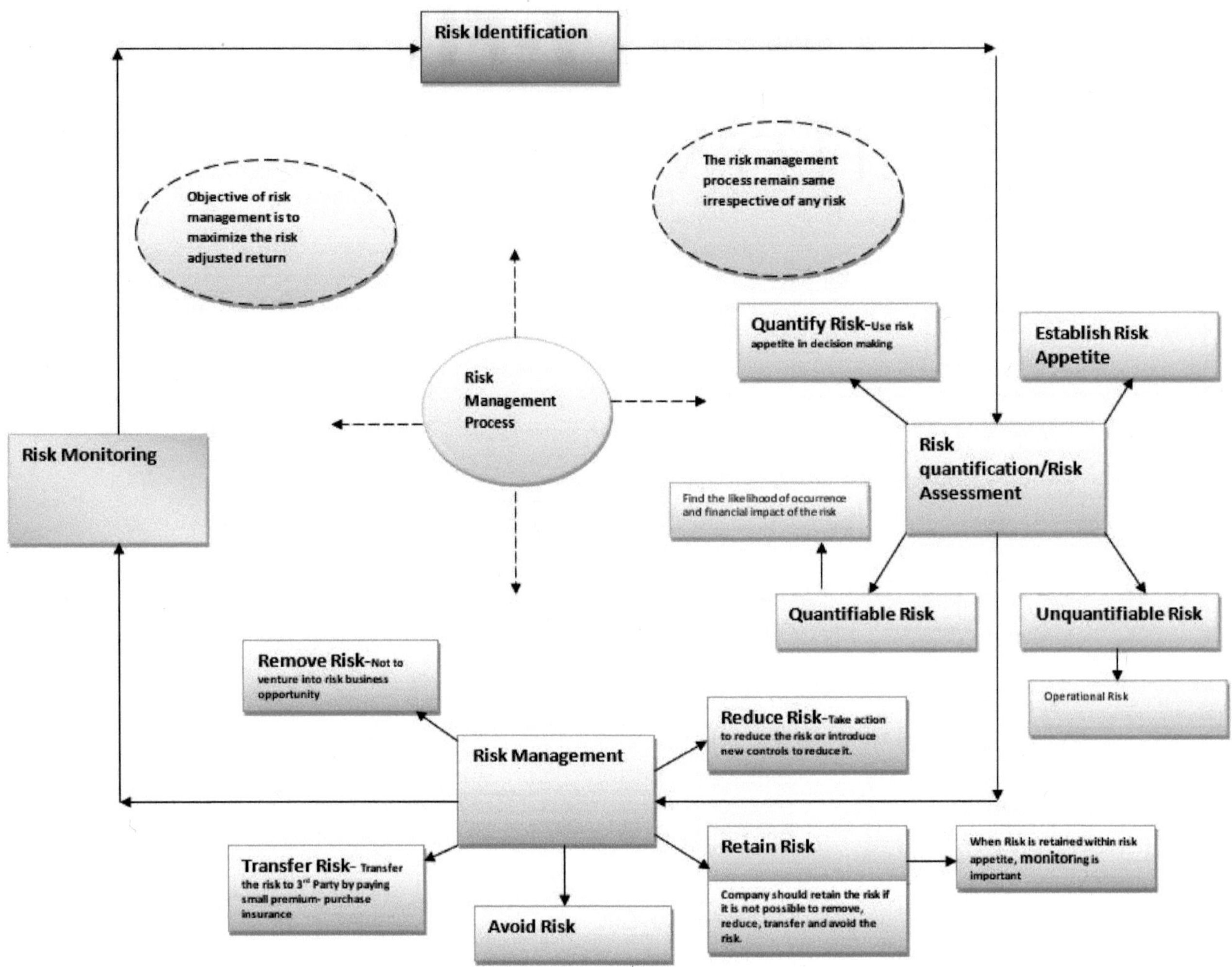

Risk Management Process

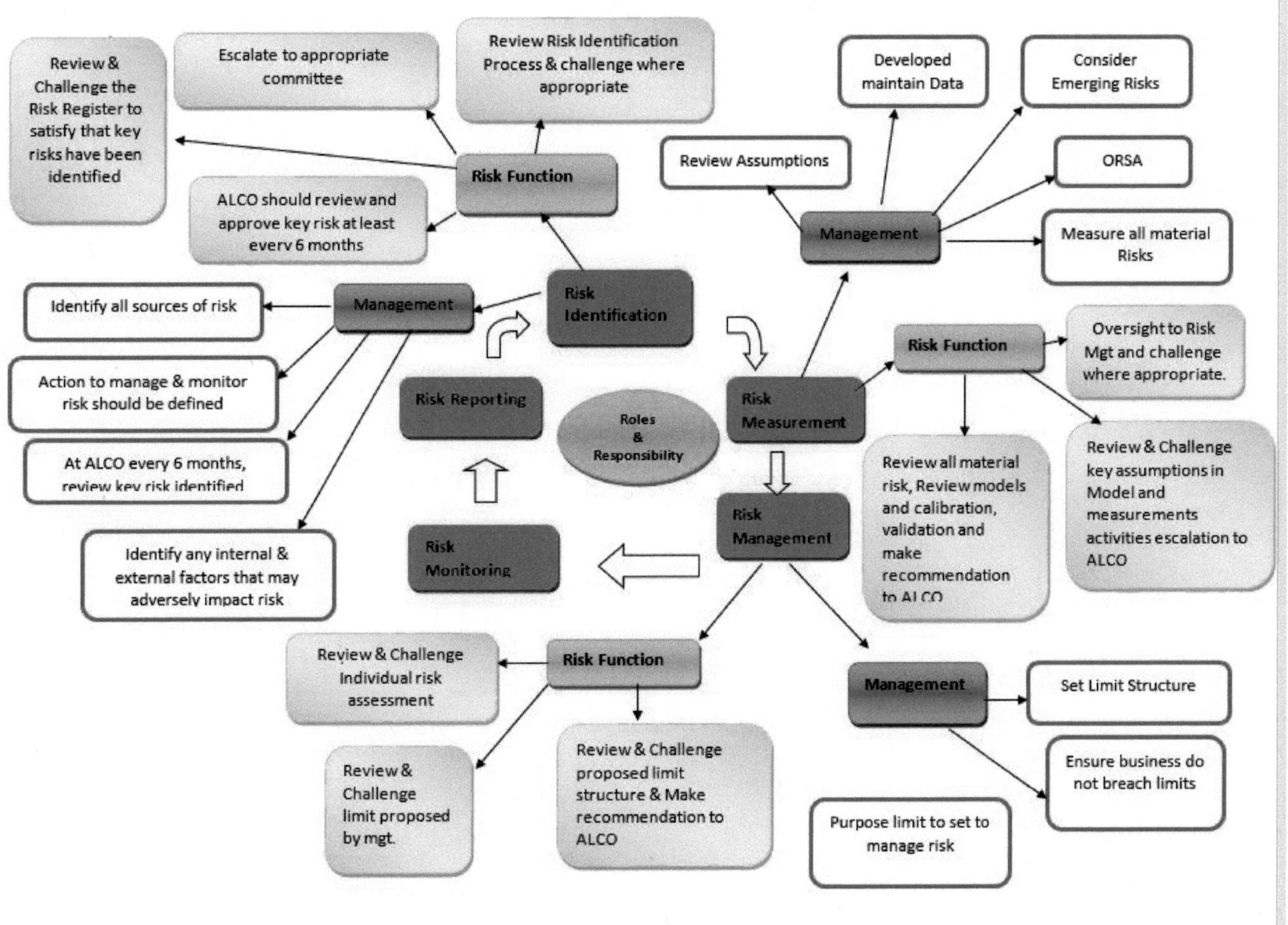

Detailed Risk Management Process

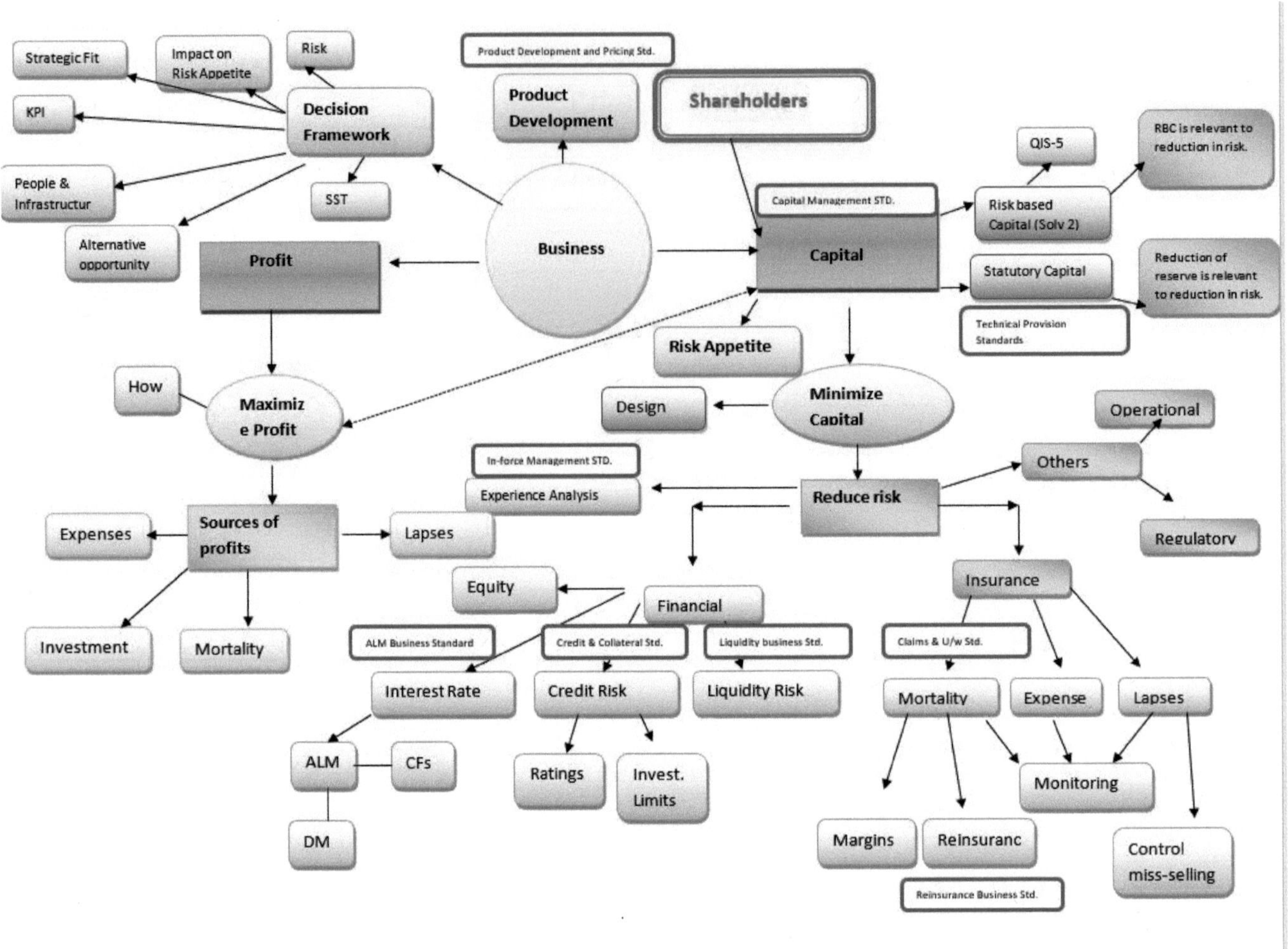

Risk Management Model in Life Insurance

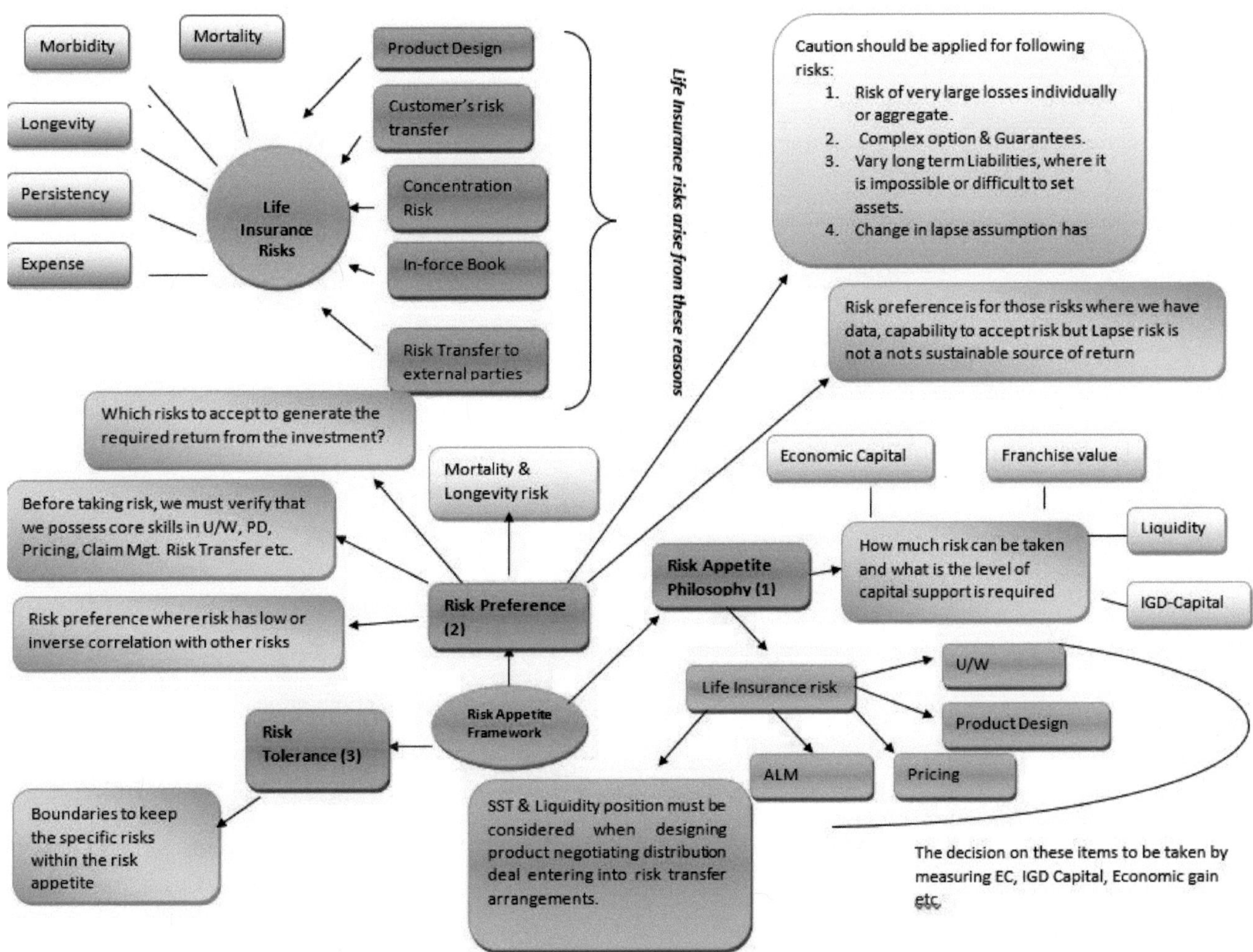

Life Insurance Risks

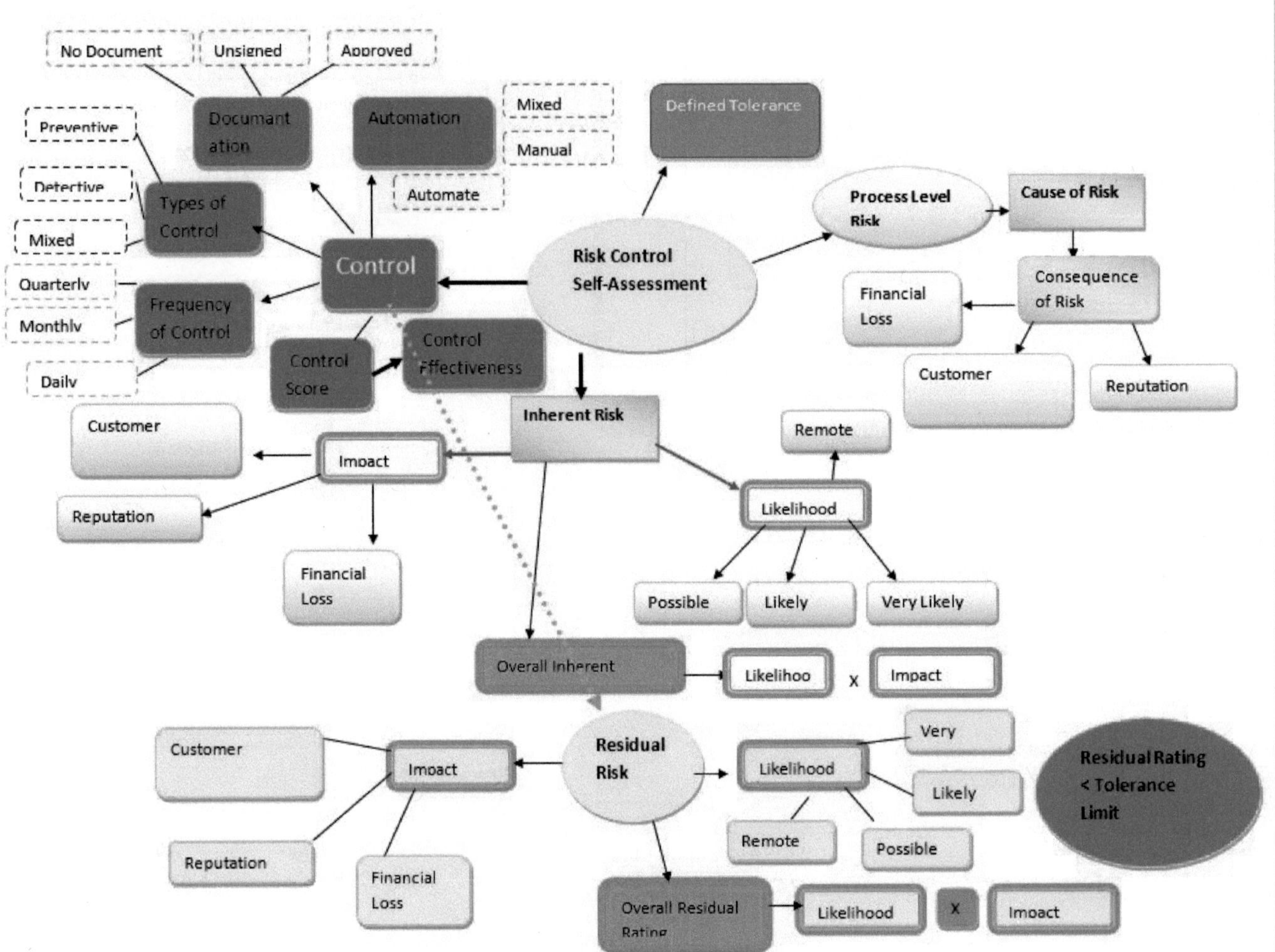

Risk Control Self Assessment (RCSA)

Printed by Libri Plureos GmbH in Hamburg,
Germany